Regulation and the Credit Rating Agencies

T0359041

This book examines the transgressions of the credit rating agencies before, during and after the recent financial crisis. It proposes that by restricting the agencies' ability to offer ancillary services there stands the opportunity to limit, in an achievable and practical manner, the potentially negative effect that the Big Three rating agencies – Standard & Poor's, Moody's and Fitch – may have upon the financial sector and society moreover. The book contains an extensive and in-depth discussion about how the agencies ascended to their current position, why they were able to do so and ultimately their behaviour once their position was cemented.

This work offers a new framework for the reader to follow, suggesting that investors, issuers and the state have a 'desired' version of the agencies in their thinking and operate upon that basis when, in fact, those imagined agencies do not exist, as demonstrated by the 'actual' conduct of the agencies. The book primarily aims to uncover this divergence and reveal the 'real' credit rating agencies, and then on that basis propose a real and potentially achievable reform to limit the negative effects that result from poor performance in this industry. It addresses the topics with regard to financial regulation and the financial crisis, and will be of interest to legal scholars interested in the intersection between business and the law as well as researchers, academics, policymakers, industry and professional associations and students in the fields of corporate law, banking and finance law, financial regulation, corporate governance and corporate finance.

Daniel Cash is a lecturer in law at Aston University, UK.

Routledge Research in Corporate Law

Available titles in this series include:

Regulation and the Credit Rating Agencies

Restraining Ancillary Services

Daniel Cash

NEW YORK AND LONDON

First published 2019
by Routledge
52 Vanderbilt Avenue, New York, NY 10017

and by Routledge
2 Park Square, Milton Park, Abingdon, Oxon OX14 4RN

First issued in paperback 2020

Routledge is an imprint of the Taylor & Francis Group, an informa business

Library of Congress Cataloging-in-Publication Data
Names: Cash, Daniel (Law teacher)
Title: Regulation and the credit rating agencies :
restraining ancillary services / Daniel Cash.
Description: Abingdon, Oxon ; New York, NY : Routledge, 2018. |
Series: Routledge research in corporate law | Includes index. |
Based on author's thesis (doctoral – Durham University, 2017) issued
under title: The Regulation of Credit Rating Agencies : An Analysis of the
Transgressions of the Rating Industry and a Measured Proposal for Reform.
Identifiers: LCCN 2018018286 | ISBN 9780815363996 (hbk)
Subjects: LCSH: Rating agencies (Finance)–Law and legislation.
Classification: LCC K1114.7 .C37 2018 | DDC 346.07/3–dc23
LC record available at https://lccn.loc.gov/2018018286

ISBN 13: 978-0-367-58803-8 (pbk)
ISBN 13: 978-0-8153-6399-6 (hbk)

Typeset in Galliard
by Out of House Publishing

Dedicated to my Mother, Jane.

Contents

Acknowledgements

There are many people that I would like to thank for their support during the construction of this work, but there are many who have had a small, yet significant, impact upon my development; listing them all here would take more than this page, but a small group of my colleagues deserve a mention, as their support in providing a soundboard for ideas as the project developed proved to be very important indeed and I am particularly grateful. However, I would like to begin by thanking Mr Chris Riley; Chris highlighted for me the importance of incorporating different approaches into one's development and I will be forever grateful for the extraordinarily valuable lessons I learned while under his stewardship. In the same vein, I would like to express my sincerest gratitude for the vital lessons learned while speaking with Professor David Held. I am a diligent subscriber to the notion that to be a success one must first humble oneself and then seek to find and learn from someone who demonstrates the very characteristics one would like to, one day, demonstrate; being able to witness his humility, his compassion and ultimately his dedication to people's development, has left a lasting impression and forms the foundation for my own approach to life – I am genuinely grateful to have such a role model.

Last, but certainly not least, I would like express my sincerest gratitude for the support of my mother, Jane. Getting to this point has been quite a journey – probably worthy of a book or two in itself! – and it simply would not have been possible without the remarkable support that she has provided for me. While a mother's support can be imagined, it does not do justice to the support that was and continues to be, provided against remarkable adversity in a multitude of ways; she is a mentor, a leader, a confidante and quite simply an inspiration and somebody whose teachings I work diligently every day to spread far and wide. There are simply not enough pages in this book to express her importance to me, so I have chosen not to try. Yet, I am in full acknowledgement of my sheer fortune for having her as my mother and this work and everything else I do, is for her.

Acknowledgements

Introduction

This historic settlement makes clear the consequences of putting corporate profits over honesty in the financial markets.[1]

This statement is taken from the press release in February 2015 from the US Department of Justice (DoJ), which was announcing that the DoJ, along with 20 states, had reached an agreement with Standard & Poor's (the largest credit rating agency by way of market share) which would see it pay a record $1.375 billion as a fine for its conduct in the lead-up to the recent financial crisis. The settlement, which was to resolve allegations that 'S&P had engaged in a scheme to defraud investors in structured financial products' is by far and away the largest fine ever given to a credit rating agency. However, the statement above contains an issue that is the raison d'être for this book: are the consequences that this historic settlement 'makes clear' enough?

There is a tendency for those who are concerned with analysing the credit rating industry to focus upon the magnitude of the fines that have been imposed or on the choice between fines and other forms of punishment (such as imprisonment) but, although each of those issues have some validity when assessing the ratings industry, they both miss the essential point which is this: *how* and *why* were the agencies able to transgress so destructively? Endeavouring to understand the nature and the causes of their transgressions is essential if we are to properly explain what went wrong or to offer *plausible* suggestions for better regulating the agencies in the future. This book endeavours to examine the forms and causes of misconduct in the credit rating industry, but it is important to note however that the nature of the misconduct is complex and its causes are multiple. Yet and to foreshadow my argument a little, I suggest that one key component in explaining the agencies' misbehaviour includes the fact that the largest agencies established non-essential ancillary service divisions in the lead-up to the crisis. Their doing so and the levels of income such services generated, almost entirely

---

1 Department of Justice 'Justice Department and State Partners Secure $1.375 billion Settlement with S&P for Defrauding Investors in the Lead Up to the Financial Crisis' [2015] Department of Justice: Office of Public Affairs (3 February).

nullified and continues to do so, any 'consequence' that may be derived from the fines that are being predominantly used by the 'State' to discipline the industry.

As a result, the credit rating agencies have been left to proceed in a manner that is a genuine threat to the public interest. The notion of 'public interest' will be dissected throughout Chapter 2 but, for this author, the aim is to *protect* the public and make large-scale social damage a thing of the past; it is simply not an acceptable part of life that the misdemeanours of financial actors should have such a devastating impact upon the lives of citizens. The reverence attached to the 'historic fine' means that for the authorities *their work is now done* with regard to disciplining Standard & Poor's. However, the profits garnered by their ancillary service division, S&P Capital IQ, means that a division that has no bearing on the accuracy of their credit ratings has protected the income from their bottom line; this is simply not a deterrent against future transgressions.

So, the protective capacity afforded to the agencies via their ancillary service divisions is the target for the reform proposal that concludes this work. This is primarily because while other proposals may be more gratifying (i.e., heavier fines or prison sentences for offenders) only small and incremental proposals are *practicable* because, ultimately, the ratings industry is extraordinarily embedded, resourceful and protected.

In order to understand why this proposal of absolute removal is optimal, we will embark upon an analysis that will describe who the agencies are and why they are deemed to be important. Having done this it will then be advanced that the agencies actually operate in a different manner than how they *ought* to, which results in the conclusion that any reform proposals or, indeed, any analysis of the ratings industry, must be focused predominantly upon what they *actually* do, rather than what we may *desire* them to do; any use of the *desired* version of events in analyses should only be used to gauge the severity of the agencies' transgressions. We shall see examples of when the *actualities* of the rating industry have not been considered enough by legislators and regulators, which has led consistently to inefficiencies that have been exploited by the rating agencies. The most important aim is to curb this exploitation and reducing their capability to absorb the only discipline deemed appropriate is a workable way of doing so.

In order to reach this goal of establishing a reform proposal that would see the agencies' capability to absorb financial penalties reduced, we must answer a number of important questions. For the purposes of clarity, those questions are:

> **Question 1** – What is the current role and status of the ratings industry and why does that role require regulation?
>
> **Question 2** – What was the regulatory landscape that surrounded the ratings industry *prior* to the financial crisis?
>
> **Question 3** – What lessons can we learn about the effectiveness of that pre-crisis regulation?
>
> **Question 4** – What regulatory reforms were introduced as a response to the financial crisis and what has been their effectiveness?

Question 5 – How does the provision of ancillary services support the agencies' ability to transgress and what effect would the prohibition of ancillary service provision have upon that capacity?

These questions will be answered in turn and, essentially, provide the structure of the book. While the chapters will examine certain issues, there is an underlying sentiment that will reveal itself as we progress through the examination and that is one of *focus*. It is very important that we remain focused in our investigations into the financial elite, because the façade that is constantly advanced only serves to continue the ability to transgress at the cost of society. In this book, the focus is on an extremely narrow section of the financial sector and that is extremely important. It is important because large-scale examinations and reforms too easily attract scorn and derision for attempting to alter the *system*, which as an ideal is naturally bound to deter or frighten. Rather, we should aim to perform an incrementally based step-by-step approach to change, simply because it is more palatable. Aiming to promote systemic change is as noble as anything else, but it is not *practical*. It is on that basis that this examination proceeds.

Bibliography

United States Department of Justice 'Justice Department and State Partners Secure $1.375 Billion Settlement with S&P for Defrauding Investors in the Lead Up to the Financial Crisis' [2015]. www.justice.gov/opa/pr/justice-department-and-state-part-ners-secure-1375-billion-settlement-sp-defrauding-investors [accessed 14/12/15].

1 A primer on the credit rating domain

Introduction

In essence, the primary role of the rating agencies is to assist a range of investors in making informed investment decisions.[1] In theory, the expert research and analysis conducted by the agencies protects investors from 'unknowingly taking credit risk'.[2] However, the vast losses incurred throughout the financial crisis, particularly those involving investments in highly rated financial products,[3] means that to assess the reality of the rating industry's role is a particularly worthwhile endeavour.

This chapter, therefore, represents a primer on the credit rating industry. The incredible effect that the ratings agencies have[4] means that if we are to analyse the

---

1　Neil D. Baron 'The Role of Rating Agencies in the Securitisation Process' in Leon T. Kendall and Michael J. Fishman (ed.) *A Primer on Securitization* (MIT Press 2000) 81.

2　ibid.

3　The financial crisis, triggered by the collapse of Lehman Brothers in 2008, encapsulated the essence of a collapsed economy, including financial sectors such as financial services, automobiles and even states and countries. For an informative overview of one of the largest collapses on record see Financial Crisis Inquiry Commission *Financial Crisis Inquiry Report* (GPO 2011). In the report (xxv), the Commission made it very clear that the crisis simply could not have occurred without the facilitation of the rating agencies: 'We conclude the failures of credit rating agencies were essential cogs in the wheel of financial destruction'. With regard to the losses experienced as a result of the crisis more generally, finding even an approximate figure is extremely difficult, probably due to the fact that the effects of the crisis are still continuing to unfold and that collecting and comparing global data is notoriously difficult. Just some attempts to approximate the damage include: the US Treasury, that in 2012 estimated the 'lost household wealth' in the US alone to be $19.2 trillion, see the United States Department of the Treasury *The Financial Crisis Response: In Charts* (2012); a former S&P Chief Credit Officer estimating global losses to be in the region of $15 trillion, see Al Yoon 'Total Global Losses from Financial Crisis: $15 Trillion' [2012] *The Wall Street Journal* (1 October); and the Government Accountability Office that estimated the losses to be in the region of $22 trillion, comprising the lost output ($13 trillion) and the paper wealth lost by US homeowners ($9.1 trillion), see United States Government Accountability Office *Financial Regulatory Reform: Financial Crisis Losses and Potential Impacts of the Dodd-Frank Act* (GAO 2013).

4　Charles F. Adams, Donald J. Mathieson, Garry Schinasi *International Capital Markets: Developments, Prospects and Key Policy Issues* (International Monetary Fund 1999) 101 'credit rating agencies have been viewed by many market participants as having a strong impact on both the cost of funding and the willingness of major institutional investors to hold certain types of securities'. For further analysis on the role of the agencies in the marketplace see Dieter Kerwer 'Standardising as Governance: The

intricacies of this unique industry effectively, then this elementary assessment will be extremely important. To do this, the chapter will primarily ask three questions: Who are the credit rating agencies? What is it that they do (including their role within the economy)? What is the regulatory framework that governs them?

Throughout the book there will be constant references to 'the credit rating agencies' or the 'ratings industry', but those blanket terms conceal dynamics within the ratings industry that are very important to understand. For example, an analysis of the global market share and ratings distribution (i.e. produced) within the ratings industry reveals an extraordinary concentration of power among three agencies: Standard & Poor's, Moody's and Fitch Ratings. Analysing these industry dynamics will be very important if we are to answer this chapter's second question, namely 'What do rating agencies do and what is their role within the economy?'

Although there is a lot of discussion to be had regarding the role of the industry, the validity of their position and many other aspects, what is not debatable is their current significance to the fluidity of the capital markets. With the capital markets being the foundation of the modern economy, the use of credit ratings by large institutional investors, banks and other large financial entities means that understanding the industry's role will be an important, but complex, affair.

The complexity of the role means that the task of regulating the industry is extraordinarily difficult. The incredible amount of analysis of the failings surrounding the ratings industry and their role in the financial crisis perhaps points to the conclusion that regulators have failed in overcoming such a difficult task. However, in order to assess whether such an understanding is correct, it will be very important to provide a basic understanding of the regulatory framework that governs the industry and its exploits. The regulation of the ratings industry in the United States is primarily a statutory endeavour, with the Judiciary and Department of Justice being mostly concerned with elements of fraudulent or criminal behaviour.[5] As we shall see, infringements of economically concerned legislation (e.g. The Dodd-Frank Wall Street Reform and Consumer Protection Act of 2010,[6] (hereafter the 'Dodd-Frank Act')) are punished by fines from the Securities and Exchange Commission (SEC) predominantly, although the SEC does theoretically have other powers at its disposal. In establishing and understanding this regulatory environment within which the ratings industry

---

Case of Credit Rating Agencies' in Adrienne Windhoff-Héritier (ed.) *Common Goods: Reinventing European and International Governance* (Rowman & Littlefield 2002).

5 The Department of Justice entered the regulatory picture when it found Standard & Poor's guilty of fraudulent behaviour during the financial crisis and beyond, ultimately prohibiting the agency from conducting certain business and fining it a record $1.375 billion for losses suffered by federally insured institutions. For more see Aruna Viswanatha and Karen Freifeld 'S&P reaches $1.375 billion deal with U.S. states over crisis-era ratings' [2015] Reuters (3 February); Moody's suffered the same fate just two years later, see US Department of Justice *Justice Department and State Partners Secure Nearly $864 Million Settlement With Moody's Arising From Conduct in the Lead up to the Financial Crisis* (2017).

6 124 Stat. 1376.

operates, we will be better able to understand any perceived or potential deficiencies in the regulatory approach to the conduct of the ratings agencies.

The industry: who they are

In terms of the global market for credit ratings there are two important aspects. Firstly, the global ratings industry contains over 100 rating agencies, with the vast majority being concerned with local economies or specialised fields.[7] Secondly, this vast market is dominated by only three agencies, with Standard & Poor's, Moody's and Fitch controlling over 90 per cent of the market.[8] This dominance has been recognised as being a *de facto* oligopoly,[9] although closer analysis of the precise market share and dynamics of the financial markets hints at the existence of 'a partner monopoly' between Moody's and Standard & Poor's[10] or, to be less cynical, a cross between a duopoly and an oligopoly.[11]

Moody's Corporation is the parent company of two legally separate operating divisions: Moody's Investors Service and Moody's Analytics.[12] Moody's Investors Service (MIS) 'provides credit ratings and research covering debt instruments and securities', whereas Moody's Analytics (MA) 'offers leading-edge software, advisory services and research for credit and economic analysis and financial risk management'.[13] These services offered by Moody's Analytics are classified for regulatory purposes as 'Ancillary Services' and are defined by Moody's as 'products and services that are not Credit Rating Services and

---

7 House of Lords: European Union Committee *Sovereign Credit Ratings: Shooting the Messenger?* (The Stationery Office 2011) 24.

8 ibid; European Securities and Markets Authority 'Credit Rating Agencies 2014 Market Share Calculations for the Purposes of Article 8d of the CRA Regulation' [2014] ESMA/2014/1583; Gianluca Mattarocci *The Independence of Credit Rating Agencies: How Business Models and Regulators Interact* (Academic Press 2014) 121.

9 House of Lords (n 7); Raquel G. Alcubilla and Javier R. del Pozo *Credit Rating Agencies on the Watch List: Analysis of European Regulation* (Oxford University Press 2012) 6.

10 There is evidence to suggest this arrangement exists, in that the ratings actions of the leading two agencies have an enormous impact upon Fitch's ratings, but not vice-versa. In addition, it has been noted that Moody's tend to follow S&P's negative watch/outlook opinions, while S&P tend to follow Moody's positive outlook/watch signals, hinting at a partner monopoly, see Rasha Alsakka and Owain A. Gwilym 'Rating Agencies' Credit Signals: An Analysis of Sovereign Watch and Outlook' [2012] 21 *International Review of Financial Analysis* 46.

11 Representative estimates place S&P's market share at between 39 and 42 per cent, while Moody's is between 34.5 and 37 per cent (accounting for variations between American and European estimates). Fitch is represented at between 16 and 18 per cent, lending credence to the argument of Fitch that 'currently the industry [is] a "duopoly" since S&P and Moody's "are virtually omnipresent in the investment guidelines of investors"'. See House of Lords (n 7) 24; European Securities and Markets Authority (n 8); Robert J. Rhee 'On Duopoly and Compensation Games in the Credit Rating Industry' [2013] 108 *Northwestern University Law Review* 89 at 93.

12 Autorité des Marchés Financiers *AMF 2009 Report on Rating Agencies* (AMF 2010) 36. As a result of being a wholly owned public company, Moody's are legally required to submit annual financial reports. It is for this reason that Moody's will be the primary focus of this book, although their figures have been recognised as being representative of S&P's position.

13 Moody's *About Moody's* (2018).

which are market forecasts, estimates of economic trends, pricing analysis or other general data analysis, as well as related distribution services',[14] though it is worth noting in addition to Moody's' self-definition that MA is also the division that controls the sales and marketing efforts for the corporation as a whole.[15] Regulation in light of the recent financial crisis has ruled that the activities of the rating and ancillary entities of the ratings agencies that offer such services must be kept separated.[16]

Moody's is a particularly vast financial entity in its own right. Its total revenue for the financial year of 2016 was $3.6 billion, with an operating margin of 17.7 per cent (down from 42 per cent the year earlier because of fines and settlements);[17] commentators have traditionally been keen to note that this margin (before the penalties in 2016/17) is much higher than a host of more recognisable entities such as Google, Microsoft or ExxonMobil.[18] MIS rates approximately 130 sovereign nations, 11,000 corporate issuers, 21,000 public finance issuers and roughly 76,000 structured finance obligations. In order to do this, the firm employs nearly 10,000 people worldwide and has a presence in 33 countries.[19] Organisationally, legendary investor Warren Buffett's Berkshire Hathaway is the majority shareholder with the influential Vanguard Group also holding significant shares in the company, perhaps signifying the incredible investment opportunity that Moody's represents.

Standard & Poor's is equally as impressive, if, indeed, not more so.[20] However, while Moody's is a stand alone public corporation, Standard & Poor's is not. It represents just part of the activities of the US-based group McGraw-Hill, which also contains other businesses in the field of publishing and education.[21] Standard & Poor's, though at one time just a division of the parent company, was transformed in 2009 into a wholly owned subsidiary and contributes over $3 billion to McGraw-Hill's total revenue, providing for 44 percent of its total.[22]

Standard & Poor's also contains a division that supplies Ancillary Services to the market, via S&P Capital IQ,[23] which in a similar vein to their counterparts at Moody's Analytics, offers 'the highest quality financial intelligence covering both

---

14 Moody's *Policy for Ancillary and Other Permissible Services: Compliance* (Moody's 2012).

15 Autorité des Marchés (n 12).

16 This aspect of the regulatory framework forms the raison d'être for this book, so the regulatory requirements concerning the said separation will be covered in much greater detail in following chapters (5 and 6 predominantly). For information on Moody's regulatory disclosures concerning this separation see Moody's *MIS – MA Separation Policy* (Moody's 2011).

17 Moody's *Annual Report 2016* (Moody's 2017) 33.

18 Ross Levine 'The Governance of Financial Regulation: Reform Lessons from the Recent Crisis' [2012] 12 *International Review of Finance* 1 at 45.

19 Moody's (n 13).

20 S&P have approximately 1.2 million credit ratings outstanding, rated $4.3 trillion in new debt in 2014 alone and employs nearly 1,400 people across 26 countries, see Standard & Poor's *What We Do* (2018).

21 Autorité des Marchés (n 12) 37.

22 ibid 38.

23 Standard & Poor's (n 20).

public and private capital markets'.[24] Standard & Poor's must also disclose under regulatory rules the pre-emptive actions taken to ensure the separation of rating and commercial entities.[25]

The third component of the oligopoly that dominates the rating industry is Fitch Ratings. An amalgamation of a number of rating agencies,[26] Fitch Ratings, as part of the Fitch Group, is majority owned by the influential Hearst Corporation; Hearst increased its equity share at the expense of the previous majority holder, French conglomerate Fimalac, in 2014.[27] Fitch also has its own designated ancillary service provider in Fitch Solutions; like the comparable divisions at Standard & Poor's and Moody's, this requires separation from the commercial entities contained within the group as a whole.[28] Owing to its status as a subsidiary of both the Hearst Corporation and Fimalac, gaining any sense of the scope of the Fitch Group is particularly difficult, although Fimalac reported that in 2013 the Group generated revenues of $982 million,[29] which in itself clearly demonstrates the disparity between Fitch and the two leading agencies in the field.

As the large financial entities that dominate the capital markets are often required by regulation to utilise the ratings of rating agencies, it should come as no surprise that 'the Big Three' are all registered to both the SEC and the European Securities and Markets Authority (ESMA). It should come as no surprise because it is perhaps reasonable to assume that the state would want to formally oversee the entities that it is forcing upon large and influential market actors, although as we shall see in *A Snapshot of the Regulatory Framework*, this formal registration only took place from 2006 onwards. Apart from the Big Three, there are a few other registered agencies that may be worth mentioning, although it must be noted that the reason for their inclusion into this analysis is to fulfil the aims of providing a thorough primer of the industry; their combined market share actually makes them rather insignificant when compared to the actions of the Big Three. A.M. Best Company, for example, is recognised as being the fourth rating agency, although its specialisation in the insurance industry means that it is not in the same category as the agencies above it. As an issuer of 'fixed-instrument debt ratings that cover bonds, notes, securitisation products and other financial instruments issued by insurers and reinsurers',[30] it does have its place within the financial landscape (although the Big Three all conduct more business in the

---

24 S&P Capital IQ *Information You Need* (2015).

25 Standard & Poor's *Confidentiality, Conflicts and Firewall: Policy Statement* (Standard & Poor's 2017).

26 Autorité des Marchés (n 12) 38 The Fitch Group merged with the UK agency IBCA, a bank rating specialist, in 1997. It then acquired the fourth-largest US rating agency, Duff & Phelps and the Canadian bank rating specialist Thomson BankWatch in 2000.

27 See Fimalac *Strategic Focus* (2015); Hearst Corporation *Hearst Corporation to Increase Equity Interest in Fitch Group to 80 Percent* (2014).

28 Fitch Ratings *2015 Form NRSRO Annual Certification: Policies and Procedures Adopted and Implemented to Prevent the Misuse of Material, Non-public Information* (Fitch Ratings 2015).

29 Fimalac *Fitch Ratings* (2015)

30 AM Best *About* (2018).

Insurance field than A.M. Best). It is perhaps worth noting that A.M. Best do not offer Ancillary Services in the same manner as the Big Three, though they do employ the infamous issuer-pays revenue model.[31] On the contrary, Egan-Jones Rating Company, a smaller firm still, actively maintains the 'Investor-Pays' model, an aspect that the company has incorporated heavily into its sales pitches to differentiate itself from other rating agencies. Having started producing ratings in 1995, it is also noted for flagging the failures of Enron and WorldCom at an earlier stage than any other agency.[32] Other noted registered agencies include Dominion Bond Rating Service (DBRS), the Canadian-based agency recently acquired by the influential Carlyle Group,[33] and Morningstar Rating, which is heavily involved in Investment Advice and Management.[34]

There are, of course, a number of agencies that are predominantly concerned with the countries from which they hail.[35] However, one cannot fail to notice the dominance of the US-based agencies in the analysis above. One scholar suggests that the agencies' knowledge 'has a special salience to it because knowledge emerging from the United States has a higher global valuation than that produced by a British, Canadian or Japanese agency',[36] which may provide some analytical

---

31 The issuer-pays model is the revenue model adopted by the Big Three in the 1970s, as opposed to the 'subscriber-pays' model that was in effect up unto that point. The issuer-pays model denotes the system where the issuer of debt will contract and remunerate the agency to formulate a rating; the subscriber-pays model is paid for by individual subscribers to the reports of the rating agencies, which contain ratings, as well as reports and in-depth analysis of rating decisions. The issuer-pays model has a number of advantages and disadvantages: on the plus side it helps issuers to have more involvement in the process and disclose more beneficial information for all parties, while it also allows for the widespread dissemination of ratings information at no cost to investors which, in turn, allows the agencies to channel more resources into their operations and should, in theory, increase the accuracy of their reports. However, there are negatives which are impossible to ignore. Irrespective of any mechanisms the agencies may employ, they simply cannot guarantee insulation from the numerous conflicts of interest that are inherent within a relationship where you are paid by the people you are assessing. Ratings influence (whether perceived or actual), ratings shopping (issuers purchasing ratings from only agencies that provide favourable ratings) and a number of other elements that will be discussed throughout are aspects that are prominent in a large number of criticisms of the industry. For just some analysis on the dynamics of the revenue model see Deryn Darcy 'Credit Rating Agencies and the Credit Crisis: How the "Issuer Pays" Conflict Contributed and What Regulators Might Do About It' [2009] *Columbia Business Law Review* 2; Douglas D. Evanoff *The First Credit Market Turmoil of the 21st Century* (World Scientific 2009); Martha Poon 'Rating Agencies' in Karin K. Cetina and Alex Preda (eds) *The Oxford Handbook of the Sociology of Finance* (Oxford University Press 2012).
32 Egan-Jones Rating Company (2018).
33 Dominion Bond Rating Service *About* (2018).
34 Morningstar Rating (2018).
35 Agencies that fit this definition include the Japan Credit Rating Agency, HR Ratings de México, SA de CV, Feri EuroRating Services AG, CERVED Group S.p.A. and Axesor SA.
36 Timothy J. Sinclair 'Bond-rating Agencies and Coordination in the Global Political Economy' in A.C. Cutler, Virginia Haufler and Tony Porter (eds) *Private Authority and International Affairs* (SUNY Press 1999) 160. Naciri also notes this in addition to the fact that 71 percent of the Big Three's global revenues stem from the US, see Ahmed Naciri *Credit Rating Governance: Global Credit Gatekeepers* (Routledge 2015) 15.

reasoning behind the unmistakable dominance of the Big Three. Nevertheless, now we have identified the major components of this extraordinarily lucrative industry, it is appropriate to ask 'What is it that they do?'

The industry: what it does

A basic understanding of what the rating agencies do would be achieved by the following statement: 'A credit rating is an opinion provided by a rating agency for a fee on the credit risk or creditworthiness of the bond issue, which reflects the probability of default of that bond'.[37] In order to be thorough, however, we must ascertain what lies at the core of the agencies' business: the *bond*. This is a debt instrument issued by an 'issuer' that usually pays a fixed rate of interest over a fixed period of time,[38] though this fixed nature of the instrument is not always the way the instrument is constructed.[39] There are four issuers of bonds: 'sovereign governments and their agencies, local government authorities, supranational bodies such as the World Bank and corporations',[40] with the largest bond market being the government bond market.

Bonds usually have fixed interest rates or *coupons*; these are paid to the investor by the bond's issuer on a semi- or annual basis. The *maturity* of the bond indicates the date when the debt ceases to exist, at which time the issuer must pay the *principal* and the last remaining interest payment to redeem the bond, thus completing the process.[41] This is the foundational understanding of an arena that is defined by its complexity.

This extraordinarily large system of finance[42] has a number of theoretical positives attached to it. Corporate issuers or 'borrowers' as they may also be

---

37 Rhee (n 11) 91.

38 Moorad Choudry *Corporate Bonds and Structured Financial Products* (Butterworth-Heinemann 2004) 3.

39 For an foundational analysis of the bond and other structured finance instruments see Les Dlabay and James Burrow *Business* Finance (Cengage Learning 2007) 207; Moorad Choudry *An Introduction to Bond Markets* (John Wiley & Sons 2010); Sunil Parameswaran *Fundamentals of Financial Instruments: An Introduction to Stocks, Bonds, Foreign Exchange and Derivatives* (John Wiley & Sons 2011) 10.

40 Choudry (n 38) 3. It must be noted here that the agencies rate an issuer separately from the bond it issues. For example, in rating a bond, the agency is only concerned with the issuer's ability to repay that particular debt (although they obviously take the health of the issuing firm more generally into account). Agencies therefore have issue-specific ratings and issuer-specific ratings which each have their own defining characteristics, see Stefan Trueck and Svetlozar T. Rachev *Rating Based Modeling of Credit Risk: Theory and Application of Migration Matrices* (Academic Press 2009) 12; Scott McClesky *When Free Markets Fail: Saving the Market When It Can't Save Itself* (John Wiley & Sons 2010) 90; Giuliano Iannotta *Investment Banking: A Guide to Underwriting and Advisory Services* (Springer Science & Business Media 2010) 106; Thummuluri Siddaiah *Financial Services* (Pearson Education India 2011) 242.

41 Choudry (n 38) 3; 4.

42 Mark Mobius *Bonds: An Introduction to the Core Concepts* (John Wiley & Sons 2012) 1 'the worldwide value of all bonds outstanding was a record US$95 trillion in 2010, with about US$35 trillion in the US bond market'.

called, issue bonds to 'raise finance for major projects and also to cover on-going and operational expenses',[43] while sovereign entities use the issuance of bonds to alleviate the disparity between the expenditure requirements of the country against the income garnered from taxation, amongst other revenue streams.[44] For corporate issuers the advantages are plentiful; in addition to allowing the raising of large amounts of resources for whatever requirements they may have, it also serves the company better than raising resources through the sale of stock.[45] Not only does the system benefit the issuer, but it also benefits the investor. While the return potential of bonds is much lower than that of other investments such as stocks, this is an attractive quality to the cautious investor who may take comfort from the relative security of a bond, while they may also use the bond to anchor their investment portfolio and use the interest payments on the bonds they hold to finance more speculative movements in the stock market.[46]

These dynamics are the foundations for the modern ratings industry. The explosion of the capital markets in the 1970s meant that these dynamics would have to be integrated into the essence of the ratings industry and their methodologies subsequently aligned to them. This is because in the wake of the collapse of Penn Central in 1970, both investors and issuers required a third party who, through a perceived reputation-based level of independence, could

---

43 Choudry (n 38) 5.
44 ibid. The rating of sovereign debt is proving to be particularly important with regard to the requirements of emerging markets that are now reliant upon access to the capital markets as opposed to the banking sector, see Constantin Mellios and Eric Paget-Blanc 'The Impact of Economic and Political Factors on Sovereign Credit Ratings' in Robert Kolb (ed.) *Sovereign Debt: From Safety to Default* (John Wiley & Sons 2011) 325.
45 Mobius notes that stockholders would theoretically much prefer a bond issuance to a stock sale, noting that the sale of shares would dilute the existing stockholder's equity position and that the corporation would gain tax benefits from issuing bonds whereas they would not if they issued new stock, see Mobius (n 42) 7. The theoretical consideration behind this is called 'Capital Structure Theory' and is concerned with the positive and negative dynamics of the two different types of financing (bond and stock issuances). For more on the theory see Stephen Lumby and Chris Jones *Corporate Finance: Theory & Practice* (Cengage Learning EMEA 2003); Arvin Ghosh *Capital Structure and Firm Performance* (Transaction Publishers 2012). For more on the consideration of tax deductions being a factor in selecting a method of financing see Doron Peleg *Fundamental Models in Financial Theory* (MIT Press 2014). For further analysis on the aspect of management losing or maintaining control of the company and the methodology of obtaining finance being central to that dynamic see P.C. Tulsian and Vishal Pandey *Business Organisation and Management* (Pearson Education India 2002) 14–19; Theodore Grossman and John L. Livingstone *The Portable MBS in Finance and Accounting* (John Wiley & Sons 2009) 147. Grossman and Livingstone also talk at length about what is considered to be the seminal work in this field written by Franco Modigliani and Merton H. Miller 'The Cost of Capital, Corporation Finance and the Theory of Investment' [1958] 48 *The American Economic Review* 3. Modigliani and Miller asserted that the value of a firm stems from the 'cash-flow-generating ability' of its assets, rather than the way in which it is financed, although it must be noted that the model the two scholars use is an absolutely ideal scenario rather than a real-world consideration.
46 Mobius (n 42) 8.

signify to the marketplace the creditworthiness of firms and their debt offerings.[47] 'Informational asymmetry' is the term assigned to the informational gap that exists between investors and issuers and represents the proclaimed justification for the existence and continuous usage of the agencies' services. Investors do not have the resources to perform credit risk analysis on each of the issuers they wish to invest in as a rule; even the largest investors who do have adequate risk analysis divisions would find it ineffective to conduct such wide-ranging analysis when a third party exists to complement their own investigations.[48] Also, issuers are more inclined to share more information with a third-party assessor than they are with individual investors, in turn avoiding duplication costs in the gathering and analysis of information, which is of increasing importance given the ever-increasing complexities within the financial markets.[49]

The agencies understand this and have developed their business accordingly:

> Through research, analysis and information the nationally recognised credit rating agencies protect investors against unknowingly taking credit risk. Investment grade rating says something very specific. It says a particular instrument will pay interest and principle according to the terms of the indenture (contract). If you hold a twenty-five-year, triple-A bond to maturity, you are assured of getting 100 percent of the principal and interest on a timely basis.[50]

Though this level of certainty is a disputable notion,[51] it is theoretically correct that the inclusion of an investment-grade rating will *more-or-less* guarantee complete repayment, particularly with respect to corporate bonds.[52] The classification of what constitutes 'investment-grade' and 'non-investment-grade' (also known

---

47 Briefly, the collapse of the Penn Central Railroad company in 1970 triggered a systemic lack of trust in the creditworthiness of financial entities, meaning that (a) investors needed independent assessments of a firm's creditworthiness and (b) issuers needed a reputable and impartial party to vouch for their creditworthiness. This is the most common hypothesis for the upsurge in the industry's fortunes post-1970; for more on this, see *The Collapse of Penn Central Hypothesis*.

48 Mattarocci (n 9) 1.

49 Andrew Crockett *Conflicts of Interest in the Financial Services Industry: What Should We Do About Them?* (Centre for Economic Policy Research 2003) 42.

50 Baron (n 1) 81.

51 For a representative argument of the impossibility of guaranteeing certainty in this marketplace see Akos Rona-Tas and Stefanie Hiss 'The Art of Corporate and The Science of Consumer Credit Rating' in Michael Lounsbury and Paul M. Hirsch (eds) *Markets on Trial: The Economic Sociology of the U.S. Financial Crisis, Part 1* (Emerald Group Publishing 2010) 117. Later we will see how this notion of certainty is reputed by the industry in broader terms to limit the levels of liability it faces (see also Mattarocci (n 8) 2) and that the allure of the Triple-A rating only belongs to the corporate and sovereign issuance sectors in light of the dramatic failings of Triple-A rated securitised products in the financial crisis.

52 Iain MacNeil 'Credit Rating Agencies: Regulation and Financial Stability' in Thomas Cottier, Rosa M. Lastra, Christian Tietje and Lucia Satragno (eds) *The Rule of Law in Monetary Affairs* (Cambridge University Press 2014) 180.

as 'speculative grade') is the same amongst the Big Three, with the investment-grade rating ranging from AAA (Aaa for Moody's) through to BBB- (Baa3 for Moody's).[53] It is worth noting that a change in credit rating is by 'notch' rather than Alphabetical letter in the first instance as agencies attach *notches* to their ratings to signify more precisely their assessment of a given entity or its offerings. The notches are either '+' or '–' or '1, 2 or 3' for Moody's (this is in addition to their market signifiers that signify the sentiment of the agency towards the short-term future of the rating[54]). While it would be tempting to attach a table to this work detailing each agency's ratings for us to compare, as some scholars have done, it is important that we understand that this would be hazardous for our assessment because each agency takes different aspects into account when developing their ratings. As well as differentiating their ratings based on short- and long-term outlooks, the agencies also base their assessments on either default probability or on the concept of expected loss, which incorporates 'expected recovery in the event of default'.[55] In light of this and although a unique definition of the 'rating service' has yet to be agreed upon, the declaration that 'a rating is a synthetic judgement that summarises, using an alphanumeric scale, the main qualitative and quantitative characteristics of an issue or issuer'[56] provides us with perhaps the simplest understanding of what the main service is that the agencies provide.

Understanding the *role* of the industry is more important still. We have already discussed the vast scope and subsequent recompense of the ratings industry, factors that indicate that the opinions of an agency have a direct effect upon the global allocation of credit;[57] this has the potential to impact the costs of an issuer dramatically. This, in turn, transfers the potential effect from the individual issuer

---

53 Moody's *Rating Symbols and Definitions* (2018); Standard & Poor's *Standard & Poor's Ratings Definitions* (2017); Fitch Ratings *Rating Definitions* (2018). Rhee notes in addition to this that these taxonomical divisions which include finer divisions are not opinions of the value of a bond, merely the estimation of likelihood of default and failure to meet interest and principal payment; the value of bonds can depend on a large number of intrinsic and extrinsic factors, see Rhee (n 11) 91; Adams et al. (n 4) 102.

54 See (n 80) (Christina E. Bannier and Christian W. Hirsch 'The Economic Function of Credit Rating Agencies – What Does the Watchlist Tell Us?' [2010] 34 *Journal of Banking & Finance* 3037).

55 Alcubilla and del Pozo (n 9) 59. See also John P. Hunt 'Rating Agencies and Credit Insurance' in H.K. Baker and Gerald S. Martin (eds) *Capital Structure and Corporate Financing Decisions: Theory, Evidence and Practice* (John Wiley & Sons 2011) 300, who confirms that Moody's ratings reflect the expected loss and S&P's reflect the risk of default. Hunt goes on to make the point that 'although the agencies do not assert that their ratings are comparable across agencies, regulations and users often treat ratings as comparable', a sentiment that draws explicit warning from Stebler who suggests that any results from a comparative study 'should be interpreted with due care'; see Roman Stebler 'Performance and Consistency of Credit Ratings in Structured Finance' in Simone Westerfeld, Beatrix Wullschleger and Pascal Gantenbein (eds) *Proceedings of the Second International Conference on Credit Analysis and Risk Management* (Cambridge Scholars Publishing 2014) 163.

56 Mattarocci (n 8) 2.

57 Naciri (n 36) 44.

to the marketplace as a whole, perhaps meaning that the opinions of the agencies are, in effect, macroeconomic factors,[58] not just unrelated judgements.

This issue of 'judgement' is also an important factor to consider. The position of the agencies within the marketplace, between issuer and investor, has led people to conclude that the agencies are, in essence, auditors, similar to accountants or securities analysts. Pallante opines that the 'third-party' dynamic of the agencies' position is what relates the ratings industry to the industries of recognised auditors,[59] although others have maintained that 'ratings are not audits of the entities being rated, nor are they designed to catch or prevent fraud'.[60] While this claim may be somewhat true, at least in the most rigid sense, it is somewhat 'disingenuous'.[61] It is perhaps disingenuous because, as Darbellay makes clear, the regulatory rules established by the Dodd-Frank Act 'result from the appreciation that CRAs play a fundamentally commercial role, thereby implying that they have to be subject to similar standards to other gatekeepers such as auditors and securities analysts'.[62] So, while they are not explicitly regarded as 'auditors' in the traditional sense, their positioning between issuers and investors has dictated that they are treated as such.

This position between the two pillars of the modern economy – the issuer and the investor – is a fascinating one. The dynamic between them is precarious at times and the services offered by the agencies help each party to protect and advance their position. Alcubilla and del Pozo note that there are three main aspects to the agencies' role with regard to issuers and investors. First, they help mitigate the fundamental information asymmetry between the two parties. Second, the agency problem that is inherent within the modern economy can *potentially* be solved. With the largest investors being institutional investors (e.g. pension funds, life insurers etc.), the ratings of the agencies can be used by the investors (or indeed regulators) to dictate what investments the managers of the institutional investor (agent) can make on their behalf, which is one reason why most institutional investors are restricted to investing in AAA rated bonds and securities only.[63] Thirdly, the scholars suggest that the ratings can solve collective action problems in that the dispersed investors can use the ratings as a trigger for debt restructuring without the administrative efforts that would be needed in the absence of the centralised views of the agencies.[64]

58 Manfred Gartner, Bjorn Griesbach, Florian Jung 'PIGS or Lambs? The European Sovereign Debt Crisis and the Role of Rating Agencies' [2011] 17 *International Advances in Economic Research* 288.

59 Tony Pallante *From Your Wallets to Their Pockets: Understanding the Credit Crisis: Privatizing Profits and Socializing Losses* (iUniverse 2008) 108.

60 L.J. Rodriguez 'The Credit Rating Agencies: From Cartel Busters to Cartel Builders' in William A. Niskanen *After Enron: Lessons for Public Policy* (Rowman & Littlefield 2007) 219.

61 Jonathan R. Macey *Corporate Governance: Promises Kept, Promises Broken* (Princeton University Press 2010) 114.

62 Aline Darbellay *Regulating Credit Rating Agencies* (Edward Elgar 2013) 69.

63 Rhee (n 11) 91.

64 Alcubilla and del Pozo (n 9) 5.

The role the industry plays in the capital markets is important, but it can only really be understood when analysed in conjunction with how the market participants both use and view them. The investors, irrespective of their requirements (whether long- or short-term) use the ratings of the agencies as a common standardised benchmark to measure the credit risk of securities, while issuers request ratings only because investors use them. By paying the price for the ratings, issuers in turn lower their cost for placing their securities in the marketplace, by way of reducing interest-rate payments.[65] Issuers also benefit from the arrangement by conveying to the market the effect of information that is confidential, via the authority of the intermediary (the rating agency).[66]

It has been noted that it may be useful to think of the issuers as the agencies' 'suppliers', while investors are their 'consumers'.[67] Because issuers rely upon the agencies to ensure the lowest rate of interest possible by way of a top-tier rating, issuers usually prefer to have more than one rating attached to their bond issuance, with there being examples of issuances containing three ratings in order to prove their creditworthiness to the market. Conversely, investors usually require fewer ratings, particularly institutional investors, as it has been argued that these sophisticated investors use the ratings as additional inputs into an already complicated risk analysis machine rather than the sole criteria for an investment decision. In this sense there is such a thing as too much information.[68] This notion of issuers being 'suppliers' has had an effect upon how they conduct their business; Crockett notes that issuing companies often structure their issuances to achieve a desired rating. They also create special-purpose entities that are specifically tailored for a designated investor who may have restrictions on what they can invest in which, in turn, would reduce their borrowing costs.[69]

While the processes of the agencies may seem to place the advantage with the issuer, the investor also uses ratings to their advantage, perhaps even more so. The usage of 'rating triggers' are particularly useful for the investor when entering into contract with a borrower. These contractual provisions may include such aspects as the right to terminate the credit availability, accelerate credit obligations or force the borrower to post collateral in the event of a rating change (downgrade).[70] Though this has the potential to encourage a liquidity crisis on a vast scale, it nevertheless offers protection to the investor in a relationship where their resources are at stake.

---

65 ibid 12.
66 Mattarocci (n 8) 1; Crockett (n 49) 43.
67 H.K. Baker and Sattar A. Mansi 'Assessing Credit Rating Agencies by Bond Issuers and Institutional Investors' [2002] 29 *Journal of Business Finance & Accounting* 1368.
68 ibid 1395.
69 Crockett (n 49) 41.
70 Alcubilla and del Pozo (n 9) 13. The scholars note that most triggers are relatively harmless for the issuer, with increased interest rates providing a common example.

The rating process

The rating process differs between the leading agencies. Some agencies may follow the process of analysts forming reports based upon qualitative and quantitative factors, which they then submit to a rating committee for final evaluations. Though most agencies have rating committees, some agencies tend to place more emphasis upon statistical modelling programmes which results in a more mechanical process.[71] This reliance upon statistical modelling has been recognised as being central to the structured finance instrument rating process.[72] We have already seen how the dynamics of the oligopoly are affected by disparities between the rating processes, with Standard & Poor's and Moody's being defined by their differing characteristics.[73] However, MacNeil argues that although there are clear differences in their approach to rating, there are three distinct similarities between the rating agencies. The first is that the ratings are characterised by the agencies as 'an ordinal measure of credit risk rather than specific estimates of credit risk metrics such as default probability or expected loss'. Next, all three agencies distinguish between investment- and non-investment grade – which they do. Finally, that rating stability is the primary objective of all of the CRAs[74], which in light of the financial crisis has become a point of debate.

Nevertheless, each agency does have its own procedure, but many aspects are indeed common. First, the agency will have statistical models that contain algorithms to predict the statistical outcome of a given scenario (e.g what may happen to an airline if the price of oil rose to $100 per barrel).[75] When an issuer requests a rating for their issuance, an analyst (or perhaps more depending on a number of factors) is assigned to that issuance. Analysts usually concentrate on just one or two industries, which allows for an accumulation of specific expertise.[76] The analyst then uses their expertise and whatever methods they deem appropriate, which may involve liaising with the management of the issuer,[77] to formulate a report which is presented to a convened rating committee. Rating committees vary according to the size and sensitivity of that particular rating.

The rating committee

The rating committee is championed as a vital part of the process. After the committee hears and debates the rating proposed to it by the analyst, it then casts a vote on what should be the final rating. This process is designed so that no one

---

71 Alcubilla and del Pozo (n 9) 18.
72 Clark R. Abrahams and Mingyuan Zhang *Credit Risk Assessment: The New Lending System for Borrowers, Lenders and Investors* (John Wiley & Sons 2009) 227.
73 See n 10.
74 MacNeil (n 52) 179.
75 McClesky (n 40) 89.
76 Trueck and Rachev (n 40) 14.
77 ibid.

individual can have undue influence over the rating process. It is also championed as being the antidote to the issuer-pays conflict of interest, as agencies maintain that the committee has no revenue goal and therefore cannot be influenced by the will of the agency. However, McClesky rightly points out that it could be argued that although it is true that the analysts do not have specific revenue goals, their first- and/or second-level supervisors do, thus diminishing the desired effect.[78] Once the committee has come to an agreed rating, the issuer is given the option of appealing the decision based upon the delivery of new information; the appeal process usually only spans a day or two.[79] After this period the rating is either released to the public or given to the issuer to release as an official corporate rating.

Signalling to the market

In order to have a greater range of flexibility with regard to their placing of the ratings within the economic cycle, agencies have addendums to their ratings. These signals are attached to the ratings to signify to the investor the agencies' belief in the current and future creditworthiness of the issuer and/or the issuance. These addendums fall into two categories and have different purposes. First, there is the *rating outlook*, which represents the agency's opinion on the development of the credit rating over the medium term. Then there is the *rating watchlist*, which is a stronger, more concerning statement for the issuer and focuses upon a much shorter time horizon, usually around three months.[80] The watchlist comes into effect when a deviation from an expected trend either takes place or is expected to take place, in which case additional information is required based upon the given scenario.[81] Bannier and Hirsch note that while rating downgrades alert the market to issuers' lack of *capability* to maintain their credit quality, 'watchlist-downgrades inform market participants of borrowers' lack of *success* in the attempt to do so'.[82]

These market signifiers are of crucial importance in the capital markets as the fluidity of the marketplace requires constant attention. Any delay in action or information could cost those exposed to certain circumstances vast sums of

---

78 McClesky (n 40) 90. It must be noted that there are procedures in effect to lessen this predicament, including reverse voting (junior analysts vote first so as not to be influenced by senior members) and all documents that assisted the committee in coming to a decision must be retained for SEC inspection. Ramirez also states that 'another former ratings agency employee stated that senior managers "intimidated" analysts and wanted employees who were "docile" and "afraid to upset the investment banks". Rating analysts often achieved higher bonus compensation based upon the performance of the ratings firm'; see Steven A. Ramirez *Lawless Capitalism: The Subprime Crisis and the Case for an Economic Rule of Law* (New York University Press 2014) 85.
79 Trueck and Rachev (n 40) 14.
80 Christina E. Bannier and Christian W. Hirsch 'The Economic Function of Credit Rating Agencies – What Does the Watchlist Tell Us?' [2010] 34(12) *Journal of Banking & Finance* 3037–3049.
81 Trueck and Rachev (n 40) 15.
82 Bannier and Hirsch (n 80) 3048.

money; this is clearly evident within the securitisation process.[83] Though this chapter will not go into tremendous detail regarding the securitisation process, it is worth mentioning the role of the industry[84] as in so doing, we may then be able to better understand the regulatory analysis that follows.

Asset securitisation involves the pooling of a certain category of loans into a pool that is then sold to investors. The interest and principal payments of these loans are paid to investors in a particular order, dependent upon which *tranche* (French for 'slice') of the pool they purchase (this process is known as 'credit enhancement', as it allows the agencies to attach higher ratings to the product as a whole and thus make it more marketable). Credit rating agencies give the most secure tranches their highest rating, which in turn encourages risk-averse and regulatory-constrained investors to partake in the process.[85] The pool is divided into particular categories of tranches, with the senior category being followed by the mezzanine tranches and then finally by the equity tranches, with the investors in the equity tranches the least likely to be paid in the event of a pool-wide default. For the process to work, investors must invest into each division of the pool. With regard to residential mortgage-backed securities that came to define the financial crisis, the banks invested in the senior tranches, the insurance industry invested in the mezzanine tranches (still rated A by the agencies) and the hedge funds invested in the equity tranches, chasing the huge returns their clients demanded of them.[86]

It is worth noting the fee structure that agencies adopted, primarily through this extraordinary and complicated[87] process. In 2007, a representative fee for a long-term corporate bond issue ranged from 2 to 4.5 basis points of the principal for each year the rating was maintained and 12 basis points for Collateralised Debt Obligations (structured finance instruments used in the securitisation process).[88] A basis point represents 1/100th of 1 per cent (e.g. an issue of $1

---

83 For a more extensive assessment of the mechanics of securitisation see John Deacon *Global Securitisation and CDOs* (John Wiley & Sons 2004); Vinod Kothari *Securitization: The Financial Instrument of the Future* (John Wiley & Sons 2006) 4–5. With regard to the importance of information to the process of securitisation, Queisser notes that

> the absence of price signals will lead to the misallocation of resources and to a bundling of risk. Intermediation through different channels will improve resource allocation since corporate bond and equity markets will give price signals which reflect risk-levels and provide information to market participants.

See Monika Queisser 'The Role of Pension Funds in the Stabilisation of the Domestic Financial Sector' in Douglas H. Brooks and Monika Queisser (eds) *Financial Liberalisation in Asia: Analysis and Prospects* (OECD Publishing 1999). See also Essvale Corporation *Business Knowledge for IT in Islamic Finance* (Essvale Corporation Limited 2010) 81 for a similar assessment of the importance of information to the securitisation process.

84 See Frank J. Fabozzi, Anand K. Bhattacharya and William S. Berliner *Mortgage-backed Securities: Products, Structuring and Analytical Techniques* (John Wiley & Sons 2010); Marco Pagano and Paulo Volpin 'Credit Ratings Failures: Causes and Policy Options' [2010] 25 *Economic Policy* 62.

85 Mark Zandi *Financial Shock: Global Panic and Government Bailouts – How We Got Here and What Must Be Done to Fix It* (FT Press 2009) 117.

86 ibid.

87 Richard C. Koo *The Escape from Balance Sheet Recession and the QE Trap: A Hazardous Road for the World Economy* (John Wiley & Sons 2015) 124.

88 Naciri (n 36) 16.

billion would cost the issuer $1.2 million at 12 basis points). Though this rate looks inconsequential, the trillions of dollars' worth of securitised products that were rated during such a short period demonstrates the precise reason for the record-breaking revenues collected by the agencies since the turn of the century. For corporate and sovereign issues the fees are much more modest, though still extremely lucrative.[89]

Credit rating agencies and issuers: a two-way street

It is worth considering that although the issuers depend on the agencies to facilitate the distribution of their issuances throughout the capital markets, agencies depend upon the issuers to maintain their position. While it is argued that agencies preserve the value of their ratings by maintaining a good reputation for the accuracy of their service,[90] this remains a controversial issue, as we shall see in the following chapters. However, what is true, is that despite the criticisms of the agencies, their reputation is dependent upon the truthful disclosure from the issuing party.[91] Though there are regulations to force this from the issuer, the agencies are still at the mercy of the issuing party, a fact proven by the Enron scandal.[92]

In addition to this, there are two competing views as to the informational value of the ratings produced by the agencies. One side argues that the agencies are specialists in procuring and processing financial information, ultimately generating previously unknown information for the financial marketplace. The counteracting argument is that the agencies merely process publicly available information that results in a general lagging in the financial marketplace with

---

89 Moody's and S&P have listed prices of 3.25 basis points on issues going up to $500 million, with a maximum fee of $125,000 (S&P) and $130,000 (Moody's). Both firms then charge an additional two basis points on amounts exceeding $500 million, see Tony Van Gestel and Bart Baesens *Credit Risk Management: Basic Concepts: Financial Risk Components, Rating Analysis, Models, Economic and Regulatory Capital* (Oxford University Press 2008) 153. Sovereign fees tend to range from $60,000 to $100,000, see Naciri (n 36) 16.

90 Howell E. Jackson 'The Role of Credit Rating Agencies in the Establishment of Capital Standards for Financial Institutions in a Global Economy' in Eilis Ferran and Charles A.E. Goodhart (eds) *Regulating Financial Services and Markets in the 21st Century* (Hart Publishing 2001) 312.

91 Orkun Akseli 'Was Securitisation the Culprit? Explanation of Legal Processes Behind Creation of Mortgage-backed Sub-prime Securities' in Joanna Gray and Orkun Akseli (eds) *Financial Regulation in Crisis? The Role of Law and the Failure of Northern Rock* (Edward Elgar Publishing 2011) 11.

92 For analysis of the Rating Agencies' involvement in the collapsing of Energy giant Enron Corporation in 2001 see Jonathan R. Macey 'A Pox on Both Your Houses: Enron, Sarbanes-Oxley and the Debate Concerning the Relative Efficiency of Mandatory Versus Enabling Rules' (2003) 81 *Washington University Law Quarterly* 329; Claire A. Hill 'Regulating the Rating Agencies' (2004) 82 *Washington University Law Review* 43. For more on the collapse more generally see Denis Collins *Behaving Badly: Ethical Lessons from Enron* (Dog Ear Publishing 2006); Malcolm S. Salter *Innovation Corrupted: The Origins and Legacy of Enron's Collapse* (Harvard University Press 2008); Frank Partnoy *Infectious Greed: How Deceit and Risk Corrupted the Financial Markets* (Profile Books 2010).

respect to information.[93] While these arguments each have merit, the introduction of 'regulatory reliance' fundamentally altered the character and trajectory of the industry and, because of that, we need to understanding the regulatory dynamic governing the rating industry.

A snapshot of the regulatory framework

On the one hand, credit ratings are used by regulators to affect other parts of the economy. For example, banking regulators have, since the 1930s, required that banks only hold assets that are considered 'investment grade' by the leading rating agencies (it is acknowledged that after the Dodd-Frank Act this is, technically, no longer the case); this may be known as 'regulatory usage' of credit ratings. On the other hand, it is the regulation *of* the credit rating agencies, which dictates actions they must take to be considered as a registered and usable rating agency.

Credit ratings have a variety of uses in terms of regulatory usage and are utilised by regulatory agencies across a broad spectrum of financial industries. They are used to identify or classify assets, provide a credible evaluation of the credit risk associated with assets purchased as part of a securitisation offering, determine disclosure requirements and also to determine prospectus eligibility, though the most common usage by the authorities is to use them to determine capital requirements.[94] This is in relation to the usage of the ratings to designate the permissible or required investments of certain financial institutions, like banks or institutional investors.[95] The ratings are used to ensure that risks are 'properly managed, disclosed and priced, as well as supported by sufficient capital to protect certain classes of claims holders, including depositors and policy holders'.[96] This concept of protection is also witnessed by the fact that structured securities are rated by 'one or more credit rating agencies, especially when they are sold to retail (non-professional) investors'.[97]

With regard to the regulation *of* the credit rating agencies and in keeping with the complexity that seems to be inherently attached to the provision of credit ratings, the regulatory environment is and perhaps always has been, a complicated affair. One of the main reasons for this is that until 2006, the ratings industry was not extensively or directly regulated. Before this, it was subject to being used in regulations and legal considerations regarding a number of different areas of the economy, but was never directly regulated while being elevated to such an influential position. For example, before the Great Depression

93 Roman Kräussl 'The Impact of Sovereign Rating Changes During Emerging Market Crises' in Michael Frenkel, Alexander Karmann and Bert Scholtens (eds) *Sovereign Risk and Financial Crises* (Springer Science and Business Media 2013) 92.
94 Alcubilla and del Pozo (n 9) 16.
95 ibid 17; United States Senate, Permanent Subcommittee on Investigations *Wall Street and the Financial Crisis: Anatomy of a Financial Collapse* (GPO 2011) 27.
96 Crockett (n 49) 43.
97 Alcubilla and del Pozo (n 9) 17.

it was the judiciary who were mainly involved with any sort of 'oversight' of the industry, although this mostly took the form of actions against the agencies for defamation arising out of the content of their publications.[98] In the wake of the Great Depression, regulators such as the Comptroller of the Currency began to incorporate the ratings of the agencies into their regulations of certain financial markets,[99] embedding them into important financial sectors while the industry remained free from direct regulation. This practice continued, with the industry being directly excluded from the landmark pieces of legislation that defined the post-Depression era.[100] In 1973, the Securities and Exchange Commission (SEC) promoted 'Rule 15c3–1' (later promulgated in 1975), which had the effect of attaching the ratings of the agencies to the Net Capital requirements that constrained brokers and dealers by way of 'haircuts'.[101]

This rule, however, subsequently introduced the first element of regulation concerning the industry directly (although to call it regulation is slightly misleading). In order to clarify which agencies' ratings were to be used when formulating the 'haircuts', the SEC attributed the term 'Nationally Recognised Statistical Rating Organisation' (NRSRO) to a small number of agencies[102] through a process known as the 'no-action letter', which entailed SEC staff not recommending 'enforcement action against broker-dealers who used the agency's ratings for purposes of complying with the net capital rule'.[103] This

98 The 'Reports' of the Credit Reporting Agencies, the precursor to the modern-day rating agency and the ratings of the very early rating agencies such as John Moody's Companies, Standard Statistics and Henry Poor's Company, were regularly the object of the judiciary's considerations in libel cases. For more on this fascinating era for the industry see Marc Flandreau and Gabriel G. Mesevage 'The Untold History of Transparency: Mercantile Agencies, the Law and the Lawyers (1851–1916)' [2014] *Enterprise and Society* 220. The vast majority of the cases held that the products of the agencies did not represent 'privileged communications' owing to the fact that the agencies could not guarantee that the details could be restricted to the purchasing subscriber. The authors detail the methods used by the agencies to circumvent this legal barrier.

99 In 1931 the Comptroller of the Currency John W. Pole began a procedural change in the Office's valuations of bonds in national bank portfolios, namely that bonds held by these banks rated below the BBB threshold could no longer be held and had to be written off, for more see Herwig P. Langohr and Patricia T. Langohr *The Rating Agencies and Their Credit Ratings: What They Are, How They Work and Why They are Relevant* (John Wiley & Sons 2010) 429; Marc Flandreau and Joanna K. Sławatyniec 'Understanding Rating Addiction: US Courts and the Origins of Rating Agencies' Regulatory Licence (1900–1940)' [2013] 20 *Financial History Review* 238.

100 The Banking Act of 1933 and the Securities and Exchange Act of 1934 only specified that the regulations of the given regulatory body (the OCC) be confirmed by those laws.

101 17 CFR 240.15c3-1; H. David Kotz, the Inspector General for the SEC from 2007 to 2012, describes a 'haircut' in relation to Rule 15c3-1 as the 'Rule that requires that a broker-dealer, when computing net capital, deduct from its net worth a certain percentage of the market value of its proprietary securities position, known as a "haircut"'; see H. David Kotz 'The SEC's Role Regarding and Oversight of Nationally Recognised Statistical Rating Organisations' [2009] *Securities and Exchange Commission: Report of the Inspector General* 458.

102 The term was declared by the SEC in the amendments to Rule 15c3-1, see *Notice of Revision Proposed Amendments to Rule 15c3-1 under the Securities Exchange Act of 1934*, Release No 34-10, 525, 1973 SEC LEXIS 2309 (29 November 1973).

103 Alcubilla and del Pozo (n 9) 6.

attribution in turn conferred the NRSRO status throughout all other US statutes and regulations where it was deemed appropriate.

This was the environment up until 2005. The emphasis then began to change for a number of reasons, although two are logically more relevant than any others. First, it has been widely noted that while rating agencies are not technically set up to detect fraudulent activity, their performance in the Enron scandal was far from desirable, particularly as up until four days before declaring bankruptcy Enron's debt was still rated as 'investment grade' by all of the major agencies.[104] When we include the involvement of the ratings industry in the Asian financial crisis of the late 1990s,[105] together with the fact that the Big Three's revenues and profits have consistently risen since the turn of the century, it is clear to see why legislators felt the need to introduce legislation to this industry for the first time.

The Credit Rating Agency Duopoly Relief Act of 2005[106] was primarily concerned with the resolving of what was recognised as a 'Catch-22' situation whereby new entrants to the industry had to be nationally recognised to gain a licence, yet could not be nationally recognised without having been granted a licence. The Duopoly Relief Act's proposed resolution was to remove the SEC's designation system and introduce a system whereby an agency that had been registered and operating for no fewer than three years could be granted NRSRO status.[107] The Duopoly Relief Act also sought to increase the capability of the SEC to interfere with the processes of the agencies, in spite of the Act's admonition of the SEC for its role in creating an artificial barrier to entry. However, this was vehemently opposed and eventually diluted in the final version of the Act so that the SEC could not interfere with aspects such as rating methodology. The Act was eventually enacted in 2006.

The Credit Rating Agency Reform Act of 2006 was enacted to 'improve ratings quality for the protection of investors and in the public interest by fostering accountability, transparency and competition in the credit rating agency industry'.[108] The CRA Reform Act recognised both the importance of the industry to the health of the economy, in what it termed its importance to 'interstate commerce' that the SEC required 'statutory authority to oversee the industry' (something which the SEC had been calling for itself).[109] It granted the SEC this authority by requiring all NRSROs to officially register with the SEC for the first time.

However, with the CRA Reform Act being retroactive, in that it was promoted as a result of findings from the Sarbanes-Oxley Act of 2002[110] (SOX), it did not

---

104 See Hill (n 92). See also Macey (n 92) for further analysis of the failings of the CRI in relation to Enron's collapse.
105 For detailed analysis on the ratings agencies' involvement in the crisis see Giovanni Ferri, Li-Gang Liu and Joseph Stiglitz 'The Procyclical Role of Rating Agencies: Evidence from the East Asian Crisis' [1999] 28 *Economic Notes* by Banca Monte dei Paschi di Siena SpA 3 335–55.
106 HR 2990.
107 Langohr and Langohr (n 99) 452.
108 120 Stat 1327.
109 ibid.
110 116 Stat 745.

prepare the regulatory environment for what was to happen just two years later. In fact, the only mention of mortgage-backed securities in the CRA Reform Act was that agencies were prohibited from threatening an issuer with a ratings downgrade or withdrawal in the event that it was not to rate the entire pool of assets (a process referred to as 'notching').[111]

The legislative framework surrounding the ratings industry was therefore strengthened by the Dodd-Frank Act, which was a wide-ranging piece of legislature enacted in direct response to the systemic crisis experienced in 2007/8. With regard to the ratings industry, the Dodd-Frank Act was particularly extensive, amending numerous elements of the Securities and Exchange Act of 1934 that had been the dominant statute up unto that point (taking into consideration numerous amendments throughout the years, of course). Just some of the highlights of the Dodd-Frank Act included removing regulatory reliance upon the ratings of the industry by way of striking references to NRSROs within laws and regulations; increasing disclosure to the SEC; increasing internal compliance structures; changes in the rules governing the relationship between agency members and issuer members; and, crucially, the removal of legislative protection regarding their liability against legal action (in that the products of the agencies do not merely represent 'journalistic opinions' unreservedly protected by the First Amendment, as was previously the case), although there are many more. The Dodd-Frank Act also instructed the SEC to introduce the Office of Credit Ratings, to 'monitor the activities' and conduct examinations of registered NRSROs to 'assess and promote compliance with statutory and Commission requirements'.[112]

The legislation covering the practices of the rating agencies is therefore administered and monitored by the regulatory body, the SEC; non-compliance with these rules may be subject to fines or a withdrawal of registration. However, the presence of potentially fraudulent activities concerning the rating agencies' role in the securitisation process[113] means that these punishments are simply not appropriate, in theory. When fraudulent activities are suspected, with there being enough evidence to indict, the US Department of Justice (DoJ) is apparently the body that enters the regulatory framework. The issue of fraudulent activity within the financial markets comes under the collaborative mandate of the Financial Fraud Enforcement Task Force,[114] with the DoJ taking the lead

---

111 See n 108.

112 Securities and Exchange Commission *About the Office of Credit Ratings* (2018).

113 The Senate committee charged with investigating the causes of the crisis referred to the word 'fraud' 157 times during their investigation across the whole spectrum of the financial arena with respect to the financial crisis, leading senior figures to question the lack of prosecutions as a result, see Judge Rakoff's comments in Frank Vogel 'Top Bankers Evaded Financial Crisis Justice – and Will Never Be Prosecuted For Their Crimes' [2014] *The Huffington Post* (14 January).

114 The Financial Fraud Enforcement Task Force was created in 2009 by President Barack Obama and consists of 20 US governmental agencies mandated to combat and prosecute financial fraud. For more information on the task force and its composition see Financial Fraud Enforcement Task Force *About the Task Force* (2015).

role in prosecuting those accused.[115] The difference in penalty is no different it appears, given the recent settlement between the DoJ and Standard & Poor's when S&P was fined a record $1.375 billion for its role in the losses of federally insured institutions;[116] Moody's reached a settlement totalling $864 million on almost identical charges.[117] During the S&P investigation, S&P had accused the US Government of indicting the agency simply because it had lowered the United States' sovereign rating, which perhaps indicates the level of effrontery that exists within the Big Three. Unfortunately, as part of the settlement S&P were allowed to deny any violations of the law, although it did sign a statement of facts acknowledging that its executives delayed implementing new models that produced more negative ratings in 2005.[118] This was accompanied by an agreed-upon apology by S&P for accusing the government of foul play.

Although this book is predominantly focusing upon the regulatory framework surrounding the ratings industry in its host jurisdiction, the United States, one international body is seemingly important to the framework in terms of setting standards that national legislators then incorporate. The International Organisation of Securities Commissions (IOSCO) is an international body which was founded in 1983 and based in Madrid, Spain. It 'brings together the world's securities regulators and is recognised as the global standard-setter for the securities sector'.[119] Before the crisis, it laid out its principles regarding the rating industry, first in 2003 with its 'Statement of Principles Regarding the Activities of the Credit Rating Agencies' and then in 2004 with its 'Code of Conduct Fundamentals for Credit Rating Agencies'.[120] IOSCO has affirmed four key principles: that rating actions should reduce information asymmetry; should be independent; should pursue transparency and disclosure; and should maintain in confidence all non-public reports.[121]

While the principles are important, it is the Code of Conduct Fundamentals that is of most interest. Revised in 2008 and again in 2015,[122] it originally prescribed that the CRAs should each 'adopt, publish and adhere to its Code of Conduct'.[123] This is demonstrable of the issues that surrounded the ratings industry prior to 2006. The Code of Conduct Fundamentals, as well as the Principles, are referred to as 'Soft Law'[124], meaning that they are not legally binding. IOSCO allows

---

115 Department of Justice *Offices of the United States Attorneys: Securities Fraud* (2015).

116 See (n 5).

117 US Department of Justice *Justice Department and State Partners Secure nearly $864 Million Settlement with Moody's Arising from Conduct in the Lead up to the Financial Crisis* (2017).

118 Viswanatha and Freifeld (n 5).

119 IOSCO *About* (2018).

120 Langohr and Langohr (n 99) 443.

121 ibid.

122 IOSCO *Code of Conduct Fundamentals for Credit Rating Agencies* (2015).

123 Langohr and Langohr (n 99) 443.

124 Chris Brummer and Rachel Loko 'The New Politics of Transatlantic Credit Rating Agency Regulation' in Tony Porter (ed.) *Transnational Financial Regulation After the Crisis* (Routledge 2014) 161.

for a great deal of discretion on behalf of the agencies in light of this fact[125] and operates a 'comply-or-explain' principle with regard to the adherence of their prescribed regulations.[126] While one could be forgiven for thinking that such a permissive framework would lead to non-compliance, the agencies were already in compliance (and even more so) with the proposed regulations before they were enacted by IOSCO,[127] which may hint at the level at which the proposals were pitched.

In the aftermath of the crisis the organisation revised their regulations with the 2008 version of the Code of Conduct Fundamentals. In that version they sought to strengthen the rules aimed at preventing or limiting conflicts of interest; the separation of analysts from the commercial side of the ratings business; and rating methodology transparency with particular regard to the separate definition of rating symbols for structured products.[128] While their regulations may be non-binding, they did have a tremendous effect on regulations that were being constructed at the time, particularly in the US and the European Union(EU). This multi-lateral approach is perhaps indicative of the complexity involved in regulating this unique industry.

Conclusion

The aim of this chapter was to provide a primer on the credit rating industry. Having established this elementary foundation, we can now embark upon more complex arguments regarding the nature of the industry and the provision of ratings, all for the purposes of introducing a reform proposal that may be able to address deficiencies in the provision of ratings and redress the industry's role in the economy for the good of the wider public. Now that we have been introduced to the rating industry and the complex relationship that exists between its agencies, the issuers of debt and the investors who invest their resources into that dynamic, the *theoretical* rationale for the existence and continued development of the agencies is perhaps clear. However, there are a number of questions raised when it comes to the *reality* of that relationship, with a number of differing influential forces at play between the parties; while on many occasions the ratings are used to protect, there are also many where the ratings are used to manipulate and exploit certain 'gaps' within the financial system. On that basis, the regulation of the industry is a fascinating study and the continued criticism of the

125 Tony Porter 'Introduction: Post-crisis Transnational Financial Regulation and Complexity in Global Governance' in Tony Porter (ed.) *Transnational Financial Regulation After the Crisis* (Routledge 2014) 14.

126 Lucia Quaglia *The European Union and Global Financial Regulation* (Oxford University Press 2014) 88.

127 Brummer and Loko (n 124) 162.

128 Quaglia (n 126) 88. Today the agencies attach additional symbols to their structured finance ratings to differentiate it from their corporate bond ratings, see Moody's (n 53) 4 for the addition of 'sf' to structured finance ratings.

regulatory framework which governs the ratings industry suggests as much. The response to the era-defining financial crisis has had a number of effects. First, it has illustrated the serious flaws that existed before the crisis. The sheer number of aspects included in the Dodd-Frank Act concerning credit rating agencies suggests that the regulatory framework pre-crisis was simply not good enough; the understanding that the industry was not *directly* regulated before 2006 is perhaps shocking in itself. Second, it has illustrated the response that is viewed by those who can affect change as being appropriate or achievable. In finding that the leading agencies conducted their business fraudulently, deceiving and failing large and important institutional investors, the fact that the only viable option available to the United States DoJ was a combined $2.239 billion fine is perhaps representative of the state of affairs, particularly when we consider that the DoJ was originally seeking to fine S&P alone $5 billion.[129] The fact that continued claims of deliberate fraudulent activity have not resulted in any criminal prosecutions is telling. What it may also represent is the parameters within which any reform proposal aimed at correcting imbalances within the Ratings Industry should be placed.

The next task for us is to address what may be termed the 'normative': to identify what role the credit rating agency *ought* to play, both in terms of what is expected from them from a number of parties *and* what they themselves profess to do. Having achieved that, we can then go on to measure the extent to which, in reality, agencies have failed to measure up to this normative expectation.

Bibliography

A.M. Best *About* (2018). www.ambest.com/about/ [accessed 18/2/18].

Abrahams, C.R. and Zhang, M. *Credit Risk Assessment: The New Lending System for Borrowers, Lenders and Investors* (John Wiley & Sons 2009).

Adams, C.F., Mathieson, D.J. and Shinasi, G. *International Capital Markets: Developments, Prospects and Key Policy Issues* (International Monetary Fund 1999).

Akseli, O. 'Was Securitisation the Culprit? Explanation of Legal Processes Behind Creation of Mortgage-backed Sub-prime Securities' in Gray, J. and Akseli, O. (eds) *Financial Regulation in Crisis? The Role of Law and the Failure of Northern Rock* (Edward Elgar Publishing 2011).

Alcubilla, R.G. and del Pozo, J.R. *Credit Rating Agencies on the Watch List: Analysis of European Regulation* (Oxford University Press 2012).

Alsakka, R. and Gwilym, O.A. 'Rating Agencies' Credit Signals: An Analysis of Sovereign Watch and Outlook' [2012] 21 *International Review of Financial Analysis* 45.

Autorité des Marchés Financiers. *AMF 2009 Report on Rating Agencies* (AMF 2010).

Baker, A. 'Restraining Regulatory Capture? Anglo-America, Crisis Politics and Trajectories of Change in Global Financial Governance' [2010] 86 *International Affairs* 3.

Bannier, C.E. and Hirsch, C.W. 'The Economic Function of Credit Rating Agencies – What Does the Watchlist Tell Us?' [2010] 34 *Journal of Banking & Finance* 12.

---

129 David Fickling 'S&P, RBS Lose Appeal of Ruling Australian Towns Misled' [2014] Bloomberg (6 June).

Baron, N.D. 'The Role of Rating Agencies in the Securitisation Process' in Kendall, L.T. and Fishman, M.J. (ed.) *A Primer on Securitization* (MIT Press 2000).

Brummer, C. and Loko, R. 'The New Politics of Transatlantic Credit Rating Agency Regulation' in Porter, T. (ed.) *Transnational Financial Regulation after the Crisis* (Routledge 2014).

Choudry, M. *An Introduction to Bond Markets* (John Wiley & Sons 2010).

Choudry, M. *Corporate Bonds and Structured Financial Products* (Butterworth-Heinemann 2004).

Collins, D. *Behaving Badly: Ethical Lessons from Enron* (Dog Ear Publishing 2006).

Credit Rating Agency Duopoly Relief Act of 2005 HR 2990.

Credit Rating Agency Reform Act of 2006 Pub. L. 109–291, 120 Stat 1327.

Crockett, A. *Conflicts of Interest in the Financial Services Industry: What Should We Do About Them?* (Centre for Economic Policy Research 2003).

Darbellay, A. *Regulating Credit Rating Agencies* (Edward Elgar 2013).

Darcy, D. 'Credit Rating Agencies and the Credit Crisis: How the "Issuer Pays" Conflict Contributed and What Regulators Might Do About It' [2009] *Columbia Business Law Review* 2.

Deacon, J. *Global Securitisation and CDOs* (John Wiley & Sons 2004).

Department of Justice *Offices of the United States Attorneys: Securities Fraud* (2015). www.justice.gov/usao/priority-areas/financial-fraud/securities-fraud [accessed 10/9/15].

Dlabay, L. and Burrow, J. *Business Finance* (Cengage Learning 2007).

Dodd-Frank Wall Street Reform and Consumer Protection Act of 2010 Pub. L. 111–203, HR 4173.

Dominion Bond Rating Service *About* (2018). www.dbrs.com/about [accessed 18/2/18].

Egan-Jones Rating Company (2018). www.egan-jones.com/ [accessed 18/2/18].

Essvale Corporation *Business Knowledge for IT in Islamic Finance* (Essvale Corporation Limited 2010).

European Securities and Markets Authority 'Credit Rating Agencies 2014 Market Share Calculations for the Purposes of Article 8d of the CRA Regulation' [2014] ESMA/2014/1583.

Evanoff, D.D. *The First Credit Market Turmoil of the 21st Century* (World Scientific 2009).

Fabozzi, F.J., Bhattacharya, A.K. and Berliner, W.S. *Mortgage-backed Securities: Products, Structuring and Analytical Techniques* (John Wiley & Sons 2010).

Ferri, G., Liu, L.G. and Stiglitz, J.E. 'The Procyclical Role of Rating Agencies: Evidence from the East Asian Crisis' [1999] 28 *Economic Notes* by Banca Monte dei Paschi di Siena SpA 3.

Fickling, D. 'S&P, RBS Lose Appeal of Ruling Australian Towns Misled' [2014] Bloomberg (6 June). www.bloomberg.com/news/articles/2014-06-05/s-p-rbs-lose-appeal-on-ruling-they-misled-australian-investors [accessed 10/09/15].

Fimalac *Fitch Ratings* (2015). www.fimalac.com/Fitch-ratings-GB.html [accessed 13/12/15].

Fimalac *Strategic Focus* (2015). www.fimalac.com/strategic-focus.html [accessed 13/12/15].

Financial Crisis Inquiry Commission *Financial Crisis Inquiry Report* (Government Printing Office 2011).

Financial Fraud Enforcement Task Force *About the Task Force* (2015). www.stopfraud.gov/sf/about-task-force [accessed 16/2/18].

Fitch Ratings *2015 Form NRSRO Annual Certification: Policies and Procedures Adopted and Implemented to Prevent the Misuse of Material, Non-public Information* (Fitch Ratings 2015).

Fitch Ratings *Rating Definitions* (2018). www.fitchratings.com/site/definitions [accessed 18/2/18].

Flandreau, M. and Mesevage, G.M. 'The Untold History of Transparency: Mercantile Agencies, the Law and the Lawyers (1851–1916)' [2014] *Enterprise and Society* 220.

Flandreau, M. and Sławatyniec, J.K. 'Understanding Rating Addiction: US Courts and the Origins of Rating Agencies' Regulatory License (1900–1940)' [2013] 20 *Financial History Review* 3.

Gartner, M., Griesbach, B. and Jung, F. 'PIGS or Lambs? The European Sovereign Debt Crisis and the Role of Rating Agencies' [2011] 17 *International Advances in Economic Research* 288.

Grossman, T. and Livingstone, J.L. *The Portable MBS in Finance and Accounting* (John Wiley & Sons 2009).

Hill, C.A. 'Regulating the Rating Agencies' [2004] 82 *Washington University Law Review* 1.

House of Lords: European Union Committee *Sovereign Credit Ratings: Shooting the Messenger?* (The Stationery Office 2011).

Hunt, J.P. 'Rating Agencies and Credit Insurance' in Baker, H.K. and Martin, G.S. (eds) *Capital Structure and Corporate Financing Decisions: Theory, Evidence and Practice* (John Wiley & Sons 2011).

Iannotta, G. *Investment Banking: A Guide to Underwriting and Advisory Services* (Springer Science & Business Media 2010).

IOSCO *About* (2018). www.iosco.org/about/?subsection=about_iosco [accessed 18/2/18].

IOSCO *Code of Conduct Fundamentals for Credit Rating Agencies* (2015). www.iosco. org/library/pubdocs/pdf/IOSCOPD482.pdf [accessed 18/2/18].

Jackson, H.E. 'The Role of Credit Rating Agencies in the Establishment of Capital Standards for Financial Institutions in a Global Economy' in Ferran, E. and Goodhart, C.A.E. (eds) *Regulating Financial Services and Markets in the 21st Century* (Hart Publishing 2001).

Kerwer, D. 'Standardising as Governance: The Case of Credit Rating Agencies' in Windhoff-Héritier, A. (ed.) *Common Goods: Reinventing European and International Governance* (Rowman & Littlefield 2002).

Koo, R.C. *The Escape from Balance Sheet Recession and the QE Trap: A Hazardous Road for the World Economy* (John Wiley & Sons 2015).

Kothari, V. *Securitization: The Financial Instrument of the Future* (John Wiley & Sons 2006).

Kotz, H.D. 'The SEC's Role Regarding and Oversight of Nationally Recognised Statistical Rating Organisations' [2009] 458 Securities and Exchange Commission: Report of the Inspector General.

Kräussl, R. 'The Impact of Sovereign Rating Changes during Emerging Market Crises' in Frenkel, M., Karmann, A. and Scholtens, B. (eds) Scholtens, B. *Sovereign Risk and Financial Crises* (Springer Science and Business Media 2013).

Langohr, H.P. and Langohr, P.T. *The Rating Agencies and Their Credit Ratings: What They Are, How They Work and Why They are Relevant* (John Wiley & Sons 2010).

Levine, R. 'The Governance of Financial Regulation: Reform Lessons from the Recent Crisis' [2012] 12 *International Review of Finance* 1.

Lumby, S. and Jones, C. *Corporate Finance: Theory & Practice* (Cengage Learning EMEA 2003).

Macey, J.R. *Corporate Governance: Promises Kept, Promises Broken* (Princeton University Press 2010).

Macey, J.R. 'A Pox on Both Your Houses: Enron, Sarbanes-Oxley and the Debate Concerning the Relative Efficiency of Mandatory Versus Enabling Rules' [2003] 81 *Washington University Law Quarterly* 329.

MacNeil, I. 'Credit Rating Agencies: Regulation and Financial Stability' in Cottier, T., Lastra, R.M., Tietje, C. and Satragno, L. (eds) *The Rule of Law in Monetary Affairs* (Cambridge University Press 2014).

Mattarocci, G. *The Independence of Credit Rating Agencies: How Business Models and Regulators Interact* (Academic Press 2014).

McClesky, S. *When Free Markets Fail: Saving the Market When It Can't Save Itself* (John Wiley & Sons 2010).

Mellios, C. and Paget-Blanc, E. 'The Impact of Economic and Political Factors on Sovereign Credit Ratings' in Kolb, R. (ed.) *Sovereign Debt: From Safety to Default* (John Wiley & Sons 2011).

Mobius, M. *Bonds: An Introduction to the Core Concepts* (John Wiley & Sons 2012).

Modigliani, F. and Miller, M.H. 'The Cost of Capital, Corporation Finance and the Theory of Investment' [1958] 48 *The American Economic Review* 3.

Moody's *About Moody's* (2018). www.moodys.com/Pages/atc.aspx [accessed 18/2/18].

Moody's *Annual Report 2016* (Moody's 2017) http://s21.q4cdn.com/431035000/files/doc_financials/annual/2016/2016-Annual-Report-vFINAL.PDF [accessed 16/2/18].

Moody's *MIS – MA Separation Policy* (Moody's 2011). www.moodys.com/sites/products/ProductAttachments/Compliance/9-9-2011/SP13372_MIS%20-%20MA%20Separation%20Policy_Sept_06_2011%20Final.pdf [accessed 18/2/18].

Moody's *Policy for Ancillary and Other Permissible Services: Compliance* (Moody's 2012). www.moodys.com/sites/products/ProductAttachments/Compliance/9-9-2011/SP13347_Policy%20for%20Ancillary%20and%20Other%20Permissible%20Services.pdf. [accessed 18/2/18].

Moody's *Rating Symbols and Definitions* (2018). www.moodys.com/Pages/amr002002.aspx [accessed 18/2/18].

Morningstar Rating (2018). www.morningstar.com [accessed 18/2/18].

Naciri, A. *Credit Rating Governance: Global Credit Gatekeepers* (Routledge 2015).

Pagano, M. and Volpin, P. 'Credit Ratings Failures: Causes and Policy Options' [2010] 25 *Economic Policy* 401–431.

Pallante, T. *From Your Wallets to Their Pockets: Understanding the Credit Crisis: Privatizing Profits and Socializing Losses* (iUniverse 2008).

Parameswaran, S. *Fundamentals of Financial Instruments: An Introduction to Stocks, Bonds, Foreign Exchange and Derivatives* (John Wiley & Sons 2011).

Partnoy, F. *Infectious Greed: How Deceit and Risk Corrupted the Financial Markets* (Profile Books 2010).

Peleg, D. *Fundamental Models in Financial Theory* (MIT Press 2014).

Porter, T. 'Introduction: Post-crisis Transnational Financial Regulation and Complexity in Global Governance' in Porter, T. (ed.) *Transnational Financial Regulation after the Crisis* (Routledge 2014).

Quaglia, L. *The European Union and Global Financial Regulation* (Oxford University Press 2014).

Queisser, M. 'The Role of Pension Funds in the Stabilisation of the Domestic Financial Sector' in Brooks, D.H. and Queisser, M. (eds) *Financial Liberalisation in Asia: Analysis and Prospects* (OECD Publishing 1999).

Ramirez, S.A. *Lawless Capitalism: The Subprime Crisis and the Case for an Economic Rule of Law* (New York University Press 2014).

Rhee, R.J 'On Duopoly and Compensation Games in the Credit Rating Industry' [2013] 108 *Northwestern University Law Review* 86–138.

Rodriguez, L.J. 'The Credit Rating Agencies: From Cartel Busters to Cartel Builders' in Niskanen, W.A. *After Enron: Lessons for Public Policy* (Rowman & Littlefield 2007).

Rona-Tas, A. and Hiss, S. 'The Art of Corporate and The Science of Consumer Credit Rating' in Lounsbury, M. and Hirsch, P.M. (eds) *Markets on Trial: The Economic Sociology of the U.S. Financial Crisis, Part 1* (Emerald Group Publishing 2010).

S&P Capital IQ *Information You Need* (2015). www.capitaliq.com/home/what-we-offer/information-you-need.aspx [accessed 11/10/15].

Salter, M.S. *Innovation Corrupted: The Origins and Legacy of Enron's Collapse* (Harvard University Press 2008).

Sarbanes-Oxley Act of 2002 116 Stat. 745.

Securities and Exchange Commission *Office of Credit Ratings – About* (2018). www.sec.gov/about/offices/ocr/ocr-about.shtml [accessed 18/2/18].

Siddaiah, T. *Financial Services* (Pearson Education India 2011).

Sinclair, T.J. 'Bond-rating Agencies and Coordination in the Global Political Economy' in Cutler, A.C., Haufler, V. and Porter, T. (eds) *Private Authority and International Affairs* (SUNY Press 1999).

Standard & Poor's *Confidentiality, Conflicts and Firewall: Policy Statement* (2017). www.standardandpoors.com/en_US/delegate/getPDF?articleId=1903360&type=COMMENTS&subType=REGULATORY [accessed 18/2/18].

Standard & Poor's *Standard & Poor's Ratings Definitions* (2017). www.standardandpoors.com/en_US/web/guest/article/-/view/sourceId/504352 [accessed 18/2/18].

Standard & Poor's *What We Do* (2018). www.spratings.com/en_US/what-we-do [accessed 18/2/18].

Stebler, R. 'Performance and Consistency of Credit Ratings in Structured Finance' in Westerfeld, S., Wullschleger, B. and Gantenbein, P. (eds) *Proceedings of the Second International Conference on Credit Analysis and Risk Management* (Cambridge Scholars Publishing 2014).

Trueck, S. and Rachev, S.T. *Rating Based Modeling of Credit Risk: Theory and Application of Migration Matrices* (Academic Press 2009).

Tulsian, P.C. and Pandey, V. *Business Organisation and Management* (Pearson Education India 2002).

United States Department of Justice *Justice Department and State Partners Secure Nearly $864 Million Settlement With Moody's Arising From Conduct in the Lead up to the Financial Crisis* (2017). www.justice.gov/opa/pr/justice-department-and-state-partners-secure-nearly-864-million-settlement-moody-s-arising [accessed 16/2/18].

United States Department of the Treasury *The Financial Crisis Response: In Charts* (2012).

United States Government Accountability Office *Financial Regulatory Reform: Financial Crisis Losses and Potential Impacts of the Dodd-Frank Act* (GAO 2013).

United States Senate, Permanent Subcommittee on Investigations *Wall Street and the Financial Crisis: Anatomy of a Financial Collapse* (GPO 2011).

Van Gestel, T. and Baesens, B. *Credit Risk Management: Basic Concepts: Financial Risk Components, Rating Analysis, Models, Economic and Regulatory Capital* (Oxford University Press 2008).

Viswanatha, A. and Freifeld, K. 'S&P reaches $1.5 billion deal with U.S. states over crisis-era ratings' [2015] Reuters (3 February). www.reuters.com/article/us-s-p-settlement-idUSKBN0L71C120150203 [accessed 6/7/15].

Vogel, F. 'Top Bankers Evaded Financial Crisis Justice – and Will Never Be Prosecuted For Their Crimes' [2014] *The Huffington Post* (14 January). www.huffingtonpost.com/frank-vogl/rakoff-wall-street-prosecutions_b_4589648.html [accessed 6/9/15].

Yoon, A. 'Total Global Losses from Financial Crisis: $15 Trillion' [2012] *The Wall Street Journal* (1 October). https://blogs.wsj.com/economics/2012/10/01/total-global-losses-from-financial-crisis-15-trillion/ [accessed 16/3/18].

Zandi, M. *Financial Shock: Global Panic and Government Bailouts – How We Got Here and What Must Be Done to Fix It* (FT Press 2009).

2 The divergence between the *actual* and the *desired*

Introduction

This chapter will begin by doing two things. First, it will establish what certain parties who are irrevocably tied to the agencies *would be reasonably expected to desire from the agencies*. It is worth pausing for a moment here to make this point as clear as is possible: the first half of the chapter describes the desires of issuers, investors and the state, as if they were purely acting how one may reasonably expect them to, almost in the mode of a survey. For example, when we see the desired situation for the state, it is entirely reasonable that the state would want to advance the fortunes of society and not actively seek to harm it, with the state being the manifestation of society. While these *quintessential* positions are admittedly contentious in certain areas (e.g. *how* the state should seek to advance the fortunes of society may be different to different people), it is a useful foundation for us to show the *divergence* that exists with regard to the ratings industry. That divergence will be demonstrated when we go through *The Actual Situation*, because we shall see that nearly all of the parties act in a very different manner to how one may reasonably believe that they should; this, then, provides us with the basis to assess whether legislation considers the *actual* performance and character of the parties or whether it looks to bring about the *desired* situation while ignoring the *actual*, which will inevitably result in no development at all.

With what is to be reasonably expected of these parties being established in the first three subsections, the second aim of *The Desired Situation* will then be met. The *normative* aspect of this chapter actually lies in the subsection *'Public Interest' or 'Public Protection'?*, because all that went before it (i.e. the desired situation for issuers, investors and the state, all essentially form a survey of what any rational thinker may expect of each party). However, in the second half of the chapter, the focus will be on declaring what should be the way forward for economic reform in general. This takes the form of discussing what is meant by the term 'public interest', because it is a concept that is easily manipulated to serve certain people to the detriment of the public at large. So, with that in mind, the call will be for a change in sentiment with regard to economic reform, so that the notion of 'public protection' is placed at the forefront of legislators' thinking to safeguard the most vulnerable in society from the iniquities of the financial sector.

Essentially, the point of this chapter is not to establish how far the agencies have deviated from what they *ought* to be doing in order to paint a fatalistic picture. The point is that to have any chance of implementing impactful change for the protection of the public we must understand how powerful, entrenched and callous the agencies are; we must understand our point of departure if we are to arrive at our desired destination.

The *desired* situation

Before we proceed, the point established in the introduction to this chapter must be repeated. What follows, in terms of the desired situation for issuers, investors and the state, is purely *what one may reasonably expect these parties to desire*, given the pressures that affect their outlook (i.e. investors want returns on their investment and the state wants to reduce its costs while maintaining economic safety). Ultimately, it will help our understanding of what can be done to reform the agencies if we start by understanding the environment within which they operate; as these three parties represent the most important aspects of the environment to the largest rating agencies, understanding what they *ought* to expect will show us how the agencies *ought* to act, which is the foundation required for developing this notion of there being a divergence that needs to be incorporated into rating agency reform.

The desired *situation for issuers*

In the first chapter it was established that credit rating agencies serve a number of important functions with regard to the advancement of an issuer. Initially, we saw how companies would need to engage with credit rating agencies to enter the capital markets. Just one reason why a company would want to enter the capital markets in order to raise funds to meet financial requirements is because it represents a viable alternative to issuing stock in the company which, as a system of financing operations, has a number of potentially undesired consequences.[1] Additionally, once the company has decided that it will attempt to raise capital through the issuance of bonds rather than stocks, it requires the rating of a rating agency to signal its capacity to repay its obligations and, in turn, lower its rate of interest upon its payments to the creditor.[2]

This issue of reducing the interest payments upon its debt is obviously a crucial aim for any company issuing bonds in the capital market. If we take the quintessential issuer and analyse how it would ideally look at the capital markets, then it is reasonable to come to the conclusion that the aim would be to signal the capacity of the company to repay its debts to the entirety of the marketplace and thus allow it to have maximum exposure to the marketplace, which would theoretically have the effect of driving down its interest payments due to the wide

1 See *The Industry: What It Does* (n 45).
2 ibid.

variety of potential creditors. Therefore, what is referred to as 'Signalling Theory' is an important aspect for us to consider.

When we analysed the concept of 'information asymmetry' earlier it was done under the guise of the credit rating agencies reducing that asymmetry for investors, in terms of providing a rating that simplified and standardised complex financial information about issuing companies and their bonds.[3] Synergistically, the same role of the ratings industry positively affects the issuer. While reducing informational asymmetry allows investors to theoretically invest with greater confidence in the levels of risk they are undertaking, it also allows issuers access to investors and allows them to drive their interest payments down depending upon the quality of rating they can attract. Rousseau notes that the sheer presence of a high-quality credit rating – AAA for example – denotes not only the capacity of the company to repay its debt, but its position within the economy as the high cost of obtaining a rating for low-standard issuers makes it highly likely that only a large and successful entity is able to achieve such a high rating in the first place;[4] there are very few companies in the world who hold such high credit ratings.[5]

So, 'Signalling Theory' basically details the process whereby issuers who have good credit can communicate this fact to investors to receive a higher market valuation.[6] This is done by issuers divulging sensitive information to a third party (the rating agency) who can then 'transform' this into information which reveals the *implications* of that information without revealing its detailed *content*.[7] This process relies upon both publicly available information and the amount of detail divulged by the issuing company; it is usual practice that the Investment Relations Officer of a given firm will have a very close relationship with the rating agency and will provide detailed information while also communicating why certain decisions have been taken by the management of that organization.[8]

There is, however, a danger for issuers when issuing new debt instruments, which is why it is extremely important for them that reputable and trusted rating agencies rate their issuances. It is important for a number of reasons. First, the cost of obtaining a rating is particularly high. Second, excessive issuance by a company has the potential to 'portray' an air of financial difficulty or the need of the business to avoid traditional financing options (i.e. financing from banks with (theoretically) strict lending practices).[9] So, reducing the cost (by way of reduced

---

3 Mattarocci (n 8) 1.
4 Stéphane Rousseau 'Enhancing the Accountability of Credit Rating Agencies: The Case for a Disclosure-based Approach' [2005] *Capital Markets Institute* 8.
5 At the time of writing only three American-based companies hold AAA ratings: Johnson & Johnson; Microsoft; and ExxonMobile Corp, see Mark Morelli 'These 3 Companies Have Debt Rated "AAA" But Not All Are Buys' [2015] Seekingalpha.com
6 Yair Listokin and Benjamin Taibleson 'If You Misrate, Then You Lose: Improving Credit Rating Accuracy Through Incentive Compensation' [2010] 27 *Yale Journal on Regulation* 96.
7 Gianluca Mattarocci *The Independence of Credit Rating Agencies: How Business Models and Regulators Interact* (Academic Press 2014)1.
8 Steven M. Bragg *Running an Effective Relations Department: A Comprehensive Guide* (John Wiley & Sons 2010) 169.
9 Mattarocci (n 8) 18.

interest payments) by obtaining a high rating from a reputable agency alleviates any concerns regarding the motive for issuing in the first place, thus making their securities more marketable.[10]

As one can plainly see, the *desired* situation with regard to the issuer is irrevocably dependent upon trust. Issuers rely upon the trust that investors have in the capability of rating agencies to produce impartial financial information, whereas the rating agencies must rely upon the issuers to reveal the correct (and full) information so that they can formulate accurate ratings, thus preserving the agencies' reputation. However, this understanding of what is *desired* is just that; in reality the situation is widely different, as we shall see in The *Actual* Situation below.

The desired *situation for investors*

As the majority of investors, of varying levels of capability, have expansive portfolios, the inclusion of highly rated investments allow them to balance their portfolios so that riskier ventures are counterbalanced by the low-yield but highly dependable interest payments accrued from highly rated debt issuances.[11] This concept of providing relative security for an investor was repeated when we assessed the notion of 'agency'. In analysing how dispersed shareholders (and stakeholders) of large institutional investors (e.g. pension funds and mutual funds) sought to control the actions of their managers, we saw how shareholders utilise credit ratings to impose restrictions on the investment opportunities with which managers can engage.[12] Investors can also use 'rating triggers' to determine a point at which the issuing company must forfeit the original agreement and settle what is owed with the creditor. We learned that the reason for this was to protect the creditor against an issuing company whose ability to repay its debt is tumbling (i.e. once the debtor falls below a certain level (rating), repayment (or a restructured agreement) is put into effect).[13]

It should already be clear that, for the investor, credit ratings are an intrinsic part of their operations. Ultimately, investors *desire* a number of things, arguably perfectly reasonable things, from the rating agency. First, they require impartiality in order to be able to trust the ratings of the agencies; as was asserted above, trust is the underlying principle for the efficient administration of this entire process. They also require transparency[14] so as to be able to check the workings of these third parties – who they do not pay for the service –to maintain a level of trust to keep the process going. They also require timely information, as the entire system is predicated upon the understanding that 'securities are traded quickly'.[15]

---

10 Neil D. Baron 'The Role of Rating Agencies in the Securitisation Process' in Leon T. Kendall and Michael J. Fishman (ed.) *A Primer on Securitization* (MIT Press 2000) 83.

11 See *The Industry: What It Does* (n 46).

12 ibid (n 63).

13 ibid (n 70).

14 Thummuluri Siddaiah *Financial Services* (Pearson Education India 2011) 260.

15 Baron (n 10).

They require all of these aspects mainly to assist them with their aim of making the *right* investment for their operation. What is right for the investor and how they will utilise the ratings produced by the agencies is dependent upon their capability; this is often referred to as the difference between a 'sophisticated' and an 'unsophisticated' or 'retail' investor.[16] Retail investors will invariably combine the ratings of the agencies with other statistical features, such as the rate of return, to select the best investment opportunities for their position.[17] Mattarocci notes that 'the user considers the mean default rate related to the rating class and computes the expected return corrected for the default risk for each available instrument'.[18] For sophisticated investors, the analytical role of the ratings is supplementary; it is often the case that these investors have specialised and dedicated offices charged with examining risk within the marketplace (often to a greater extent than the rating agencies themselves).[19]

It is worth pausing here to consider an exercise, which contemplates what the situation would be if credit rating agencies did not exist. Although, there are many factors which make this exercise theoretical, it is still worthwhile to imagine the theoretical role of the agencies. Husisian argues that if rating agencies did not exist, then the capital markets would be plagued with high information costs. These would inhibit action from investors which is, of course, the driving force of the modern economy. He continues by stating that to find profit opportunities within the capital markets

> the investor must spend time and money evaluating the riskiness and potential return of various investment opportunities. The returns from investing in research, however, are likely to be too small to justify much investment. The returns are small because the debenture landscape is so cluttered with differing issues that risk evaluation is very difficult.[20]

This alludes to the fact that the rating agencies, in a perfect scenario, act to facilitate the fluidity of the capital markets, by allowing investors to participate in the process by making it economically viable to do so.

Credit rating agencies are clearly important to the investor. However, when we analyse the perfect model, this raises questions about how important rating agencies are for sophisticated investors, although that analysis is not appropriate for this section. Yet, ideally, they are vital to facilitating the fluidity of the marketplace. If we then consider that modern society is intrinsically attached to the market and its fortunes, the importance of the rating agencies becomes

---

16 The differentiation between the two categories is far more complex than this simple understanding and also has a long legal history. For more on the legal history of the differentiation and its impact, see Jennifer G. Hill 'Images of the Shareholder – Shareholder Power and Shareholder Powerlessness' in Jennifer G. Hill and Randall S. Thomas (eds) *Research Handbook on Shareholder Power* (Edward Elgar Publishing 2015) 58.

17 Mattarocci (n 7) 11.

18 ibid.

19 ibid.

20 Gregory Husisian 'What Standard of Care Should Govern the World's Shortest Editorials? An Analysis of Bond Rating Agency Liability' [1989–90] 75 *Cornell Law Review* 410.

abundantly clear. It is this notion of structural (and therefore societal) importance that forms the next part of this section.

The desired *situation for the state*

These two pillars of modern society – the issuer and the investor – are clearly
important for us to examine with regard both to the financial system and the
conduct of the rating agencies. However, the role of the state in facilitating and
now *unreservedly* protecting, the economy makes it perhaps the most important
element to consider. We saw in Chapter 1 how the marketplace requires constant attention and how any delays with regard to information or structurally
impactful decisions can cost vast sums of money for interested parties (and sometimes parties that do not have a direct stake in these financial dealings, such as the
general public).[21]

The assumed and attributed position of the state as the lender of last resort
(LOLR) makes the state's position the most difficult, the most dynamic and
the most important. Langley succinctly suggests that 'it is only because of
(state) sovereignty that the endemic crisis tendencies of finance do not realise
the ultimate collapse of money, markets and capitalism'.[22] If were are to accept
this understanding, then it is clear that we must acknowledge the potential
effect that this dynamic may have upon the likelihood of establishing impactful
reforms which may protect the public more, as opposed to facilitating economic
movement (many would argue that these are the same thing); this understanding
raises the question of where the state's priority lies.

The events of the financial crisis made it abundantly clear that the maintenance
of the market is the absolute priority. This relates to the widely held notion that
a wider social benefit will be the natural result of the maintenance of the market,
which is often cited as the rationale for intervening in financial matters, usually at
a great cost to society (e.g. quantitative easing leading to austerity measures).[23]

When discussing the notion of the 'state' and the 'system', it is very difficult
not to move into the direction of theories concerned with capitalism. The intricacies of the social system referred to as capitalism are extraordinarily complex and
require much more analysis than we can afford here. Yet, one line of reasoning
may allow us to move into assessing why the credit rating industry has become
so prominent. Tae-Hee Jo suggests, with regard to his systemically centred analysis of business cycles, that business enterprise and the state actively pursue the
same goal – 'the stability of the economic system and the existing social order'.[24]

21 See *Signalling to the Market* (n 83).
22 Paul Langley *Liquidity Lost: The Governance of the Global Financial Crisis* (Oxford University Press
   2015) 19.
23 ibid 16.
24 Tae-Hee Jo 'A Heterodox Microfoundation of Business Cycles' in Joëlle J. Leclaire, Tae-Hee Jo
   and Jane Knodell (eds) *Heterodox Analysis of Financial Crisis and Reform: History, Politics and
   Economics* (Edward Elgar Publishing 2011) 114.

As this suggests a common goal, it is interesting that he then notes that 'the state regulates markets primarily in order to protect private enterprises from the macro-uncertainty and -instability'.[25] If this is so, that the state's highest priority is the protection of private enterprise, then the natural question to ask in light of this understanding is how would the state go about performing such a vital task? There are two issues here that will move us towards our analysis of the credit rating industry. First, while this society is undoubtedly defined by the market, there are other important elements of society that the state must give its attention to, with societal welfare, threats to its citizens' safety (e.g. from terrorism) or dynamics between sovereign states being good examples. The second issue is that, as we have already seen above, the onset of the credit rating industry's dramatic rise coincided with the explosion of the capital markets in the 1970s.[26] This explosion had the effect of increasing the macro- and micro-instability within the system due to the rapid increase in participants within the financial system (which increased the systemic exposure to risk) and the amounts being traded (which increased the severity of that risk and the consequences of failure).[27] These factors contributed to a lessening of the state's capability to fulfil its protectionist obligations.

Therefore, with its capability to protect the system by using its own means declining because of external factors like those mentioned above, the state responded reasonably (in theory) by seeking to outsource these responsibilities to specialist market actors (in the same way investors would constrain mutual fund managers). In continuing our analysis in the section from within the *quint-essential* parameters set earlier, there are a number of valid reasons for why the state would want to recruit and incorporate specialist third parties into the financial stability framework. If we use the example of the credit rating industry, the ability to define the parameters that certain financial sectors can operate within (as we saw earlier with the 'haircut' requirement for broker-dealers[28]) is arguably 'understandable from a public policy standpoint'.[29] It is even more understandable if we were to accept, as the House of Lords suggests,[30] that credit ratings are considered: to be easy to use; easily accessible; independent; relatively stable; have a successful track record; and are ultimately non-discriminatory in their publications to the market. This ability to set and maintain prudential standards[31] without bearing the entirety of the cost related to that role is obviously an attractive proposition for the state.

---

25 ibid 117.
26 See *The Industry: What It Does* (n 47).
27 Jo (n 24) 117.
28 See *A Snapshot of the Regulatory Framework* (n 103).
29 House of Lords *Banking Supervision and Regulation: 2nd Report of Session 2008–09, Vol. 2: Evidence* (The Stationery Office 2009) 77.
30 ibid.
31 Anjali Kumar, Terry M. Chuppe and Paula Perttunen *The Regulation of Non-bank Financial Institutions: The United States, the European Union and Other Countries, Parts 63–362* (World Bank Publications 1997) 17.

The act of outsourcing this responsibility also confers a crucial responsibility upon the market actor. With reference to the credit rating industry (as with the accounting industry, to provide just one other example), this role is commonly referred to as being a 'gatekeeper'. In outsourcing this responsibility, the state requires or at least *desires* that the rating industry performs a certain number of tasks. In discussing the gatekeeping function of the credit rating industry, Mohammed Hemraj asserts that, essentially, the role is that of a decision maker, in that 'it is a gatekeeper who decides which information will go forward and which will not. Gatekeeping is, therefore, a "process of culling and crafting countless bits of information into the limited number of messages that reach people every day" … this process determines not only which information is selected, but also what the content and nature of the message, such as news [or ratings], will be'.[32] Similarly, Coffee defines the gatekeeper as 'some form of outside or independent watchdog or monitor – someone who screens out flaws or defects or who verifies compliance with standards or procedures'.[33].

It is worth noting that the state does not just have one financial gatekeeper in its arsenal; different gatekeepers have different tasks which, theoretically, should all contribute to a tightly knit regulatory framework that is much less expensive for the state to coordinate than to shoulder the responsibility itself. For example, credit rating agencies are continually at pains to declare that their purpose is not to detect fraud within organisations;[34] that role in the framework has been afforded to the accounting industry. So, while rating agencies are not expected to detect fraud, the state does *desire* that they provide market-based verification to assist investors when making allocation decisions,[35] in addition to providing benchmarks for certain market actors. However, with that trusted position comes a certain power, which usually stems from the penalties that arise from non-compliance with that particular gatekeeper. For example, should an agency withhold its cooperation or consent,[36] then not only would an issuer's interest payments rise with a lower rating, but larger investors cannot even attempt to purchase debt that is not of a certain category of rating. This means that a large amount of capital is not available to poor-quality issuing companies.

Their position as a gatekeeper is just one element to why rating agencies are considered to be very important by the state. When we consider the state's mandate as discussed earlier, namely that they must seek to protect and advance the system, then the reasons for *desiring* that the agencies perform their tasks to the best of their ability are clear and reasonable. Their verifying role, when combined

---

32 Mohammed Hemraj *Credit Rating Agencies: Self-regulation, Statutory Regulation and Case Law Regulation in the United States and European Union* (Springer 2015) 4.

33 John C. Coffee *Gatekeepers: The Professions and Corporate Governance* (Oxford University Press 2006) 2.

34 See *The Industry: What It Does* (n 60).

35 Mads Andenas and Iris H.Y. Chiu *The Foundations and Future of Financial Regulation: Governance for Responsibility* (Routledge 2013) 193.

36 Coffee (n 162).

with the availability of their products, mean that they are vital in allowing access to the capital markets (this is where the term 'gatekeeper' is directly appropriate), allowing a wide range of entities access to the markets. This is touted as increasing both the fluidity and the health of the economy.[37] The tendency to promote the perceived relationship between economic health and societal health makes this aspect of the rating agencies' role very important indeed.

Mattarocci notes that perhaps the key role within the economy for the credit rating agencies is that the information they produce has the theoretical effect of increasing the overall amount of information within the marketplace more generally, while also making the prices of financial instruments more consistent with the real risk-return profile of the issuer and issue,[38] thus reducing the potential for any price imbalance within the marketplace. This notion of balance is something that one may rationally expect the state to pursue in its management of the economy.

Yet, a surface level analysis does not reveal the issues that arise with this arrangement. For example, rating agencies must be independent to be justifiably considered as an acceptable form of what has come to be termed 'quasi-governance'.[39] This, then, raises the questions 'If they are not (at least perceived to be) independent, then does that affect the authority of the state?' and 'If the state's authority is reduced by outsourcing, who is then influencing the direction of the market?'

The state, therefore, has a number of factors that it should be considering, all of which *should* translate to the protection *and* advancement of society. However, the *protection* of society and the *advancement* of society are not the same thing. For far too long it has been the prevailing theory that if the market is prepared favourably for advancement, then society will also analogously advance. Now, before we discuss the *actual* situation with regard to investors and the state in relation to the rating industry, it is important to address this notion of 'public interest'.Coming to a clear understanding as to what one means by this, in terms of society overall, allows for the reasons for one's actions to become clear.

'Public interest' or 'public protection'?

It is widely held that the agencies' output and the regulation of them, is in the 'public interest'.[40] Yet, if we apply a critical lens to this understanding, then the question must be what connotations does the attachment of that term have upon the effectiveness of regulating such an important part of the financial system?

37 James Ciment 'Credit Rating Agencies' in James Ciment (ed.) *Booms and Busts: An Encyclopedia of Economic History from Tulipmania of the 1630s to the Global Financial Crisis of the 21st Century* (Routledge 2015) 192.
38 Mattarocci (n 8) 18.
39 Andenas and Chiu (n 35).
40 Herwig P. Langohr and Patricia T. Langohr *The Rating Agencies and Their Credit Ratings: What They Are, How They Work and Why They are Relevant* (John Wiley & Sons 2010) 429.

When legislators consider what may be in the public interest, within what framework are they operating? It is argued here that any decision that is taken by legislators or any of the powerful for that matter, are done so within the parameters of the marketplace, rather than society. The effect of this is that we are left exclusively valuing the *measurable*, rather than regulating for the *valuable*.[41]

While this view may be contentious, given the dominance of the market upon everyday life, it is certainly not original. In describing the reasons why this market-centric view is problematic, Feintuck states that 'the frame of reference of the market is too narrow to encompass properly a range of social and political values which are established in liberal democracies and can be seen as constitutional in nature'.[42] It is absolutely essential that we remember that the economy is not a natural phenomenon, to which we are all indebted. As Sunstein correctly declares: 'markets should be understood as a legal construct, to be evaluated on the basis of whether they promote human interests, rather than as part of nature and the natural order...'.[43]

This dominance of the market ideal on everyday consciousness, at least in the modern context, has been attributed to a clear alteration in thought that blossomed in the 1980s, shared between the British Government headed by Margaret Thatcher and the US Administration led by Ronald Reagan. This ideal of economic efficiency driving regulatory policy[44] is the foundation to what Feintuck views as the purposefully created divergence between the interests of the *citizen* as a consumer and the interests of the citizen as a *consumer*;[45] this helps us to understand the point made earlier regarding what one may mean when they say they are making decisions with the 'public interest' in mind – is it in their interests as a consumer or a citizen? The market-centred theories that underpin this movement are many, as we shall see later,[46] and they are dominant, but they are not absolute.[47] What appears to be the case is a clear theoretical and philosophical divide between those who seek to incorporate fundamental human values into society and those who perceive there to be little need to focus on such large-scale endeavours, following the sentiment declared by Margaret Thatcher that there is 'no such thing as society'.[48]

---

41 Mike Feintuck 'Regulatory Rationales Beyond the Economic: In Search of the Public Interest' in Robert Baldwin, Martin Cave and Martin Lodge (eds) *The Oxford Handbook of Regulation* (Oxford University Press 2012) 45.

42 Feintuck (n 41) 39.

43 Cass Sunstein *Free Markets and Social Justice* (Oxford University Press 1999) 5. Linarelli concurs, noting that 'Financial markets are, however, totally of our doing. We create them. Our social practices and our actions determine who gets what, who loses and who gains'; see John Linarelli 'Luck, Justice and Systemic Financial Risk' [2015] 34 *Journal of Applied Philosophy* 331.

44 Cento Veljanovski 'Economic Approaches to Regulation' in Robert Baldwin, Martin Cave and Martin Lodge (eds) *The Oxford Handbook of Regulation* (Oxford University Press 2012) 25.

45 Feintuck (n 41) 59.

46 See *Deregulation – A False Diagnosis*.

47 For just some scholars who oppose the market-based view see Feintuck (n 41); Mark Sagoff *Price, Principle and the Environment* (Cambridge University Press 2004); Sunstein (n 43).

48 Feintuck (n 41) 60.

For the viewpoints that *are* concerned with the notion of society, there are two interesting concepts for our discussion. The first is the notion of 'steward-ship' which, admittedly, is usually attributed to environmental concerns. As Lucy and Mitchell tell us, the concept is derived from religion, focusing on the Bible, with the concept stemming from the relationship between man and God in rela-tion to the Earth. The notion of 'stewardship' has been enlarged from this initial understanding of man having absolute domain over the resources of the planet (i.e. '... have dominion over the fish in the sea and over the fowl in the air and over every living thing that moveth upon the earth') to one where man is not despotic, but rather seeks to act responsibly and, rather than do it for God, does it for the wider human community.[49] Feintuck correctly attaches the notion of 'future generations' to this concept of stewardship,[50] which is particularly relevant to the discussion here; we must consider more than just what we can see and that includes future generations as well as those who are cast adrift by society because of destructive finance.

This cross-generational sentiment is both the greatest strength of the ideal of stewardship and yet its greatest weakness.[51] It is a weakness for the advancement of the ideal because it is arguably impossible to come to a consensus regarding what future generations may require or even what they may want. It is for this reason that the call here to eradicate fundamental social ills that are the result of destructive finance are so basic; it was noted earlier in the introduction that one cannot have absolute knowledge regarding what is best for everyone but, problems such as homelessness or poverty, are so basically inexcusable that any calls for them to remain would make for fascinating reading.

The second viewpoint that *is* concerned with society is one aspect of 'public interest' which is usually classified in a trio of accounts. The three accounts of the public interest – the preponderance, the common interest and the unitary account – are all understandings developed by Virginia Held in 1970,[52] which address the notion of public interest and how to satisfy it. However, for the purposes of this discussion, we will focus mainly on the *Unitary Account*; the pre-ponderance account describes that the public interest is 'equivalent to the greatest sum of individual interests',[53] while the common interest account is defined by the understanding that 'what is in the public interest is *always* in one's individual interests (although the reverse is not necessarily true).[54]

The unitary account, however, holds that the public interest 'can be formulated without recourse to individual interests at all and, second, that the assertion that something is in the public interest is an assertion that it is

---

49 William N. R. Lucy and Catherine Mitchell 'Replacing Private Property: The Case for Stewardship' [1996] 55 *The Cambridge Law Journal* 583.
50 Feintuck (n 41) 58.
51 Lucy and Mitchell (n 49) 590.
52 Virginia Held *The Public Interest and Individual Interests* (Basic Books 1970) 42.
53 Lucy and Mitchell (n 49) 588.
54 ibid 591.

universally morally right or good'.[55] Also, the unitary account differs to that of the others because it recognises that determining what is in the 'public interest' is a purely normative endeavour. Lucy and Mitchell continue by stating that the account holds that there can be no conflict between individual interest and the public interest; in the case of conflict, one must be mistaken.[56] It is here, though, that the potential problems with this mode of thought begin to appear because, as Held identifies, 'to assert that someone involved in such conflicts is always misguided or that one of any two conflicting positions must be evil, is to close one's sensitivities to the actualities of human affairs'.[57] This idea of an ideal being in the interests of the public, based on a moral footing and that conflicting ideas must be 'wrong', has a long history; it has been associated with some of the most revered philosophers like Plato, Aristotle and Hegel. However, it has also been (rightly) associated with the Soviet Union and Nazi Germany as the basis for their persecutions of non-conformists or those classified as 'different' and to the Church with its persecution of female healers (witches), to provide just three examples.[58]

The call here, that we should consider eradicating a number of social ills when deliberating on economic reform, is most likely classified as falling within the unitary account. The examples given above of Nazi Germany, the Soviet Union and the Church, are excellent examples of the power of man to warp the notion of the public interest, which is why the call here is so basic, perhaps even rudimentary. The notion that we must strive to eliminate the connection between financial crises and social ills like homelessness, suicide, mass unemployment, family breakdown and even cancer-related deaths,[59] is *almost* impenetrable to the iniquities of man. Therefore, it is claimed here that we must operate on the basis of reducing the social damage that destructive finance causes and develop a reform proposal to assist in that aim – it is perhaps better to think of this ideal as 'public protectionism', rather than striving for what is in the 'public interest'.

---

55 ibid 594.
56 ibid.
57 Held (n 52) 156.
58 Mike Saks *Professions and the Public Interest: Medical Power, Altruism and Alternative Medicine* (Routledge 2005) 37–9.
59 For details on the links between the financial crisis and these social ills see: (Homelessness) Aoife Nolan *Economic and Social Rights after the Global Financial Crisis* (Cambridge University Press 2014); (Suicides) Aaron Reeves, Martin McKee and David Stuckler 'Economic Suicides in the Great Recession in Europe and North America' [2014] *The British Journal of Psychiatry* 246; (Mass Unemployment) United Nations *The Global Economic and Financial Crisis: Regional Impacts, Responses and Solutions* (United Nations Publications 2009) 7; OECD *OECD Employment Outlook 2015* (OECD 2015); (Family Breakdown) Brian Nolan, Wiemer Salverda, Daniele Checchi, Ive Marx, Abigail McKnight, István G. Tóth and Herman Van de Werfhorst *Changing Inequalities and Social Impacts in Rich Countries: Thirty Countries' Experiences* (Oxford University Press 2014) 722; (Cancer Mortality) Mahiben Maruthappu, Johnathan Watkins, Aisyah M. Noor, Callum Williams, Raghib Ali, Richard Sullivan, Thomas Zeltner and Rifat Atun 'Economic Downturns, Universal Health Coverage and Cancer Mortality in High-income and Middle-income Countries, 1990–2010: A Longitudinal Analysis' [2016] *The Lancet* (online, 25 May).

The *actual* situation

As was stated in the concluding remarks of the last section, the issue here is that this 'perfect' situation is idealistic. What is *desired* by these parties is proving to be unachievable in the real world. Nevertheless, this has not stopped the incessant quest to attain it, which is the reason why this chapter plays an important role in communicating the idea of 'realignment'. In this section we will see that the *actual* version of events is plagued with imbalances that warp the resulting outputs. Even a cursory analysis of the *actual* will reveal that the divergence between the *actual* and *desired* is so far apart that it makes the concept of attempting to achieve the *desired* without addressing the *actual* a clearly fruitless endeavour. The reasons for this wide divergence will be covered in the next chapter; for now, there are some important aspects of the *actual* which need to be clarified before we progress any further.

So, certain elements need to be clarified in light of this analytical framework that will constrain the following section. First, not all investors partook in the pre-crisis securitisation system that was at fault so, in that sense, the issues raised within this section are not absolutely representative of the relationship between 'the investor' and 'the agency'. Similarly, the Residential Mortgage-Backed Securities (RMBS) market was dominated by only a few issuers, which had the effect of changing the dynamic between 'the issuer' and 'the agency'.[60] In this sense more specifically, the relationship between the issuers of asset-backed securities and the agency during the build-up to the financial crisis is not precisely representative of the usual relationship between the issuer and the agency. What makes the assessment in this section relevant, despite these issues regarding representativeness, is that the financial crisis is, in itself, representative of a situation that can cause systemic damage, which has obvious benefits for normative analyses. It also serves to highlight, in an extreme fashion, the disposition of the rating agencies (the term 'Big Three' has been purposefully omitted here as (allegedly) other rating agencies also partook in this systemic abuse of their position).[61]

Therefore, even though there have been claims that the rating agencies can, on occasion, even act against the issuer, by not factoring the constitution of the creditor in the arrangement[62] into their analysis, it will be more appropriate to

60 Lawrence J. White 'The Credit-rating Agencies and the Subprime Debacle' in Jeffrey Friedman (ed.) *What Caused the Financial Crisis?* (University of Pennsylvania Press 2011) 233.
61 Egan-Jones Ratings Co. was barred by the SEC in 2012 from rating asset-backed and government securities for 18 months, for the reason that one of their founders, Sean Egan, consciously made misrepresentations to the SEC when the company was applying to gain NRSRO status in 2008 (thus apparently demonstrating their determination to receive some of the residual money that was available before the system completely ground to a halt). See Securities and Exchange Commission 'Egan-Jones Rating Co. and Sean Egan Charged with Making Material Misrepresentations to SEC' [2012] Press Release (2012–75). There is, however, some doubt as to the legitimacy of this action by the SEC; for more see *A Reality Check*.
62 Elmar Altvater and Margot Geiger 'Exiting the multiple crises through 'green' growth?' in Andreas Exner, Peter Fleissner and Lukas Kranzl (eds) *Land and Resource Scarcity: Capitalism, Struggle and Well-being in a World without Fossil Fuels* (Routledge 2013) 19.

focus on the effects of the rating agencies on two parties: the investor and the state. While the majority of investors can quite rightly claim to be victims of the agencies' conduct, there is a line of reasoning that suggests that investors, particularly the sophisticated investors, have no real claim to being an innocent victim in the process, given their expertise. Also, while the state is presumed to be solely interested in systemic balance and safety, there is a staggering amount of evidence to suggest that the state lies behind almost every crisis, which creates the fertile ground for such devastating damage (whether they do this knowingly or unknowingly is inconclusive). This research, particularly with regard to the state, has important connotations for what may be possible in terms of reform, so further investigation will be important.

Where loyalties lie – the relationship between the investor and the agency

To start with, one of the main reason for the divergence between expectation and reality, in this particular relationship, is the fact that rating agencies are predominantly paid by issuers under the issuer-pays model and therefore have a 'vested interest'.[63] While agencies will contest that under normal conditions the conflict of interest inherent in this model is relatively small and also manageable,[64] the dynamics of the RMBS market that dominated the financial landscape for over a decade prior to the financial crisis alters that perception immeasurably.

Within the securitisation process, the RMBS products needed to be endorsed by financial entities, predominantly investment banks, through a process known as 'underwriting'.[65] However, the size and scale of these products meant that only a handful of companies had the capability to perform such a vital function, which leads to perhaps the underlying issue with regard to the distasteful conduct of the rating agencies. The SEC noted that while 22 different 'arrangers' (issuers of asset-backed securities) underwrote subprime RMBS deals (based on a sample of 642 deals), 12 arrangers accounted for 80 per cent of the total number of that sample, in both number and dollar volume. Furthermore, for 368 Collateralised

---

63 Faruk Ülgen 'Financial Liberalism and New Institutional Environment: The 2007–08 Financial Crisis as a (De)Regulatory Deadlock' in Patrick O'Sullivan, Nigel F.B. Allington and Mark Esposito (eds) *The Philosophy, Politics and Economics of Finance in the 21st Century: From Hubris to Disgrace* (Routledge 2015) 381. Also, de Lange argues that there are many social and financial ties that lead agencies to favour issuers over shareholders (and investors); chief among which is the fact that 90 per cent of their revenue comes from issuers, see Deborah E. de Lange *Cliques and Capitalism: A Modern Networked Theory of the Firm* (Palgrave Macmillan 2011) 124.

64 Neuman discusses in further detail some evidence that suggests that the sheer amount of business courted by the agencies reduces the likelihood that one issuer may provide enough business to influence the direction or policies of the rating agency, see Nicole B. Neuman 'A "Sarbanes-Oxley" for Credit Rating Agencies? A Comparison of the Roles Auditors' and Credit Rating Agencies' Conflicts of Interests Played in Recent Financial Crises' [2010] 12 *University of Pennsylvania Journal of Business Law* 921.

65 For a comprehensive guide to 'underwriting' and the importance of investment banks to the modern incarnation of this process see Giuliano Iannotta *Investment Banking: A Guide to Underwriting and Advisory Services* (Springer Science & Business Media 2010).

Debt Obligation (CDO) products accounted for by the sample taken from the Big Three, of the 26 different arrangers who underwrote these products only 11 accounted for a total of 92 per cent of these deals at 80 per cent of the dollar value (12 of the 13 largest RMBS underwriters were also the 12 largest CDO underwriters which served to further concentrate the underwriting function).[66] The SEC went on to make the obvious deduction that 'the combination of the arrangers' influence in determining the choice of rating agencies and the high concentration of arrangers with this influence appear to have heightened the inherent conflicts of interests that exist in the "issuer pays" compensation model'.[67]

This dynamic-altering detail is where our analysis of how the agencies differed so much from what was expected of them can begin. We have already seen how the dynamic changed for the credit rating industry in the early to mid-1970s when the SEC inducted them formally into the regulatory framework.[68] Having grown at an unprecedented rate as a result of this induction, the agencies were in a prime position to take advantage of the next external factor, the explosion of the asset-backed securities (ABS) market. Partnoy noted that having been invented in the mid-1970s, the total issuance of ABSs in 1987 stood at just $9 billion. Yet, just ten years later the total issuance would be between $100 and $150 billion. In 1995 alone, the total issuance was just over $109 billion.[69] This extraordinary rate of increase would be the signal for all the concerned parties within the securitisation chain to begin positioning themselves to take maximum advantage of their respective positions.

Writing in 1999, Partnoy describes a process that demonstrates the issuers' preparedness to manipulate the rating agencies into giving favourable ratings for the structured products being sold, even to the extent that the largest issuers had a 'side-business' which advised clients on how to prepare and 'window dress' their products before courting the agencies for the required ratings.[70] Partnoy suggests that this highlights the fact that the issuers considered the agencies to be easily manipulated. However, while this notion is indeed revealing, particularly given how long this process must have been going on, hindsight suggests that, rather than being manipulated by devious issuers, the rating agencies were completely willing participants in the larger scheme.

Tymoigne and Wray suggest that the Basel I regulations,[71] put forward in 1988 which were to be fully enacted by 1992, were the main motive for innovations in the field of security underwriting.[72] The major players within the securitisation

---

66 Barry Leonard *Summary Report of Issues Identified in the Security and Exchange Commission Staff's Examinations of Select Credit Rating Agencies* (DIANE Publishing 2009) 32.

67 ibid.

68 *A Snapshot of the Regulatory Framework* (n 103).

69 Frank Partnoy 'The Siskel and Ebert of Financial Markets? Two Thumbs Down for the Credit Rating Agencies' [1999] 77 *Washington University Law Quarterly* 664.

70 ibid 675.

71 Bank for International Settlements *International Convergence of Capital Measurement and Capital Standards* (BIS 1988).

72 Eric Tymoigne and Larry Wray *The Rise and Fall of Money Manager Capitalism: Minsky's Half Century from World War Two to the Great Recession* (Routledge 2013) 141.

process quickly realised that the credit rating agencies would take centre stage in the process as a result of the regulations, so 'major innovations had to occur in the credit rating methods because asset-backed bonds cannot be issued without ratings'.[73] Unfortunately, rather than being prudent and accepting the great responsibility that came with this pivotal role, the agencies actively went out of their way to incorporate models that were suspect in order to garner the business of the concentrated issuers. Initially, they simply set arbitrary default correlations and default rates based on data available for proxy securities.[74] However, the sheer number of individual assets (mortgages within the RMBS products) that were being packaged together meant that agencies required a method that would both reduce the time it took to come to a decision about the underlying risk and also give the desired rating that their clients demanded. That method was to be the 'Gaussian Copula Formula'.[75]

This formula, which under specific conditions was able to produce a single number that was apparently representative of the underlying risk of all the collected claims within the product,[76] was perfect for the rating agencies in meeting their clients' demands. However, even though the formula was fully incorporated into the rating system of the major agencies in August 2004, the formula had crucial limits and the agencies knew it. The issue was that while the formula allowed them to rate these exotic financial products, they were doing so with little or no underlying data. In order to rectify this potentially fraudulent behaviour, the agencies turned to the financial markets for assistance, taking their signals from Credit Default Swaps (CDS) and Equity Default Swaps (EDS) premia, meaning that the amount of protection buyers in securities were paying in premiums was now being factored into the rating process on large pools of individual claims.[77] The issue with this approach, however, was that the premia of the CDSs and the EDSs were themselves dependent upon the underlying credit ratings. This resulted in a highly procyclical, unreliable and completely inappropriate system of finance that was inherently destined to collapse, leading Tymoigne and Wray to liken the system to a Ponzi scheme.[78]

Clearly, at that point, the protection of investors (or the taxpaying public) was the last thing on the minds of the agencies. Put simply, the agencies were

---

73 ibid.
74 ibid.
75 The full title of the formula is the Gaussian Copula Formula, developed by Dr David X. Li. Farrell explains that the equation is used to predict and quantify, for the goal of setting a price, the effects of individual elements so that correlations can be determined (thus providing the opportunity for rating agencies to suggest the risk exposure on thousands of claims with just one symbol), see Joseph P. Farrell *Babylon's Banksters: The Alchemy of Deep Physics, High Finance and Ancient Religion* (Feral House 2010) 21–7. For other resources explaining and relating the Gaussian Copula Formula see Dana Mackenzie *What's Happening in the Mathematical Sciences, Vol. 8* (American Mathematical Society 2010) 40; Matthew Watson *Uneconomic Economics and the Crisis of the Model World* (Palgrave Macmillan 2014) 35.
76 Tymoigne and Wray (n 72) 142.
77 ibid.
78 ibid.

determined to meet the requirements of only one party: the one who paid the most. There is a technical argument that these agencies should not act in such a mercenary-like manner because their reputation could suffer;[79] although there are a number of factors that have contributed to the decreasing effect of this 'reputational capital' deterrent, as we will see throughout this chapter. Furthermore, Tymoigne and Wray cite a former employee of Moody's who suggests that a cultural change took place that completely altered its mindset (and we can safely infer that the other members of the Big Three would follow suit with it being an oligopoly/duopoly).[80]

In what is arguably the most important study conducted on the ratings industry, purely for the fact that, as an entity, the United States Senate can acquire information that no-one else can, its Permanent Subcommittee on Investigations' report on the causes of the financial crisis makes for compelling reading. Within this report the notion of cultural change around the turn of the millennium is repeated. The report states that a number of analysts who worked for Moody's during the 1990s and into the 2000s informed the subcommittee that a 'major cultural shift took place at the company around 2000', from being academically oriented and conservative in its ratings to anything but.[81] Rather unfortunately, the subcommittee, acting on reference from the members of Moody's, attribute this cultural shift to the rise of Brian Clarkson, who would go on to become its Chief Operating Officer. However, this timeline coincides with the arrival of a much more influential figure, which gave the clearest signal of all in the corridors of power that there was serious money to be made in this era.

One of the world's richest people and widely regarded as one of, if not the, greatest investor of modern times is Warren Buffett.[82] In 1999, Buffett's Berkshire Hathaway purchased Dun & Bradstreet. The interesting aspect was that Dun & Bradstreet was not considered to be a great investment at the time because its business of credit reporting was not particularly profitable, even though it was the ancestor of the modern-day ratings industry. Buffett rarely invests in a speculative manner and Dun & Bradstreet was not his primary target. Dun & Bradstreet had purchased Moody's in 1962 after John Moody's death[83] and in 1999 was the parent company of an entity that, as we have already seen, was the key to unlocking the extraordinary profits that were available in the markets. In an incredible demonstration of stock arbitrage, something Buffett is famous for, he increased his stake in Dun & Bradstreet

---

79 Howell E. Jackson 'The Role of Credit Rating Agencies in the Establishment of Capital Standards for Financial Institutions in a Global Economy' in Eilis Ferran and Charles A.E. Goodhart (eds) *Regulating Financial Services and Markets in the 21st Century* (Hart Publishing 2001) 312. For more on what is referred to as the 'reputational capital' view see Hemraj (n 32) 16; Aline Darbellay *Regulating Credit Rating Agencies* (Edward Elgar 2013) 126.

80 Tymoigne and Wray (n 72) 142.

81 United States Senate, Permanent Subcommittee on Investigations *Wall Street and the Financial Crisis: Anatomy of a Financial Collapse* (GPO 2011) 273.

82 Richard Phalon *Forbes Greatest Investing Stories* (John Wiley & Sons 2004).

83 Charles R. Geisst *Encyclopaedia of American Business History* (Facts on File 2006) 111.

to 24 million shares for a price of $499 million (at $21 a share), which gave him the power to spin-off the company; the spin-off subsequently took place in September 2000. Under the conditions of the spin-off, Buffett's shares in Dun & Bradstreet were converted into 24 million shares of the standalone Moody's Corporation, which also left him with 12 million shares in Dun & Bradstreet. In the following three years Buffett sold his 12 million shares in Dun & Bradstreet for an average price of $30 a share, resulting in a total of $360 million. This incredible move reduced his overall cost in the stock of Moody's to $139 million or just *$5.56 a share*.[84]

The reason why this information has been included is because it is vital for our understanding of the aims of the credit rating agencies in the pre-crisis era. Rather than attributing the cultural change to internal managers, this is clear evidence that shows the world's most influential people were scrambling to be a part of what was about to happen. What it also does is identify for us that the only consideration of the agencies was profit; Buffett does not invest to contribute to societal balance. This incessant quest for profit is at odds with everything that was required of the agencies as we saw in the last section. There are many examples of the agencies actively operating *against* both the interests of the investor and systemic stability although, at this stage, it would be helpful to continue to focus on the incredible collusion between the agencies and the small number of issuers who brought the world to its knees.

Collusion

Prior to the Dodd-Frank Act of 2010 the largest investors were legally bound to invest only in products that were rated at least investment-grade, if not simply AAA. Also, many money managers were bound by the investors they represented to invest only in highly rated products, which relates to the agency-related benefits of credit ratings as we discussed earlier.[85] The clear issue here is that in order to tap into this lucrative market, issuers needed the very highest of ratings for their 'exotic' products. It is worth noting that the majority of investors at this level were 'institutional investors', which means that they were usually representing a large number of policy holders or individual investors (e.g. pension funds or mutual funds). That these entities were bound to *only* invest in securities deemed worthy by rating agencies is indicative of the responsibility placed upon the agencies. If we operate for a moment using the hypothesis that rating agencies are *only* concerned with profit and their own advancement, then these factors of issuers willing to pay extraordinary amounts; investors being forced to go through the agencies to invest in securities; and a system that meant even if the agencies' reputational capital was reduced they would still survive; all contribute to a seemingly inevitable result. As Senator Richard

---

84 Mary Buffett and David Clark *Warren Buffett and the Art of Stock Arbitrage: Proven Strategies for Arbitrage and Other Special Investment Situations* (Scribner 2010).
85 *The Industry: What It Does* (n 63).

Shelby declared in the aftermath of the crisis: '...it seems to me that money is trumping ethics...'.[86]

The fact that the agencies clearly colluded with the concentrated issuers of these 'exotic' or more precisely 'toxic' financial products is widely recognised.[87] Farlow, in an excellent analogy that suitably describes the whole situation, states that

> just as the manufacturers of meat products find clever ways to make the last extruded and most unprepossessing, bits of offal taste quite palatable, the manufacturers of structured products worked closely with the credit rating agencies to make sure that the bits that got into each rating tranche just about made the grade.

In continuing this notion of a Ponzi-like system, he continues by stating

> by such a ruse, structured products had on average more favourable ratings than corporate bonds. So long as plenty of buyers were prepared to take the financial products that oozed out of the end – often referred to as collateralised debt obligations – this was an ideal vehicle to pull in more funds to feed the creation and sale of yet more financial products.[88]

While the role played by the investors is important and will therefore be covered shortly, the fact still remains that the rating agencies circumvented all of their professional standards to participate in this Ponzi-like scheme.

'Stockholm syndrome'

In the last chapter we saw how the structure of the securities was created so that different classes of investors could simultaneously invest in them.[89] In fact, the differing levels were absolutely crucial to maintaining the system and garnering the huge levels of investment that the system was devised for. This structuring is called 'subordination', which is just one aspect of what are collectively known as 'credit enhancements'.[90] As was stated earlier, the aim of subordination was to be able to advertise each section of the security as being protected from suffering from losses with relation to the investor's regulatory constraints, so AAA investors were to be protected first from suffering losses while the predominantly unregulated hedge funds could invest in the lowest (equity) tranche, which contained the possibility of high returns but little protection. The issue for the issuers was that they did not want to spend unnecessarily to be as efficient (and profitable) as possible, thus it was vital that they liaised with the rating agencies to calculate

---

86 United States Senate, Committee on Banking, Housing and Urban Affairs *The Role and Impact of Credit Rating Agencies on the Subprime Credit Markets* (GPO 2009).

87 Robert Kolb's work is just one piece that is representative of a wider understanding, see Robert W. Kolb *The Financial Crisis of Our Time* (Oxford University Press 2010) 177.

88 Andrew Farlow *Consequences of the Global Financial Crisis* (Oxford University Press 2013) 62.

89 *Signalling to the Market* (n 87).

90 United States Senate (n 81) 251.

the minimum amount of protection required so that the higher tranches could receive the required ratings to lure the regulatory constrained investors; the rating agencies duly obliged.[91] The same aim can be seen when we understand that the issuers would arrange the product so that the total amount of revenue expected to be garnered from the product was much more than was to be paid out to each tranche, also known as 'over-collateralisation'.[92] The resulting excess was to be factored into the equity tranche to absorb losses first which, in theory, would amount to more protection for the higher tranches. Again, the issuers needed to know the minimum amount of collateral needed that would enable the agencies to award the ratings required and leave the excess to be removed from the process.

The extraordinary fees that were being paid by these issuers meant that the emphasis of the Big Three was solely on meeting the requirements of the issuers, with those from the agencies surveyed for the Senate report confirming that there was a strong emphasis 'on relationships with issuers and investment bankers',[93] as opposed to researching new and potentially more accurate and efficient rating approaches. In developing an extraordinarily appropriate analogy, the employees at S&P demonstrated their frustration through internal e-mails at what they referred to as 'a kind of Stockholm syndrome'. The employee complained that 'they've become so beholden to their top issuers for revenue they have all developed a kind of Stockholm syndrome which they mistakenly tag as Customer Value creation'.[94] The Senate report goes on to confirm this notion by detailing that, on a number of occasions, the result of an issuer complaining about rating methodologies, criteria or even rating decisions was that they were often granted exceptions or favourable treatment,[95] even sometimes without having requested it.[96]

The report declares that some of the factors that fell into this category of increased assistance included rating models that failed to include the relevant mortgage performance data, unclear and highly subjective criteria that was to be used in producing ratings, failing to apply updated rating models to existing rated transactions and a failure to adequately staff the relevant departments which resulted in a reduction in the effectiveness of rating and surveillance services (at a time when the agencies were recording record revenues).[97] The point made here regarding the agencies being *aware* of underlying problems in the mortgage market is very important. The report found that even though the agencies were fully aware of the high-risk nature of the loans being issued,[98] the lax lending standards and

91 ibid.
92 ibid.
93 ibid 274.
94 ibid 277.
95 ibid 280.
96 ibid 284. This section of the report details a deal between UBS and S&P on a 'Vertical CDO' were rating analysts were showing frustration that their managers were going out of their way to accommodate UBS despite little pressure to do so from the bank and very little cooperation on their behalf. This incident is indicative of their mind-set during this period.
97 ibid 244.
98 The highest-risk loans were (are) what is known as 'NINJA' loans, which stands for 'No Income No Job or Assets'. For more on this extraordinarily awful approach to finance see Whitney Tilson and Glenn Tongue *More Mortgage Meltdown: 6 Ways to Profit in These Bad Times* (John Wiley & Sons 2009) 12.

even outright mortgage fraud, they simply continued to issue the ratings that were required to get these products entered into the system. The committee concluded that the agencies did this because 'it was not in the shortterm economic self-interest of either Moody's or S&P to provide accurate credit ratings for high risk RMBS and CDO securities'.[99] This damning evidence continued; only six months prior to the collapse did Moody's begin to factor in the quality of the mortgage originators and servicers, while S&P did not factor these elements in at all.[100]

Before we move on to analysing some of the actual cases of this negligent and fraudulent approach to conducting their business, one revelation from an S&P employee deserves to be mentioned. In the last chapter (under the heading *The Rating Committee*) we saw how the rating committee is championed by the agencies and their supporters as being the one process that guarantees rating analysts' independence and should inspire confidence from the rating's users that the process is free from bias or external influence. With what we are learning about the ethical conduct of the agencies, the following should come as no surprise:

> Two years earlier, in May 2005, an S&P analyst complaining about a rating decision wrote: 'Chui told me that while the three of us voted "no", in writing, that there were 4 other "yes" votes... [T]his is a great example of how the criteria process is NOT supposed to work. Being out-voted is one thing (and a good thing, in my view), but being out-voted by mystery voters with no "logic-trail" to refer to is another... Again, this is exactly the kind of backroom decision-making that leads to inconsistent criteria, confused analysts and pissed-off clients'.[101]

Rather than inserting their institutional preference into the rating process at the decision stage, which is so obvious that it has the potential to backfire, the management at S&P cleverly realised that it was not necessary to intervene at such a late and pronounced stage; one can simply interfere and set the parameters at the beginning so that the desired rating will *always* result as a matter of policy. The question is, on the back of all this evidence of transgressive behaviour, what is or at least should be, the appropriate punishment for what is evidenced wrongdoing?

Appropriate punishment?

In the aftermath of the financial crisis, senior officials within the United States Judiciary were questioning why there had been no convictions for crimes

---

99 United States Senate (n 81) 244. This sort of fraudulent negligence can also be seen in the extraordinary case of Moody's who, in 2007, discovered that a bug in their computer models had generated ratings for products in 2006 which resulted in Aaa ratings, which upon correction should have been up *four notches lower*. The ratings in question were not corrected, see Kolb (n 87) 219.
100 ibid 252.
101 ibid 294.

committed during the financial crisis, even though the Senate subcommittee charged with investigating the collapse referred to the word 'fraud' on no fewer than 157 occasions.[102] In actual fact, at the time of writing there has only been *one* instance of someone being given a custodial sentence for their involvement in the financial crisis, although this figure represents those from the very large and well-known banks; in terms of convictions relating to the financial crisis the Inspector General of the Troubled Asset Relief Program (TARP) confirms that, as of 2016, 35 bankers have been sent to prison for their crimes, albeit from local banks.[103] Yet, this brings us to an important issue which unfortunately cannot be addressed here; the overwhelming issues attached to the concept of 'white-collar crime' dictates that to study a topic with an entire field devoted to it would not be appropriate.[104] So, while this section will not analyse the intricacies involved with prosecuting 'white-collar criminals', it will examine the most impactful 'punishments' that have been administered against the rating agencies, which are few and far between.

In preparation for the next section which seeks to examine the *actual* role of the state, this section promotes the idea that the agencies are being treated leniently by regulators. This idea is based on two aspects: first, that no-one from the agencies has been prosecuted for what seems, to all intents and purposes, consciously fraudulent behaviour; second, that aside from the issues surrounding fining corporate entities rather than prosecuting individuals, the levels of these fines are in no way a deterrent against future fraudulent behaviour, particularly as the agencies have sought to take advantage of their position and develop extra-curricular-type revenue sources which serve to buffer the effect of the fines (e.g. the Ancillary Service Provision).

Rhinebridge (and Cheyne Finance) SIVs

So far we have heard about the rating agencies doing all that they could to enable the concentrated issuers to take their RMBSs and CDOs to the market-place quickly and with minimal investigation into the assets at the heart of these

102 For Judge Rakoff's comments see *A Snapshot of the Regulatory Framework* (n 113).

103 See Nicholas Ryder *The Financial Crisis and White Collar Crime: The Perfect Storm?* (Edward Elgar Publishing 2014) 159 for just one account of the conviction of Credit Suisse's Global Head of Structured Credit Trading Kareem Serageldin, who was sentenced to serve two and a half years in prison. For Christy Goldsmith Romero's comments on the rate of convictions for bankers more generally see Chris Isidore '35 bankers were sent to prison for financial crisis crimes' [2016] CNN (28 April).

104 The field that is concerned with the examination of white-collar crime is extensive and has a variety of perspectives. For just some resources that may be representative see David Weisburd and Elin Waring *White-collar Crime and Criminal Careers* (Cambridge University Press 2001); Petter Gottschalk *White-collar Crime: Detection, Prevention and Strategy in Business Enterprises* (Universal Publishers 2010). For some perspectives specifically concerned with the financial crisis see Ryder (n 103); Mathieu Deflem *Economic Crisis and Crime* (Emerald Group Publishing 2011); Nicholas Ryder, Umut Turksen and Sabine Hassler *Fighting Financial Crime in the Global Economic Crisis* (Routledge 2014).

complex financial products. However, the cases of 'Rhinebridge' (and 'Cheyne Finance') are representative of a slightly different situation. These Structured Investment Vehicles (SIVs), amongst a number of others, were in fact *created*, *operated* and *rated* by the Big Three, as opposed to simply providing a supposedly third-party verification of their creditworthiness.[105] On this basis, two institutional investors initiated legal action against Moody's, S&P and Morgan Stanley for a variety of charges, including misrepresentation and breach of fiduciary duty. For the purposes of this section only the Rhinebridge case will be assessed, although the Cheyne Finance case is almost identical.

Before we understand the intricacies of the case and its conclusion, a small detour would be very useful indeed. Although it will also be factored into the next section regarding the state, there is one aspect of the regulations surrounding this level of SIV operation that demonstrates why understanding the *actual* is vitally important, rather than being lost and deluded in the pursuit of the *desired*. SIVs are special purpose vehicles that borrow money from investors and then invest in longer-term securities with varying levels of income-producing assets packaged within them. Judge Scheindlin, who was presiding over the case, surmised that 'the SIV business model resembles that of a bank in that its goal is to earn a spread between its borrowing interest rate and its lending interest rate. Like banks, SIVs have both assets and liabilities'.[106]

Earlier, the claim was made that 'behind almost every crisis lays the state'. While this may seem controversial, it was also declared that whether they do this knowingly or not is inconclusive, simply because it is extraordinarily difficult to uncover the underlying rationale for promoting policy changes within a government. The reason why this is important in this case is that the claimants, King County and the Iowa Student Loan Liquidity Corporation, are what is referred to as 'Qualified Institutional Buyers' (QIBs), as declared by Rule 144A of the Securities Act of 1933 (it should be stated however that the Rule was adopted in 1990, not 1933).[107] The rule essentially dictates that only entities who own over $100 million in investable assets may be sold to by brokers or dealers who are operating in accordance with Rule 144A; entities that have over $100 million in investable assets are usually institutional investors. What should be clear here is that the state has funnelled institutional investors, who are socially embedded, into a dishonourable system of finance where *they are the only available targets*. When we understand this, while also remembering the despicable practices that were integral to this system of finance, then the state must be held

---

105 *King County, Washington and Iowa Student Loan Liquidity Corporation v IKB Deutsche Industriebank AG, Moody's Investors Service, Inc., The McGraw Hill Companies, Inc., Fitch, Inc. and Morgan Stanley & Co. Incorporated* [2012] 863 FSupp2d 288 (4 May).

106 ibid.

107 *Securities Act of 1933* Pub. L. 73-22, 48 Stat 74 Rule 144A. The classification is also known as 'Qualified Purchasers' under the *Investment Company Act of 1940* Pub. L. 76-768 2(a)(51)(A). Although part of the Securities Act the Rule was adopted by the SEC in 1990 to 'spur further development of the U.S. private placement market'; see William K. Sjostrom 'The Birth of Rule 144A Equity Offerings' [2008] 56 *UCLA Law Review* 410.

up to a thorough examination; this is not simply a case of a dishonourable financial culture on Wall Street or in the City of London.

The judge declared that 'the Rating Agencies collaborated with IKB and Morgan Stanley to draft key selling documents, determine which assets the SIV could hold and what structural protections to put in place and investigate and recommend securities for the SIV's portfolio';[108] these are not aspects that the agencies declare are part of their operations. Not only did they 'help', they also had the right to veto management changes, veto funding changes, modify its operations and set its investment guidelines (which they did). As the judge concludes, 'the Rating Agencies did not merely provide ratings; rather, they were deeply entrenched in the creation and operation of Rhinebridge'.[109]

For our assessment of the *actual* situation between investors and the agencies and the divergence that exists between what is required and what is delivered, what the judge discussed next in the case is extremely illustrative of these issues. The SIV issued varying products for investment, like nearly all SIVs do, ranging from CDOs to more focused products like 'Senior Notes'. Senior Notes, in this instance, was the term used for short-term commercial paper that had maturities of up to 364 days; these notes were given the highest possible ratings by the agencies. In displaying their callous and contrived nature, the agencies 'knew that the Senior Notes could only be offered to QIBs and QPs (Qualified Purchasers)'.[110] Even worse, not only did the agencies recognise this, but the claimants also informed the agencies that 'they relied on credit ratings to make investment decisions'.[111]. A phrase that comes to mind here is 'like lambs to the slaughter'.

With the belief in the rating scales being that AAA-rated entities were extremely unlikely to default on their obligations,[112], the AAA rating given to the Rhinebridge SIV on or about 27 June 2007 was inexplicably downgraded to 'junk' or 'non-investment grade' on 18–19 October 2007. So, in fewer than four months the SIV was left almost worthless. As a result, the claimants initiated legal action for the purposes of finding the defendants guilty of causes of action for negligence, negligent misrepresentation, breach of fiduciary duty, as well as aiding and abetting with respect to those claims. In the 7 June hearing, the Judge dismissed all the claims except negligent misrepresentation, allowing that claim to proceed. However, as we shall see, the agencies would do anything not to appear in court. The airing of their business and potentially being found guilty as a result prompted them to continue an approach they have always utilised,[113] which is to

---

108 *King County* (n 105).

109 ibid.

110 ibid.

111 ibid.

112 As we saw earlier, the agencies themselves viewed the structural finance ratings differently to the corporate ratings (which coincidentally are extraordinarily accurate), although this was not communicated to the investors, an aspect which has been corrected since the crisis, see *A Snapshot of the Regulatory Framework* (n 127).

113 There are a variety of legal (and illegal) approaches that the rating agencies' predecessors established which have been continually utilised by the agencies, including silent settlements and

find a resolution that is private in nature by any means necessary. Before the case could be heard, the defendants, Moody's, McGraw-Hill and Morgan Stanley, settled with the claimants for a total of $225 million divided between them, with the details of the settlement remaining private.[114] The agencies did exactly the same thing in the Cheyne Finance case.[115]

A rational person may be forgiven for assuming that the agencies, having partaken in a systemic pilfering of investors' resources, would have stopped such detestable practices once the hubris of the era had come to a crashing standstill and their role had been found out. However, we shall now see that their manipulative and deceitful practices continued unabated after the height of the financial crisis, which may lead to an understanding that the penalties and attack on their reputation were completely ineffective and, most importantly, that examining the *nature* of the agencies is imperative, rather than categorising their actions as part of a wider degeneration of ethical standards.

The SEC's Cease and Desist Order against S&P

With the financial crisis came the end of the creation of irresponsible mortgages (for the most part), such as the NINJA loans we looked at earlier.[116] However, we shall now see why the examination of the agencies and their role in the securitisation process is still important, as the financial crisis brought to an end just one source of the securitisation process, not the ills of the process itself. Between 2010 and 2011, Standard & Poor's had changed its rating methodology of certain financial instruments so that the amount of credit enhancement required to achieve an investable grade was lowered, without publicly declaring the amendment. This is telling, as we have already seen that this aspect of their

---

intimidation (the rating agencies conduct a much more subtle form of intimidation because their victims are now in a much more healthier position to defend themselves than they were in the era of the reporting agencies [contrast the case of *Patterson v Dun*, *King v Patterson* and *Beardsley v Tappan* against the modern incarnation represented by the case involving Hannover Re]). For a fascinating (re)examination of the approaches utilised by the reporting agencies see Marc Flandreau and Gabriel G. Mesevage 'The Untold History of Transparency: Mercantile Agencies, the Law and the Lawyers (1851–1916)' [2014] Enterprise and Society. For the citations of the cases: (The case report for *Patterson v Dun* has yet to be located by historians, which is extremely unfortunate given its importance to this line of enquiry – it is referenced in other cases however); *King v Patterson* (1887) 49 New Jersey Law Reports 417, 9 A. 705; *Beardsley v Tappan* 5 Blatchf. 498 (1867). With regard to the recent instance of the intimidation of the large reinsurer Hannover Re via unjustified rating downgrades see Alec Klein 'Credit Raters' Power Leads to Abuses, Some Borrowers Say' [2004] *Washington Post* 24 November; Lynn Bai 'On Regulating Conflicts of Interest in the Credit Rating Industry' [2010] 13 *New York University Journal of Legislation and Public Policy* 253; Paolo Fulghieri, Gunter Strobl and Han Xia 'The Economics of Solicited and Unsolicited Credit Ratings' [2014] 27 *The Review of Financial Studies* 2.

114 Jeannette Neumann 'Cost of Ratings Suit: $225 Million' [2013] *The Wall Street Journal*.
115 Stephen Foley 'Standard & Poor's and Moody's settle US subprime lawsuits' [2013] *Financial Times*.
116 *'Stockholm Syndrome'* (n 98).

approach was one of the main issues before the crisis, so clearly it had very little effect on the *practice* of the agencies.[117]

In order to provide some context for this claim we will now examine the SEC's recent Cease and Desist Order against S&P concerning rating certain products. The subject of this order was S&P's business of providing ratings for 'Conduit/ Fusion Commercial Mortgage Backed Securities'[118] (C/F CMBS), products that consist of geographically diversified pools of at least 20 mortgage loans made to unrelated borrowers. Rather than homes, these products contained mortgages for 'commercial properties'. For the purpose of the securitisation, this was divided into five categories: retail, office, multi-family, lodging and industrial'.[119] The subject of the SEC's investigation was S&P's methodology for calculating 'Debt Service Coverage Ratios' (DSCRs), which is the ratio of the annual net cash flow 'produced by an income-generating property, divided by the annual debt service payment required under the mortgage loans', with the ultimate aim being to provide a measure of the property's ability to cover debt service payments.[120]

The SEC noted that S&P's market position for rating these types of products had declined following the financial crisis, which had the knock-on effect of sub-duing the issuance of new CMBS products. However, the Big Three are reactionary and serve to capitalise upon trends so that they can extract as much profit as possible, even if this means relegating any ethical standard to do so. When issuers increased their CMBS output in 2010, S&P's CMBS Group decided that the fact the company's market share had not grown in sync with the level of issuance was solely due to 'conservatism of the firm's criteria' in rating CMBS products.[121] This deplorable willingness to sacrifice quality and accuracy to garner profit and not lose market share to competitors, who S&P naturally assume are also willing to lose any standards, is the clearest indicator that the agencies cannot be trusted to hold anyone's interests dear other than their own.

In a lot of these cases the fraud perpetrated by the agencies is clear, but not so completely obvious that calls for individual prosecution would have any considerable weight. The case with agencies circumventing their rating process by setting rating standards that were favourable to issuers *before* the decision process is a good example of appropriating negligence, but pinning individual fraud charges

---

117 What is meant by this is that the financial crisis affected the revenues of the agencies from structured finance deals simply because the levels of issuance of structured finance products naturally dropped in response to the crisis. The SEC note that the issuance of structured finance products bounced back from 2010 onwards (albeit at lower levels than witness pre-crisis), with the difference being that the underlying assets were of a slightly different nature. This was noted in the press briefing by the SEC concerning the Cease and Desist Order against S&P, which this section will be relying on, see Securities and Exchange Commission *Order Instituting Administrative and Cease-and-Desist Proceedings, Pursuant to Section 8A of the Securities Act of 1933 and Sections 15E (d) and 21C of the Securities Exchange Act of 1934, Making Findings and Imposing Remedial Sanctions and a Cease-and-Desist Order* [2015] Release No. 9705; 74104, File No. 3-16348.

118 ibid.

119 ibid.

120 ibid.

121 ibid.

would be very difficult, unfortunately. However, this case of the Cease and Desist Order is entirely different. DSCRs have the effect of lowering the amount of credit enhancement required to obtain a top rating and in late 2010, S&P changed its methodology for calculating DSCRs. Between February and July of 2011, S&P published eight CF CMBS reports that 'failed to describe its changed methodology' and not only did they not declare the change to interested investors, *they included DSCRs that were calculated using the prior methodology*[122] (which had the effect of portraying conservativeness that no longer existed). This was not simply an error, because on at least four out of the eight occasions the CMBS group communicated the details of the revised DSCR model to the *issuers* of the products, which not only gave the issuers a distinct advantage but also proved collusion between the agency and the issuers. For this the agency received just over $7 million for the rating of six transactions.

To compound this Faustian relationship, the senior management of S&P responded to investor questions about low credit enhancement levels by stating that the ratings were 'consistent with S&P's rating definitions', with the SEC confirming that 'these publications did not inform investors of the effect of the change in methodology on required CE levels'.[123] In a perfect environment – one free from lobbying influence – the political protection for white-collar criminals and a narrow societal definition of 'crime', the very fact of this conscious misrepresentation alone would lead to the indictment of the senior management of S&P for fraud, along with the leading figures of the CMBS division.[124] But this is not a perfect environment, which is sadly and brutally confirmed by the leniency of their punishment for this attack upon investors.

The SEC found the agency guilty of no fewer than four serious violations of major financial legislation. The punishment for this extensive crime was an overall fine of $42 million (rising to $80 million) and a 12-month suspension from the

---

122 ibid (emphasis added).

123 ibid.

124 It should be mentioned here that legal aspects such as the issues with the lifting of the 'corporate veil' would most likely come in to play in this scenario, although the US and the UK both have measures which would allow them to prosecute corporate officers, rather than just the company itself. For the UK's own assessment of its capability under law to prosecute corporate officers for financial fraud see Crown Prosecution Service '*Corporate Prosecutions*' [2015]. The US DoJ also has a dedicated division for fraud, see The United States Department of Justice 'Fraud Section (FRD)' [2015]. While the capability to prosecute corporate officers and in certain circumstances major shareholders for negligent/fraudulent behaviour exists, it is very rare that the judiciary in a given state will do so for a myriad of reasons. As there is clearly no appetite for prosecuting the officers of the CRAs and also that we are not overtly calling for such prosecutions, it would not be appropriate to envelop such an analysis here because to effectively cover the main issues would take volumes, at the very least. For just some analyses that investigate these issues further see Julie Cassidy *Concise Corporations Law* (Federation Press 2006); Reinier Kraakman, John Armour, Paul Davies, Luca Enriques, Henry B. Hansmann, Gérard Hertig and Klaus J. Hopt *The Anatomy of Corporate Law: A Comparative and Functional Approach* (Oxford University Press 2009); Angela Schneeman *Law of Corporations and Other Business Organisation* (Cengage Learning 2009) §7.6; Eilis Ferran and Look C. Ho *Principles of Corporate Finance Law* (Oxford University Press 2014) Ch. 2.

business of providing ratings on any CF CMBS transactions. The SEC did, however, allow the agency to publicly deny the findings of the SEC's investigation and admit no fault. As we have seen already and will continue to see, the agencies are determined to settle any case away from public scrutiny and are insistent upon denying any wrongdoing, primarily for the purposes of reducing any future legal action for the same offence.

This issue of leniency and inappropriate punishment is one that will be considered in Chapter 3, mainly because it is the by-product of certain aspects that are enforcing this divergence between what is *desired* and what is *actually* occurring. There are a number of instances around the world where rating agencies are being found guilty of fraudulent behaviour against investors and are being prosecuted as a result. In Australia, the courts have found the agencies (predominantly S&P) to be guilty of 'deceptive and misleading conduct', awarding a claimant $18.8 million in the process.[125] In Europe, the European Markets and Securities Authority has issued its first monetary punishment since its inception after the financial crisis, fining DBRS $33,360 for failing to comply with record-keeping requirements (concluding that the agency had 'acted negligently').[126] While these legal actions are welcome, it is clear that fines of $42 or $18 million are not going to influence the decision-making process of an entity that records revenues in the billions of dollars. In response to the $18 million fine in Australia, S&P spokesman Richard Noonan characterised the agency's view on such matters: 'It is bad policy to enforce a legal duty against a party like S&P, which has no relationship with investors who use rating opinions, yet impose no responsibility on those investors to conduct their own due diligence'.[127] While Noonan's claim of the agency having *no* relationship at all with investors is obviously not correct as we should now be aware, his claim regarding investor responsibility will certainly need to be considered before we end this section regarding the *actual* situation between the agencies and the investors. However, before we can do that there is one series of events that needs to addressed, as it resulted in the largest fine ever to be imposed upon a rating agency. The concept of fining agencies may be distasteful to some, but a breach of the billion-dollar barrier is indicative of the level of fraud/negligence that was found by prosecutors.

CalPERS

In 2009 the California Public Employees' Retirement System (CalPERS) filed a complaint against Moody's, S&P and Fitch on the grounds of negligent

---

125 This was the result of action initiated by Bathurst Regional Council (that spanned a number of cases against a number of entities). For more see *Bathurst Regional Council v Local Government Financial Services Pty Ltd (No 5)* [2012] FCA 1200; *ABN AMRO Bank NV v Bathurst Regional Council* [2014] FCAFC 65; David Fickling 'S&P, RBS Lose Appeal of Ruling Australian Towns Misled' [2014] Bloomberg (6 June).

126 Huw Jones 'EU Watchdog Imposes its First Fine on Rating Agency DBRS' [2015] Reuters (29 June).

127 Fickling (n 125).

misrepresentation and negligent interference with prospective economic advantage.[128] The claimant initiated the actions based on the rating agencies' granting of their highest ratings to three SIVs (Cheyne Finance, Stanfield Victoria Funding and Sigma Finance) in which the claimant invested during 2006. Having invested in the AAA-rated SIVs in 2006, the three SIVs subsequently defaulted on their payment obligations in 2007 and 2008, resulting in the loss of around $1 billion for CalPERS alone.

There is very little need to analyse the intricacies of this fraud by the agencies because the cases of Cheyne, Stanfield Victoria and Sigma are identical to the Rhinebridge case we assessed earlier in this section. The difference with the CalPERS case is that while the investor pursued its own lawsuit, the Department of Justice (DoJ) took action (based upon the CalPERS situation and the complaints of over 20 states for similar offences). The introduction of such a powerful entity fundamentally altered the rules of engagement for the rating agencies. While they had used their tried-and-tested legal approach to emerge relatively unscathed from the previous legal actions against them, they would surely not be able to intimidate or manipulate the United States Department of Justice in a similar manner. This is a rational conclusion to come to, although in assisting our understanding of the unique nature of the agencies, the fact that S&P decided to fight back against the DoJ is representative both of their attitude and their inherent nature.

CalPERS settled with Fitch first. The terms of the settlement are fascinating and hint at the *actual* situation of the rating industry being a duopoly, rather than an oligopoly. Under the terms of the settlement Fitch handed over confidential documents to CalPERS that would be crucial for the investor to continue to pursue its claims against Moody's and S&P; no money changed hands.[129] While it may admittedly be a stretch to claim that as members of an oligopoly the agencies would protect each other, Fitch's willingness to absolve themselves of potential financial punishment by providing the investor with crucial and unobtainable information is extraordinarily telling of the dynamics of the industry today.

Meanwhile, the DoJ had picked up on the ascent of the CalPERS case through the courts and on this occasion took the lead for CalPERS, for itself as the representative of the Federal Government and for 20 states against Standard & Poor's. After initial settlement talks broke down, the DoJ sought to sue S&P for a record $5 billion on the grounds of 'defrauding investors'. In response and in what can only be described as terribly advised or extraordinarily egotistical approach, the rating agency accused the DoJ of pursuing the lawsuit purely because it had downgraded the United States' sovereign rating shortly beforehand. This naturally riled the Attorney General Eric Holder who stated that punishing the agency was 'important to me' and dismissed the allegation as 'utter nonsense'.[130] This

---

128 Complaint for Negligent Misrepresentation under Common Law & California Civil Code §§ 1709 & 1710 & Negligent Interference with Prospective Economic Advantage at 23, *Cal Pub Employees' Ret Sys v Moody's Corp (and others)*, No CGC-09-490241.

129 Dale Kasler 'CalPERS cleared to sue ratings agencies' [2014] Sacramento Bee (15 September).

130 *A Primer on the Credit Rating Domain* (n 5). See also Ryder (n 103).

incredible approach hints at a number of potential actualities concerning the pre-sent ratings industry. First, it signifies that the agencies believe that their conduct is acceptable and does not warrant punishment. Second, it perhaps details their arrogance as a private party to go up against the state (and arguably the most powerful state in the world), particularly in the manner that they did. Last, it demonstrates their belief, founded upon continued success, that irrespective of their conduct they can find a way out of being punished by a variety of methods. However, in this instance, these factors resulted in the largest fine ever conferred upon a rating agency (albeit not the initial $5 billion that was pursued).

Through extensive dialogue the DoJ and S&P finally agreed on a settle-ment package of $1.375 billion.[131] In a settlement of the private lawsuit between CalPERS and S&P the agency paid $125 million,[132] thus taking the total outlay as of 3 February 2015 to $1.5 billion for defrauding investors. The settlement with the DoJ was split between the Federal Government ($687.5 million) and the 20 states ($687.5 million split according to an agreement between the states). The DoJ also insisted that the agency would not be able to do what it was used to doing and denying the facts. The agency admitted misrepresenting key information to investors; being aware of delinquent loans and not informing the public; and that decisions were not taken because of the potentially negative effect upon their business with paying issuers. Additionally, S&P acknowledged that 'the voluminous discovery provided to S&P by the United States in the litigation does not support their allegation that the United States' complaint was filed in retaliation for S&P's 2011 decisions on the credit rating of the United States', with the agency formally retracting the claim from the litigation.[133] CalPERS have taken action against other fraudulent actors and has been able to retrieve almost $900 million for its efforts.

Some suggested that the decision to prosecute S&P and not Moody's, who acted in exactly the same manner, is proof that the S&P litigation was a retaliation for their lowering of the United States' credit rating (Moody's did not lower the rating).[134] However, this has not proven to be the case, because in early 2017 the DoJ, in almost identical circumstances, reached a $864 million settlement with Moody's, with CalPERS reaching a private settlement agreement totalling $130 million earlier in the process.[135] For our analysis of the *actual* relationship

131 United States Department of Justice 'Justice Department and State Partners Secure $1.375 Billion Settlement with S&P for Defrauding Investors in the Lead Up to the Financial Crisis' [2015]. www.justice.gov/opa/pr/justice-department-and-state-partners-secure-1375-billion-settlement-sp-defrauding-investors

132 CalPERS 'CalPERS to Recover More than $300 Million from Standard & Poor's in Investment Ratings Settlements' [2015] www.calpers.ca.gov/page/newsroom/calpers-news/2015/recover-investment-ratings-settlements

133 United States Department of Justice (n 131).

134 *The Wall Street Journal* 'A Poor Standard of Justice' [2015] (8 February).

135 The United States Department of Justice *Justice Department and State Partners Secure Nearly $864 Million Settlement With Moody's Arising from Conduct in the Lead up to the Financial Crisis* [2017]. www.justice.gov/opa/pr/justice-department-and-state-partners-secure-nearly-864-million-settlement-moody-s-arising; James R. Koren 'CalPERS settles with Moody's for $130 million in ratings case' [2016] *LA Times* (9 March).

between the agency and the investor, these examples of Rhinebridge, Cheyne and other SIVs, together with the SEC's Cease and Desist Order against S&P (and a long list of other smaller examples), provide us with more than enough evidence to confidently claim that, in actual fact, the agencies are operating *against* the investors especially when there are substantial amounts of profit to be made from working with highly unstable financial products. This claim may be viewed as controversial or at the very least considered to be relying on extreme examples of the agencies' operations. However, it is precisely such extreme examples that demonstrate the true position of the agencies.

Are investors completely innocent?

Before this section concludes, the claims made by the S&P spokesman Richard Noonan deserve to be assessed. Is it correct to claim that investors (particularly institutional investors) were irresponsible in relying so heavily upon the ratings of the agencies? Should institutional investors take much more care when investing, as their resources are predominantly from the public and have a systemic importance? These types of questions clearly signify the reality that the investors naturally played a part in the system; the important question is whether they took these risks knowingly and are now looking for a scapegoat to facilitate the recuperation of their losses or whether they were forced into a system where those who forced them into it had not adequately checked the safety of the system first.

Andrew Farlow has suggested that the *actual* situation is closer to the first of these two scenarios. He argues that the securitisation system that dominated the pre-crisis financial landscape was an 'agreeable way to make money' and as such 'investors never asked awkward questions about the underlying collateral'.[136] While some have argued that it is more the case of investors believing in the purpose and function of the CRAs and subsequently suffering the consequences for this misplaced understanding[137], Farlow is unequivocal in his stance that, in actual fact, investors made huge returns on these fundamentally risky endeavours and they took this risk because they knew that when the defaults came they would not be punished and would be financially supported by the state; Farlow labels this scenario 'Heads they had won; tails they would win'.[138]

Apart from alluding to the 'too big to fail' issue that is dominating the modern marketplace, Farlow also makes the point that governments reaped huge financial rewards in short-term taxes that were related to the securitisation system (in addition to reaping the rewards that come with a market experiencing a large

---

136 Farlow (n 88) 62.
137 Thomas Clarke 'Corporate Governance Causes of the Global Financial Crisis' in William Sub, Jim Stewart and David Pollard (eds) *Corporate Governance and the Global Financial Crisis: International Perspectives* (Cambridge University Press 2011) 39.
138 Farlow (n 88) 62.

boom). He is arguably correct in claiming that the investors did not ask enough questions when investing the money of millions upon millions of people.[139] He is also arguably correct in claiming that the investors knew that the government, on behalf of taxpaying citizens, would rescue them if they all partook in the system. What these views do not consider is the parameters for their actions. Yes, they could have done more, but the situation regarding the legal funnelling of institutional investors into an unregulated financial system is deplorable. The actions of government-sponsored enterprises like Fannie Mae and Freddie Mac, in pursuing institutional investors and making the terms of their investment almost irresistible, is surely more important. The conscious relegation of laws that had protected the United States and arguably the world, from systemic financial collapse for over 70 years, cannot be ignored.

When assessing the conduct of the issuer, the rating agencies and the investor, it becomes quickly apparent that underneath all of the factors that are often discussed (i.e. industry dynamics organisational structure) lies the state; its approach is pivotal in deciding the navigation of the eras. We saw in *The Desired Situation for the State* that its aim should be to promote and maintain systemic balance, as its position as the guardian for public health dictates that it must foster balance within the economic realm (given the centrality of the market in modern life). In this sense, then, there are two deductions that can be made: either the state simply failed in its mandate in 2007/8, in which case we could confidently say that the financial crisis could be categorised as the largest failure of the state (as an ideal) in the modern era; or they produced the situation for a variety of reasons, which means that what we understand to be its mandate (i.e. the *desired* situation) does not exist and we should recalibrate our focus accordingly.

It was stated earlier that it is extraordinarily difficult to know if certain policies were enacted with an aim in mind, which makes proving the culpability of the state almost impossible (at least beyond any reasonable doubt). However, this should not dissuade one from assessing the actions of the state from within such parameters, as to refuse to do so would limit the analysis and distort any potential conclusions. The reform proposal that dominates this work is practicable, but controversial. It is not controversial in the sense that it is not deserved because, as we are seeing, the conduct of the agencies has been and continues to be, quite frankly appalling. It is controversial in the sense that the likelihood of it being, at the very least, considered, is solely dependent upon the state's inclination to affect lasting change in a field where societal safety is often spoken about, but rarely established.

---

139 This sentiment is not exclusive to the rating scenario. Sergakis notes that with respect to proxy advisors, investors are, in the same manner to users of credit ratings, extremely over-reliant upon proxy advisors. Again, this is because of the perceived supporting of these third-party actors by regulators, see Konstantinos Sergakis 'Proxy Advisory Firms under ESMA's Microscope: A Perfectible Regulatory Approach?' [2014] 25 *International Company and Commercial Law Review* 4.

The pivotal role of the guardian – where the emphasis lies for the state

It would be prudent to operate on the basis that the financial system, within the modern context, is certainly part of the public domain[140]. With the financial system being central within modern society, the state is charged with supervising an arena that contains organised and concentrated power, while having to balance that against the interests of dispersed and diverse entities, such as citizens. When we also consider that the globalised nature of the modern world means that financial policies can and often do, affect other countries outside of one's own jurisdiction, then the precarious nature of the state's role is clear.

However, this role is accompanied by the defining power of being able to direct the progression of the market and therefore modern society. In this section we shall see how the state, in its many forms, has arguably acted against their *desired* role as imagined by the general public and society (or at the very least the understanding of the state's quintessential role). Again, it is very important to state that whether this is done consciously or not cannot be accurately determined, but the facts can be established to build a picture of whether the approach of the state can be predicted. Peter Swan argues that understanding this dynamic of the relationship between the state and society can fundamentally alter one's philosophical parameters. For example, the financial crisis is widely held to be one of the largest *failures* of the state in modern times, however for Swan 'it was not a failure of regulatory policy, *but the very success of regulatory policy by successive administrations and Congress that had created the subprime crisis*'.[141] This incredible understanding means that while it is right to focus on the conduct of rating agencies, banks, investors and all the other culpable parties in the financial crisis, it is erroneous to focus *just* on them: if Swan's understanding is to be accepted, then they were all *actively encouraged* to do what they did.

The opposing argument may be that the state sought to increase productivity and economic output by loosening the financial constraints that had been in place since the Great Depression and that this innocent motive had been abused by dishonourable parties. However, the sheer amount of evidence that exists from recent history that proves that banks and rating agencies *will always* attempt to maximise their potential returns at the cost of reducing their ethical and moral standpoint renders that opposing argument simply invalid; their conduct was to be expected. So, while it would be imprudent to accept Swan's argument in full, it is appropriate to continue in the vein of not rejecting such a controversial but fitting idea.

---

140 Geoffrey Underhill 'The Public Good Versus Private Interests and the Global Financial and Monetary System' in Daniel Drache (ed.) *The Market or the Public Domain: Redrawing the Line* (Routledge 2005) 280.

141 Peter L. Swan 'The Global Crisis and Its Origins' in Robert W. Kolb (ed.) *Lessons from the Financial Crisis: Causes, Consequences and Our Economic Future* (John Wiley & Sons 2010) 54 (emphasis added).

Setting the scene

The power of the state to direct the market and therefore society, manifests itself through the ability to regulate the capabilities of market actors (with legislation and financial regulations). If the state deems it appropriate to ban a practice outright then that practice simply cannot continue, irrespective of the influence of the targets (we saw this with the forced separation of Commercial and Investment Banks in the 1930s – a regulatory approach that is vital for the reform proposal proposed here). Alternatively, if the state deems it appropriate to facilitate the proliferation of certain business practices, then usually that area is opened for business and tends to generate incredible activity due to the fresh potential for sizeable returns; this process is known simply as 'deregulation'.

In charting the actions of the state in the lead up to the crisis we can examine the role it plays in setting the direction of the marketplace, with the aim being to reveal patterns that can illuminate us as to their potential motives for taking particular actions. It is worth noting, before we continue, that Neil Barofsky, who was the Special (United States Treasury Department) Inspector General charged with overseeing the Troubled Assets Relief Program (SIGTARP), declared that 'I was to learn while at SIGTARP that "adopting a narrative" was a tried-and-true tactic in Washington: define the status quo as a success and ignore all evidence that suggests otherwise'.[142] This method needs to be incorporated into our understanding of the possible methods the state may use to justify their systemically concerned decisions because, should the evidence point to this being a reality – that the state actively promotes a narrative that will help it achieve a set goal irrespective of the evidence – then it will have a huge impact on our assessment of what parties the state seeks to embolden at the cost of others.

The Senate subcommittee report that has proven to be useful to our analysis so far will be useful again, as it details how, in the mid-1990s, the pieces were put in place for the systemic escalation of risk to begin. Damon Silvers, in describing these pieces with regard to the mortgage market, states that

> the pieces were in place in a deregulated mortgage market for a wholesale shift from 30-year fixed mortgages to short-term mortgages. Securitisation, largely unregulated mortgage companies driven by executive pay linked to their stock prices and regulators who did not believe in regulating at the Federal Reserve were all in place.[143]

Furthermore, the ability for large banking institutions to partake in the system was determined by key pieces of legislation, which was a crucial factor in dictating the potential size of the bubble that would inevitably burst.

142 Neil Barofsky *Bailout: An Inside Account of How Washington Abandoned Main Street While Rescuing Wall Street* (Simon and Schuster 2012) 8.
143 Damon Silvers 'Deregulation and the New Financial Architecture' in Martin H. Wolfson and Gerald A. Epstein (eds) *The Handbook of the Political Economy of Financial Crises* (Oxford University Press 2013) 439.

To briefly provide some context we have to go back to the turn of the twentieth century. At this time, the burgeoning United States was dominated by just a few expansive banking houses, chief amongst which was the empire controlled by JP Morgan.[144] However, to counter the influence of this financial oligarchy unofficially led by Morgan, the state (under the auspices of the administration of President Coolidge) enacted the McFadden Act of 1927,[145] with the aim of rebalancing the national banking market so that large overpowering banking conglomerates were not unfairly dominating the State-wide banking organisations. This prohibition on inter-state banking, however, did not have the desired effect because the large banking institutions had the distinct advantage of being able to combine the resource-generating commercial banking entities with the speculative (and potentially very profitable) investment banking entities, a system also known as 'universal banking'.

In 1929, however, the situation dramatically changed for large banking houses. Their role in the Wall Street crash, which was an important factor, but by no means the only one,[146] turned public opinion against them to such an extent that politicians sought to take impactful action against them. The politicians and legislators wanted to reduce their speculative capability, with the intention of fostering systemic balance and to make the infamously opaque banking institutions as transparent as possible (e.g. up to this point JP Morgan *had never* issued a financial report for examination).[147] To digress for one brief moment, it is worthwhile noting the famous words of Machiavelli:

144 John Pierpont Morgan's influence spread the length of the United States and even further afield. As a result there is an extensive range of literature that can provide details on the man and his legacy. For just a few resources see Daniel Alef *JP Morgan: America's Greatest Banker* (Titans of Fortune Publishing 2009); Ron Chernow *The House of Morgan: An American Banking Dynasty and the Rise of Modern Finance* (Grove/Atlantic, Inc 2010); Steven H. Gittelman *JP Morgan and the Transportation Kings: The Titanic and Other Disasters* (University Press of America 2012).

145 *An Act to Further Amend the National Banking Laws and the Federal Reserve Act (McFadden Act)* Pub. L. 69–639 HR 2 (1927).

146 Interestingly for us the dynamics within the banking industry were not the only factor that instigated the era-defining reforms. In response to the fraudulent and obscure offerings of securities that were at the heart of the Wall Street Crash, regulators (primarily the Comptroller of the Currency) incorporated the *credit rating agencies* to officially provide verification for the safety of securities being offered; the Comptroller forced certain investors to only invest in securities the agencies deemed safe. This is commonly referred to as the start of the induction of the agencies into the economy, although that understanding is misleading, as economic historians have detailed that the agencies were considered central and were also given legal status, years before the actions of the Comptroller in 1931. For more on the Comptroller's actions see *A Snapshot of the Regulatory Framework* (n 101). For why the understanding developed by Partnoy primarily is not accurate see Marc Flandreau and Joanna K. Slawatyniec 'Understanding Rating Addiction: US Courts and the Origins of Rating Agencies' Regulatory Licence (1900–1940)' [2013] 20 *Financial History Review* 3. For Partnoy's establishment of the view that 1931 signifies the creation of the agencies' 'regulatory licence' see Frank Partnoy 'How and Why Credit Rating Agencies are not Like other Gatekeepers' in Yasuyuki Fuchita and Robert E. Litan (eds) *Financial Gatekeepers: Can They Protect Investors?* (Brookings Institution Press 2007); Partnoy (n 69). For just one assessment into the fraudulent aspects of securities offerings before the Wall Street Crash in 1929 see Frank Partnoy *The Match King: Ivar Kreuger and the Financial Scandal of the Century* (Profile Books 2010).

147 Charles R. Geisst *Wall Street: A History* (Oxford University Press 1997) 201.

Whoever wishes to foresee the future must consult the past; for human events ever resemble those of preceding times. This arises from the fact that they are produced by men who ever have been and ever shall be, animated by the same passions and thus they necessarily have the same results.[148]

This sentiment was clearly not in the minds of legislators and politicians in the mid-1990s when they sought to dismantle these New Deal-era legislative principles as we shall see very shortly.

To continue, in the New Deal era of the United States, the state, under the auspices of the Roosevelt administration, sought to finally reduce the overwhelming presence of the largest banking entities.[149] In enacting the Banking Act of 1933,[150] more commonly referred to as the Glass-Steagall Act after its Senatorial sponsors and certain important sections within the Act, the state had brought an end to 'universal banking' and forced the previously almighty banking establishments to choose between registering as a commercial bank or an investment bank.[151] The State also sought to remove the redeemer-status that JP Morgan and his affiliates had donned after the Panic of 1907 intervention, arguably unenthusiastically,[152] by introducing deposit insurance which fundamentally (although not entirely) reduced the risk of national 'runs' on banking institutions.[153] This concept of facing the challenge of regulating *against* powerful entities is extraordinarily important and, arguably, should be vital to every other normative analysis of the financial sector. This incredible era initiated over 70 years of financial balance (for the most part), which has come to be referred to as the 'Quiet Period'. Gary Gorton argues that this shows that 'properly designed bank regulations can prevent financial crises for a significant period of time'.[154]

However, in adapting Gorton's and combining with it Swan's analysis from earlier, perhaps it could be stated that properly designed *deregulation* can also generate similar levels of success, albeit within a purely alternative context.

---

148 Mark T. Hebner *Index Funds: The 12-step Program for Active Investors* (IFA Publishing 2006).

149 Geisst (n 147) 230. Perhaps the best demonstration of their *influence*, in excess of their obvious power emanating from being leading bankers, can be seen when assessing the foundations of the modern-day financial lynchpin that is the Federal Reserve. For more on the fascinating insight into JP Morgan, JD Rockefeller and the Executives of Kuhn, Loeb essentially creating the Federal Reserve. See Alexander Tabarrok 'The Separation of Commercial and Investment Banking: The Morgans vs The Rockefellers' [1998] 1 *The Quarterly Journal of Austrian Economics* 1. For more general resources analysing the foundations of the Federal Reserve see Gabriel Kolko *The Triumph of Conservatism* (Quadrangle Books 1963); Murray N. Rothbard 'The Federal Reserve as a Cartelisation Device: The Early Years 1913–1930' in Barry N. Siegel (ed.) *Money in Crisis* (Ballinger 1984).

150 *The Banking Act of 1933* Pub. L. 73-66, 48 Stat 162.

151 Randall S. Kroszner and Raghuram G. Rajan 'Is the Glass-Steagall Act Justified? A Study of the US Experience with Universal Banking Before 1933' [1994] 84 *The American Economic Review* 814.

152 R. G. Donaldson 'Financing Banking Crises: Lessons from the Panic of 1907' [1993] 31 *Journal of Monetary Economics* 71.

153 Geisst (n 147) 230. This was also the reason for the creation of the Federal Reserve. For more on its truly fascinating beginnings see Tabarrok (n 149) 1.

154 Gary Gorton *Misunderstanding Financial Crises: Why We Don't See Them Coming* (Oxford University Press 2012) 4.

Irrespective of the heated debate that surrounds this issue of the relevancy of deregulation, the seemingly coordinated series of legislative events can help us to understand further the potential causes of the crisis. The Senate subcommittee, in continuing its examination across the eras suggests that up until the mid-1990s, the New Deal era statutes were having the intended effect:

> U.S. banking consisted primarily of thousands of modest-sized banks tied to local communities ... this broad-based approach meant that when a bank suffered losses, the United States could quickly close its doors, protect its depositors and avoid significant damage to the U.S. banking system or economy.[155]

However, 1994 was the beginning of the end for the Quiet Period. In that year the State, under the Clinton administration, introduced the Riegle-Neal Interstate Banking and Branching Efficiency Act of 1994,[156] with the result that banks could now begin to establish branches across the country and also buy other banks across the country. Supporters of the Act argued at the time that it would 'allow banks to become more efficient as they grew bigger, reducing costs, lowering loan rates and accelerating economic growth'.[157] We know now, with hindsight, that this was a short-sighted and dangerous analysis, although if we ignore the pleasantries of affording these supporters the protection of hindsight for just one moment, it is worth noting that it is these sorts of misguided and naive sentiments that add support to dangerous movements (and this does not just apply to financial regulation – and we shall see further evidence of this phenomena next in *Deregulation – A False Diagnosis*); the responsibility that comes with being a reputable commentator should inhibit one's prevalence for placing trust in untrustworthy sectors (the Machiavellian quote from earlier is very much applicable here).

In 1987, the same year that Alan Greenspan assumed the Chairmanship of the Federal Reserve, the 'Fed' began to allow banks to establish affiliates that dealt in short-term commercial paper securities, although they established the restriction that these dealings could not contribute more than 5 per cent of the bank holding company's revenues.[158] In 1997, the same year the Riegle-Neal Act was to be fully implemented, the Federal Reserve (still under the stewardship of Greenspan) voted to raise the limitation to 25 per cent. The Federal Reserve also allowed the Citicorp–Travelers merger which opened the floodgates for the reappearance of excessively large conglomerates. Furthermore, the State formally repealed the Glass-Steagall Act of 1933 with the Gramm-Leach-Bliley Act of 1999,[159] which essentially 'eliminated the Glass-Steagall prohibition on banks

155 United States Senate (n 81) 15.
156 *Riegle-Neal Interstate Banking and Branching Efficiency Act of 1994* Pub. L. 103–328.
157 Hersh Shefrin and Meir Statman 'Behavioural Finance in the Financial Crisis: Market Efficiency, Minsky and Keynes' in Alan S. Blinder, Andrew W. Loh and Robert M. Solow (eds) *Rethinking the Financial Crisis* (Russell Sage Foundation 2013) 124.
158 Silvers (n 143) 439.
159 *The Gramm-Leach-Bliley (Financial Services Modernisation) Act of 1999* Pub. L. 106–102, 113 Stat 1338.

engaging in proprietary trading and exempted investment bank holding companies from direct federal regulation'.[160]

The deregulatory phase was completed with the enactment of the Commodity Futures Modernisation Act of 2000,[161] which 'barred federal regulation of swaps and the trillion-dollar swap markets and which allowed U.S. banks, broker-dealers and other financial institutions to develop, market and trade these unregulated financial products'.[162] These Acts were all either developed or supported by now-infamous figures within the financial world, such as Senator Gramm,[163] Larry Summers[164] and Robert Rubin.[165]

This concerted phase of deregulation, developed by prominent members of the financial elite, is of course extremely worrying. Silvers notes that if the New Deal-era statutes were designed to smash the House of Morgan, the deregulatory phase in the late 1990s was designed to rebuild it. In fact, once the dust had settled from the turbulent period of 2007 and 2008, there were only four giant banking institutions left standing in the United States: JP Morgan Chase, Citigroup, Bank of America and Wells Fargo.[166] The lessons learned by 'FDR' in the midst of the Great Depression were conveniently forgotten. Claims such as those from James K. Galbraith, that this version of the State represents 'the predator State', are particularly hard to argue against. Galbraith defines the predator State as one that 'systematically turned regulation over to the industries to be regulated and not just to them but to their lobbies, which tended to represent the most aggressively anti-government, antiregulation and antistabilisation aspects of each industry'.[167] Yet there are those that argue against this understanding and they argue their case vehemently.

Deregulation – a false diagnosis

There is a line of reasoning, advanced by a number of prominent scholars and politicians, that suggests the argument that deregulation was a key cause of the crisis is, to put it bluntly, 'dead wrong'.[168] The protagonists of this belief are predominantly strongly pro-market and believe that government intervention should only occur when the potential effects of failure are truly large in scale.[169]

---

160 United States Senate (n 81) 16.

161 *The Commodity Futures Modernisation Act of 2000* HR 4577.

162 United States Senate (n 81) 16.

163 Eric Lipton and Stephen Labaton 'Deregulator looks back, unswayed' [2008] *The New York Times* (16 November).

164 United States Department of the Treasury *Remarks of Treasury Secretary Lawrence H Summers to the Securities Industry Association* (Treasury Press Centre 9 November 2000).

165 Silvers (n 143) 442.

166 ibid. Silvers notes that together these institutions control over 60 per cent of the assets of all US bank holding companies.

167 James K. Galbraith 'The Roots of the Crisis and How to Bring It to a Close' in Robert W. Kolb (ed.) *Lessons from the Financial Crisis: Causes, Consequences and Our Economic Future* (John Wiley & Sons 2010) 38.

168 Charles W. Calomiris 'The Subprime Turmoil: What's Old, What's New and What's Next' [2009] 2 *Journal of Structured Finance* 37.

169 ibid 32.

So, rather than castigating the state for deregulating the marketplace, this point of view castigates them for *determining* the abhorrent practices witnessed in the creation of the financial crisis through regulation rather than deregulation. As we shall now see, the leading protagonists suggest that all of those entities criticised in the wake of the collapse, from investment banks and insurers to rating agencies and mortgage brokers, were simply adhering to policies that the state had conjured up years before the crisis began.

Charles Calomiris is particularly active in promoting this notion of deregulation being a positive element rather than a negative one. Calomiris argues that the deregulation narrative adopted in the wake of the crisis 'made no sense', mostly because the involvement by banks in the sub-prime mortgage market and within mortgage securitisation was 'in no way affected by the deregulation of the last two decades'.[170] Furthermore, he argues that instead of threatening the security of the economy, deregulation *in fact* 'cushioned the financial system's adjustment to the sub-prime shock by making banks more diversified and by allowing troubled investment banks to become stabilised by becoming or being acquired by, commercial banks'.[171] He continues by suggesting that, in opposition to previous crises, where 'shocks have not been mitigated by the raising of capital by financial institutions in the wake of losses', the response of the US financial system to such a devastating collapse was an *improvement* which emanated from deregulation, consolidation and globalisation.[172] This 'improvement' (i.e. the appropriation of over half a trillion dollars of taxpayers' money to prop up a system that has been officially labelled as systemically fraudulent is, according to Calomiris, 'appropriate and allows monetary policy to be "surgical" and more flexible').[173] He also concludes that, in what he sees as a positive element, the acquisitions of Bear Sterns and Merrill Lynch by JP Morgan Chase and Bank of America respectively would not have been possible without the repealing of Glass-Steagall.

There is a slightly more palatable argument advanced by Jeffrey Friedman and Wladimir Kraus, who contest that looking solely at the role deregulation played *directly* within the securitisation process has to lead to the conclusion that this argument is deficient. The technical understanding that no bank got into trouble because of a securities affiliate is indeed true. Also, the understanding that the banks that suffered losses did so because they held low-quality mortgages which was an activity that was always permitted by Glass-Steagall is also arguably true.[174] However, even though Friedman and Krauss call for us to look beyond 'narrow intellectual horizons',[175] which is obviously a welcome call, both they and

---

170   Charles W. Calomiris 'Origins of the Subprime Crisis' in Asli Demirgüç-Kunt, Douglas D. Evanoff and George G. Kaufman (eds) *The International Financial Crisis: Have the Rules of Finance Changed?* (World Scientific 2011) 88.

171   ibid.

172   Calomiris (n 168) 7.

173   ibid.

174   Jeffrey Friedman and Wladimir Kraus *Engineering the Financial Crisis: Systemic Risk and the Failure of Regulation* (University of Pennsylvania Press 2011) 445.

175   ibid 28.

Calomiris do not follow that advice. The deregulatory phase may have not had an absolutely direct impact upon the securitisation system as Calomiris explains, but the systemic escalation of profits and risk that resulted from widespread deregulation did have a direct effect upon the potential of the inevitable collapse enveloping the global community. As we shall see after examining the next main component of this school of thought, not looking beyond such narrow intellectual horizons has perhaps made their understanding particularly dangerous with regard to capitalising upon the financial crisis to promote stark realities.

Calomiris blames 'regulatory failure', particularly with respect to the Government-Sponsored Enterprises (GSEs) like Fannie Mae and Freddie Mac and also prudential banking regulation, as the key contributor to the financial crisis. This sentiment is echoed by another prominent protagonist, Peter Wallison. Wallison, who was a prominent Republican under President Reagan, was the leading dissenting opinion in the Majority Report of the Financial Crisis Inquiry Commission. For Wallison, the fault lies with the government, not for the deregulatory measures it imposed years before the crisis, but for its housing policies instead. This is more-or-less the same argument as Calomiris' (they rely upon the same research as we shall see shortly).

He ultimately argues that the government-induced growth of the sub-prime mortgage market inevitably resulted in a decline of underwriting practices.[176] Through the Housing and Community Developing Act of 1992[177] and the re-enforcement of the Community Reinvestment Act of 1977[178] (in 1995), Wallison argues that Non-Traditional Mortgages (NTMs) became hot property and the overwhelming presence of the two GSEs meant that underwriting practices had to deteriorate to meet the legal requirement to hold such mortgages. The *stated* aim of the government was to increase the availability of loans for mortgages to middle- to low-income applicants by changing the standards for applicability (i.e. the down-payment percentage required was reduced to just 5% and the applicant only had to have a satisfactory credit history spanning the previous *12 months*).[179]

Wallison cites these figures and the fact that only Lehman Brothers ranked in the top 5 of MBS issuers at the height of the market in 2005, as being the proof for the claim that banking deregulation was not to blame for the crisis; the rest of the top five was made up of other sub-prime issuers like Fannie Mae and Freddie Mac. This ultimately led Wallison to conclude that 'it would be more accurate to say that Wall Street followed Fannie and Freddie into subprime lending rather than vice versa'.[180] This version of events advanced by Wallison details a false system, whereby the laws forced GSEs, sub-prime lenders and banks into funnelling more and more funds into the MBS market so that instead of defaults occurring earlier and the crisis coming to view, the incessant pumping of

176 Peter J. Wallison 'Dissenting Statement' in Phil Angelides *Financial Crisis Inquiry Report* (DIANE Publishing 2011) 451.
177 *The Housing and Community Development Act of 1992* HR 5334.
178 *The Community Reinvestment Act of 1977* Pub. L. 95–128, 91 Stat 1147.
179 Wallison (n 176) 454.
180 ibid 463.

funds into increasingly lower-quality loans meant that those who would normally be delinquent borrowers were able to refinance and prolong the system.

This argument is completely rational and is supported by the facts of the securitisation system and the effects of the legislation that was passed. However, in attributing blame, Wallison seeks to pardon a wide range of market actors and simply focus on the government, which is an extraordinary mistake. He argues that the Commission's report is wrong for criticising 'firms, regulators, corporate executives, risk managers and rating agency analysts' because the information about the composition of the mortgage market '*was simply not known when the bubble began to inflate*'.[181] This sentiment is particularly distasteful in light of the fraudulent behaviour by those market actors Wallison pardons. However, there is one aspect to Wallison's understanding which raises enough suspicion to warrant an alternative viewpoint; the GSEs were not completely regulated and only shared their financial information with regulators voluntarily. This is important because, in essence, their mandate was to guarantee loans for NTMs on the basis of meeting the government's quotas and regulations, not for profit. This perception, according to Wallison, led market participants to believe that the loans held by the GSEs were 'prime' loans, as their quasi-governmental status had always resulted in their conservatism in making financial decisions. What had actually happened was that in order to meet the demands of the state, the GSEs had subverted such policies and were actually holding millions more NTMs than the market knew (because they did not have to disclose their records).[182] The result of this was the contagion witnessed in the privately created MBS market, which subsequently spread across all mortgages because mortgages are all related by house prices. So, the shock at the losses in the private MBS market was amplified to a spectacular degree because the market then realised that Fannie and Freddie held many more NTMs than they had initially realised. This was why in September 2008 the placing of both Fannie Mae and Freddie Mac into conservatorship signalled the commencement of the actual 'crisis'.

So this understanding places the blame squarely at the feet of the US government. It is difficult to argue against this perception because the facts of the crisis allude to it being the correct evaluation. However, to suggest that market actors who are relied upon to *know* certain elements of the economy better than anyone else (i.e. credit rating agencies and securities analysts) simply could not have known is irresponsible. A key aspect in responsible economics is to analyse trends, not just to accept figures at face value, which is something Wallison seems to overlook; it was not impossible for rating agencies and market analysts to have known that the bubble was not based on solid foundations. The key issue here is that while it was not impossible, it was extremely *profitable* to accept figures at face value; as we have seen already: 'money triumphed over ethics'.

Wallison's viewpoints are perhaps narrow, but they are at least critical. The viewpoint held by Calomiris, however, is particularly different. While it is prudent

181 ibid 466 (emphasis added).
182 ibid.

to remain objective, it is important to use Calomiris' views (and the school of thought he represents) as an example of the dangers of misappropriating the reverence for scholarly commentary. This school of thought, which suggests that the suspension of accepted regulatory principles and the appropriation of over half-a-trillion dollars of taxpayers money to pump into irresponsible institutions is not only acceptable but should also be praised, is exceptionally dangerous. It provides the intellectual support for a societal shift that possibly may affect the direction of human history. The events of the financial crisis set an extraordinarily bad precedent; it was no ordinary 'crash'. When we align this to the fact that very few individuals have been prosecuted and that the leading figures of the process have become significantly wealthier than they already were, then the school of thought should be understood as contributing to the advancement of that agenda. Calomiris stated in 2009 that

> those of us who argued in the 1980s that nationwide branching would allow commercial banks to serve as platforms for universal banks with large relationship economies of scope can now say *we told you so* ... Bank of America, J.P. Morgan Chase and Citibank have all weathered the financial storm.[183]

Through the Troubled Asset Relief Program the three institutions received $115 billion of taxpayers' money. Those that can say we *told you so* must accept their share of responsibility for contributing to the largest and most widespread financial collapse on record.

Calomiris and Wallison pay particular attention to one source of research. Edward Pinto, who was a former executive vice president and chief credit officer for Fannie Mae until he was dismissed 'without reason' in the late 1980s,[184] is a particularly staunch critic of the GSEs and their involvement in the financial crisis, probably best characterised by his many works on behalf of the American Enterprise Institute[185] and his many testimonies to official hearings in the wake of the crash. The issue is, however, that Pinto's research is doubted in the same way as his motives. While this is presented here not to question Pinto's integrity, other scholars have.[186] Wallison himself ultimately admits that this line of reasoning is 'difficult to prove'.[187] While it is fine and arguably beneficial to the discipline that

---

183 Calomiris (n 168) 43 (emphasis added).
184 James R. Hagerty *The Fateful History of Fannie Mae: New Deal Birth to Mortgage Crisis Fall* (The History Press 2012) 203.
185 Edward J. Pinto 'Government Housing Policies in the Lead-up to the Financial Crisis: A Forensic Study' [2011] American Enterprise Institute. www.aei.org/docLib/Government-Housing-Policies-Financial-Crisis-Pinto-102110. Pinto has a number of other related works which form aspects of the scholarly output of the AEI. For more see the American Enterprise Institute.
186 Paul Krugman 'Evil > Stupid' [2011] *The New York Times* blog (15 July); Christopher Payne *The Consumer, Credit and Neoliberalism: Governing the Modern Economy* (Routledge 2012) 169; Oonagh McDonald *Fannie Mae and Freddie Mac: Turning the American Dream into a Nightmare* (A&C Black 2013) 146.
187 Payne (n 186).

theories are not discounted just because they are not 'popular', the effects of Wallison's and Calomiris' incorporation of Pinto's understanding are troubling. Unfortunately, while Wallison's dissent in the enquiry was widely criticised and was labelled as such, Calomiris' work continues to garner a following.

Coming to a unanimous conclusion is particularly difficult. It is difficult because one's understanding of this area comes not from just assessing the facts, but also by how the facts relate to one's wider perception of society. For example, the deregulation detailed in this section cannot be disputed; there were a number of legislative actions that took place within a particularly concentrated period of time which definitively illustrate a conscious period of deregulation. The issue with that, however, comes when we ask 'What was the purpose?' At first glance the divide seems straightforward. One argument is that it was to liberate constrained markets and increase efficiency by returning to a financial system centred on universal banking. We can also add that the state made a genuine attempt to increase the availability of mortgages to people who usually would not be afforded such an opportunity. Both of these endeavours are just and righteous from the perspective of societal health. However, the other argument centres on the fact that the financial crisis was the largest and most extensive financial collapse on record and irrevocably altered power structures. Perhaps more importantly, it has made the public safety net an *expectation* rather than an extraordinary solution, which alters the rules of our society completely. This argument would lead one to believe that the motives of the state and of the market actors who gained the most from the pre-crisis system were not genuine. This has to lead to the conclusion that these entities do not operate in the name of societal balance, which is a stark and chilling proclamation.

Mechanistic importance

This section will be very brief for two reasons. First, the importance of the agencies to the state in carrying out its mandate, whatever that may be, has already been established. We have seen how the agencies are important in allowing the state to form a regulatory framework for a smaller cost than if it were to do it itself; we have also seen how the agencies fit into the relationships between each market actor, which serves to make them almost indispensable within currently accepted understandings of the economy and how it should function. Second, to describe in detail why they are so important would take away from the analysis that directly follows this section. The reasons why agencies are considered to be so important are exactly the reasons why there is such a divergence between what is *desired* and what *actually* occurs. Aspects such as the need to decipher and navigate through the purposefully created complexity that defines the modern marketplace is just one reason why the state seemingly depends upon the rating agencies, despite its claims of reducing rating dependency in the wake of the crisis.

It is becoming apparent that there are two extremes that describe the role of the 'state': the first version consisting of the state aiming to protect the public through making genuine attempts to foster responsible economic growth and the second that is chiefly concerned with providing a supportive environment to financial elites so that they can make as much money as possible without bearing the cost of that inherently excessive quest. The former of these versions is safe; it is comforting to believe in and, most importantly, it contains answers. If we understand that the state was simply exploited by greedy and immoral market actors, then should the state incorporate this knowledge into its regulatory approach we should, theoretically, be free from further financial disasters. But, there is very little evidence for this being the reality. There is, however, an abundance of evidence that suggests the state acted predominantly in the interests of market actors who stood to profit immensely from the pre-crisis system, which brings us to ask why they would do such a thing.

It is admittedly a digression but arguably it is an important one because understanding the *motive* of the state may help us understand how and why it utilises the rating agencies in the manner that it does. It must be declared immediately that there is simply not enough space here to accommodate an appropriate analysis of what is known as 'Capture Theory'. However, some cursory definitions, when combined with a closer look at just one small element, may suffice for our requirements. 'Capture' in the context of regulation can be broadly defined by a regulatory agency or officer acting for the benefit of a party that is compensating it in some way, in opposition to its stated mandate (i.e. which is usually to *protect* a given entity that is at risk such as investors or the general public). A good example of capture from the financial crisis can be found in the statement of former Chairperson of the Federal Deposit Insurance Corporation (FDIC) Sheila Bair who, in an extraordinary exposé of the world of banking regulation, detailed how the problem with regard to regulators and Citicorp (as the primary example) was not just the cosy relationship between them

> but a problem of regulatory capture, in which the (Office of the Comptroller of the Currency) OCC, Office of Thrift Supervision (OTS) and the Fed all saw themselves as *advocates* for the banking industry, rather than as regulators of the industry.[188]

This one example is indicative of capture, whereby the captured agency or agencies go against their mandate and actively work *for* the party that has captured it; it is so easily forgotten that they are public servants.

Capture theories cover a wide range of aspects and advance a number of methods and reasons for how and why agencies (and therefore states in some cases) can become captured by private interests.[189] One reason that may supplement our

---

188 Adam J. Levitin 'The Politics of Financial Regulation and the Regulation of Financial Politics: A Review Essay' [2014] 127 *Harvard Law Review* 23 (emphasis added).

189 For just some of the key works on the capturing of the legislative process see Mancur Olson *The Logic of Collective Action: Public Goods and the Theory of Groups* (Schocken Books 1968); George J. Stigler 'The Theory of Economic Regulation' [1971] 2 *Bell Journal of Economics and Management Science* 3; Sam Peltzman 'Toward a More General Theory of Regulation' [1976] 19 *Journal of Law and Economics* 211; Charles E. Lindblom *Politics and Markets: The World's Political-Economic Systems* (Basic Books 1977); Theodore J. Lowi *The End of Liberalism*

analysis is known as the 'revolving door' theory.[190] The 'revolving door', which signifies the moving between different strategically important positions within the field of finance (it can apply to other fields, of course) increases the potential for success for the lobbying efforts of big business. Sriramesh notes that 'lobbyists and public relations consultants in the U.S. often use personal influence to conduct their public relations activities ... these former officials rely on the contacts they made during their tenure in government service to help their clients'.[191] This is clearly an issue; the fact that the whole lobbying system is not as transparent as it perhaps should be compounds the potential for regulatory capture to occur.

The biggest issue here is one of influence and it is common knowledge that the leading figures in the agencies concerned with financial stability (the Treasury, the Federal Reserve etc.) had predominantly moved to the agencies from the leading entities on Wall Street, so much so that the government was termed 'Government Sachs' by the press due to the number of ex-Goldman Sachs employees who were in influential positions in the government when the crisis hit.[192] If we are to accept this is as the true version of events (and one cannot deny that is true, it is just a matter if one believes it has an effect) then the *potential* effect it may have, at the very least deserves maximum attention. If regulatory leaders are sympathetic, if not absolutely supportive to their former employers' concerns (a lot of them return to the industry once their term finishes) and legislative leaders are being systematically lobbied by organised and connected parties, then it is rational to suggest that the state functions for business predominantly, not for the public whom they represent in a democracy. There will be much more on this topic in the next chapter, but for now there is an important question to be asked before we can move on: if the state operates for business, then what role do the rating agencies play in assisting the state in its business-friendly endeavours?

(WW Norton & Company 1979). For a deeper analysis of the concept see Jon Hanson and David Yosifon 'The Situation: An Introduction to the Situational Character, Critical Realism, Power Economics and Deep Capture' [2003] 152 *University of Pennsylvania Law Review* 173. For the arguments against the presence and effects of regulatory capture see Michael A. Crew and Charles K. Rowley 'Toward a Public Choice Theory of Monopoly Regulation' [1988] 57 *Public Choice* 1; Michael E. Levine and Jennifer L. Forrence 'Regulatory Capture, Public Interest and the Public Agenda: Towards a Synthesis' [1990] 6 *Journal of Law, Economics and Organisation* 167; Daniel Carpenter 'Confidence Games: How Does Regulation Constitute Markets?' in Edward Balleisen and David Moss (eds) *Government and Markets: Towards A New Theory of Regulation* (Cambridge University Press 2009); Lawrence G. Baxter 'Essay: "Capture" in Financial Regulation: Can we Channel it Toward the Common Good?' [2011] 21 *Cornell Journal of Law and Public Policy* 177.

190 For a representative analysis of the 'revolving door' theory see Andrew Baker 'Restraining Regulatory Capture? Anglo-America, Crisis Politics and Trajectories of Change in Global Financial Governance' [2010] 86 *International Affairs* 3.

191 Krishnamurthy Sriramesh 'Power, Distance and Public Relations: An Ethnographic Study of Southern Indian Organisations' in Hugh M. Culbertson and Ni Chen (eds) *International Public Relations: A Comparative Analysis* (Routledge 2013) 186.

192 Helen Deresky and Elizabeth Christopher *International Management: Managing Cultural Diversity* (Pearson Higher Education AU 2011) 53.

If we look back on what has been established already with regard to the function of the rating agencies and analyse it from the point of view of helping the state to promote and protect the interests of big business, then the centrality of the agencies to that cause quickly becomes apparent. Credit ratings allow the state to separate investors so that only the truly large, influential and resource-rich investors can partake in schemes that stand to generate the most profit for a handful of organisations. Rating agencies also govern which organisations (issuers) will be allowed to partake in such schemes by administering the required ratings for entry to a specific marketplace. While this admittedly sounds conspiratorial, we have already learned how the rating policies of the top agencies in the lead-up to the crisis became *highly* subjective, which alone means this understanding is not entirely baseless.

Again it must be stated that such conclusions will be measured on one's general and personal understandings of the economy and society. While the belief that the state operates for business and against the public may be too adversarial for some, it can at least be stated that enough evidence exists to suggest that it *may* be the case. The existence of the possibility alone should cause suspicion and force people to apply their critical faculties when assessing the power relations within our market-centric society. What can also be said, perhaps with much more authority, is that a clear divergence between what is *desired* and what is *actually* the case exists throughout the relationships in which the ratings industry plays an important part. Irrespective of the view that someone may have on the role of the state, it must be advanced universally that it has a considerable duty to protect its citizens; this is a *desired* quality. Investors can reasonably expect that rating agencies do not *actively* operate against them, as prior to 2010 the state forced them to deal with the rating agencies *exclusively*; this is a *desired* quality. But, the *actual* reality is arguably completely different, as this section has endeavoured to detail. What we need to know now is *why*? What are the key reasons that underpin and perpetuate this divergence? Finding the answer to these questions will have a direct impact on our ability to predict the potential for the reform proposal to be adopted and forms the purpose of Chapter 3.

Conclusion

Ultimately it is contested here that this divergence between what is *desired* and what is *actually* the case is both real and pervasive. The number of instances where the ratings industry operated against what may be termed as 'the public interest' and, more tellingly, against what they themselves argue is their role, is truly staggering. Whether it is brazenly operating against investors who control the savings of the vast majority of the developed world or whether it is going against the mandate that was given to it to lessen the possibility of a systemic failure, the ratings industry has acted in its own interest throughout. Perhaps what is truly desired is that the ratings industry should consider others, in some limited form, it its approach to business.

However, the ratings industry has shown no appetite to do this since it received NRSRO status in the early 1970s. It actually showed no appetite to do so before then, but the fact that they were dependent upon investors (subscribers) for their income prohibited the agencies from fully indulging in self-preservation. Today, there is no such prohibition. This notion has to be incorporated into any future regulatory proposal. Rather than hoping or anticipating that the agencies will act in a certain way, we should heed the words of Machiavelli[193] and examine their *actual* performance and the motivations that underpinned that performance; there is simply no justification for believing that the agencies will act in a socially responsible manner.

While eradicating the *actual* entirely, in terms of conflicts of interest stemming from remuneration structures or the 'revolving door' is undoubtedly desirable, it is almost impossible. There are simply too many factors at play that would inhibit such a reality coming to fruition. However, rather than seeking to eradicate the *actual* (i.e. the oligopolistic structure of the industry or the issuer-pays remuneration system) it is argued here that we acknowledge it as much as possible. What is meant by this is that *accepting* certain truths about the ratings industry (i.e. that issuers must pay for the ratings otherwise nobody else will because of the 'free-rider' problem) will allow us all to focus upon the reality of the situation rather than focusing on attaining the *desired* without any real substance (i.e. calling for increased competition for an industry defined by its oligopolistic structure to appease widespread condemnation of the agencies' performance). While some elements of the *actual* cannot be changed, like the fortified position of an industry that is nearly 180 years old or the need for third-party analysis in the bond market, other elements can be changed if we view the process of reform in the right way; it is not unreasonable to constrain the activities of such a fundamentally important sector of society, irrespective of their private status. Dictating that rating agencies cannot exploit their position by offering non-rating services is perfectly rational and represents an element of the *actual* which can so easily be changed given there is an appetite to do so. In Chapter 3 we shall see how the divergence between the desired and the *actual* came to be and how it continues. This will be a very important endeavour if we are to demonstrate clearly that what is required is a different way of looking at rating-agency reform; we must understand intently and acknowledge the reasons for this divergence if we are to reduce the potential dangers that rating agencies pose to society.

Bibliography

ABN AMRO Bank NV v Bathurst Regional Council [2014] FCAFC 65.
Alef, D. *J.P. Morgan: America's Greatest Banker* (Titans of Fortune Publishing 2009).
Altvater, E. and Geiger, M. 'Exiting the Multiple Crises through "Green" Growth?' in Exner, A., Fleissner, P. and Kranzl, L. (eds) *Land and Resource Scarcity: Capitalism, Struggle and Well-being in a World Without Fossil Fuels* (Routledge 2013).
An Act to Further Amend the National Banking Laws and the Federal Reserve Act (McFadden Act) Pub. L. 69–639 HR 2 (1927).

---

193 See (n 148).

Andenas, M. and Chiu, I.H.Y. *The Foundations and Future of Financial Regulation: Governance for Responsibility* (Routledge 2013).

Bai, L. 'On Regulating Conflicts of Interest in the Credit Rating Industry' [2010] 13 *New York University Journal of Legislation and Public Policy* 253.

Bank for International Settlements *International Convergence of Capital Measurement and Capital Standards* (BIS 1988).

Barofsky, N. *Bailout: An Inside Account of How Washington Abandoned Main Street while Rescuing Wall Street* (Simon and Schuster 2012).

Baron, N.D. 'The Role of Rating Agencies in the Securitisation Process' in Kendall, L.T. and Fishman, M.J. (ed.) *A Primer on Securitization* (MIT Press 2000).

Bathurst Regional Council v Local Government Financial Services Pty Ltd (No 5) [2012] FCA 1200.

Baxter, L.G. 'Essay: "Capture" in Financial Regulation: Can We Channel It toward the Common Good?' [2011] 21 *Cornell Journal of Law and Public Policy* 177.

Beardsley v Tappan 5 Blatchf. 498 (1867).

Bragg, S.M. *Running an Effective Relations Department: A Comprehensive Guide* (John Wiley & Sons 2010).

Buffett, M. and Clark, D. *Warren Buffett and the Art of Stock Arbitrage: Proven Strategies for Arbitrage and Other Special Investment Situations* (Scribner 2010).

Calomiris, C.W. 'Origins of the Subprime Crisis' in Demirgüç-Kunt, A., Evanoff, D.D. and Kaufman, G.G. (eds) *The International Financial Crisis: Have the Rules of Finance Changed?* (World Scientific 2011).

Calomiris, C.W. 'The Subprime Turmoil: What's Old, What's New and What's Next' [2009] 15(1) *Journal of Structured Finance* 6.

CalPERS 'CalPERS to Recover More than $300 Million from Standard & Poor's in Investment Ratings Settlements' [2015]. www.calpers.ca.gov/page/newsroom/calpers-news/recover-investment-ratings-settlements [accessed 14/12/15].

Carpenter, D. 'Confidence Games: How Does Regulation Constitute Markets?' in Balleisen, E. and Moss, D. (eds) *Government and Markets: Towards a New Theory of Regulation* (Cambridge University Press 2009).

Cassidy, J. *Concise Corporations Law* (Federation Press 2006).

Chernow, R. *The House of Morgan: An American Banking Dynasty and the Rise of Modern Finance* (Grove/Atlantic, Inc 2010).

Ciment, J. 'Credit Rating Agencies' in Ciment, J. (ed.) *Booms and Busts: An Encyclopedia of Economic History from Tulipmania of the 1630s to the Global Financial Crisis of the 21st Century* (Routledge 2015).

Clarke, T. 'Corporate Governance Causes of the Global Financial Crisis' in Sub, W., Stewart, J. and Pollard, D. (eds) *Corporate Governance and the Global Financial Crisis: International Perspectives* (Cambridge University Press 2011).

Coffee, J.C. *Gatekeepers: The Professions and Corporate Governance* (Oxford University Press 2006).

Commodity Futures Modernisation Act of 2000 HR 4577.

Community Reinvestment Act of 1977 Pub. L. 95–128, 91 Stat. 1147.

Complaint for Negligent Misrepresentation under Common Law & California Civil Code §§ 1709 & 1710 & Negligent Interference with Prospective Economic Advantage at 23, *Cal Pub Employees' Ret Sys v Moody's Corp (and others)*, No. CGC-09-490241.

Crew, M.A. and Rowley, C.K. 'Toward a Public Choice Theory of Monopoly Regulation' [1988] 57 *Public Choice* 1.

Crown Prosecution Service 'Corporate Prosecutions' [2015] (15 November). www.cps. gov.uk/legal/a_to_c/corporate_prosecutions/#a07 [accessed 18/2/18].

de Lange, D. *Cliques and Capitalism: A Modern Networked Theory of the Firm* (Palgrave Macmillan 2011).

Deflem, M. *Economic Crisis and Crime* (Emerald Group Publishing 2011).

Deresky, H. and Christopher, E. *International Management: Managing Cultural Diversity* (Pearson Higher Education AU 2011).

Donaldson, R.G. 'Financing Banking Crises: Lessons from the Panic of 1907' [1993] 31 *Journal of Monetary Economics* 69.

Farlow, A. *Consequences of the Global Financial Crisis* (Oxford University Press 2013).

Farrell, J.P. *Babylon's Banksters: The Alchemy of Deep Physics, High Finance and Ancient Religion* (Feral House 2010).

Feintuck, M. 'Regulatory Rationales Beyond the Economic: In Search of the Public Interest' in Baldwin, R., Cave, M. and Lodge, M. (eds) *The Oxford Handbook of Regulation* (Oxford University Press 2012).

Ferran, E. and Ho, L.C. *Principles of Corporate Finance Law* (Oxford University Press 2014).

Fickling, D. 'S&P, RBS Lose Appeal of Ruling Australian Towns Misled' [2014] Bloomberg (6 June). www.bloomberg.com/news/articles/2014-06-05/s-p-rbs-lose-appeal-on-ruling-they-misled-australian-investors [accessed 10/09/15].

Flandreau, M. and Sławatyniec, J.K. 'Understanding Rating Addiction: US Courts and the Origins of Rating Agencies' Regulatory License (1900–1940)' [2013] 20 *Financial History Review* 3.

Foley, S. 'Standard & Poor's and Moody's Settle US Subprime Lawsuits' [2013] *Financial Times*. www.ft.com/cms/s/0/27a59708-af46-11e2-ac6f-00144feabdc0. html#axzz3rDDouMB4 [accessed 18/2/18].

Friedman, J. and Kraus, W. *Engineering the Financial Crisis: Systemic Risk and the Failure of Regulation* (University of Pennsylvania Press 2011).

Fulghieri, P., Strobl, G. and Xia, H. 'The Economics of Solicited and Unsolicited Credit Ratings' [2014] 27 *The Review of Financial Studies* 2.

Galbraith, J.K. 'The Roots of the Crisis and How to Bring It to a Close' in Kolb, R.W. (ed.) *Lessons from the Financial Crisis: Causes, Consequences and Our Economic Future* (John Wiley & Sons 2010).

Geisst, C.R. *Encyclopaedia of American Business History* (Facts on File 2006).

Geisst, C.R. *Wall Street: A History* (Oxford University Press 1997).

Gittelman, S.H. *J.P. Morgan and the Transportation Kings: The Titanic and Other Disasters* (University Press of America 2012).

Gorton, G. *Misunderstanding Financial Crises: Why We Don't See Them Coming* (Oxford University Press USA 2012).

Gottschalk, P. *White-collar Crime: Detection, Prevention and Strategy in Business Enterprises* (Universal-Publishers 2010).

Gramm-Leach-Bliley (Financial Services Modernisation) Act of 1999 Pub. L. 106–102, 113 Stat. 1338.

Hagerty, J.R. *The Fateful History of Fannie Mae: New Deal Birth to Mortgage Crisis Fall* (The History Press 2012).

Hanson, J. and Yosifon, D. 'The Situation: An Introduction to the Situational Character, Critical Realism, Power Economics and Deep Capture' [2003] 152 *University of Pennsylvania Law Review* 173.

Hebner, M.T. *Index Funds: The 12-step Program for Active Investors* (IFA Publishing 2006).

Held, V. *The Public Interest and Individual Interests* (Basic Books 1970).

Hemraj, M. *Credit Rating Agencies: Self-regulation, Statutory Regulation and Case Law Regulation in the United States and European Union* (Springer 2015).

Hill, J.G. 'Images of the Shareholder – Shareholder Power and Shareholder Powerlessness' in Hill, J.G. and Thomas, R.S. (eds) *Research Handbook on Shareholder Power* (Edward Elgar Publishing 2015).

House of Lords *Banking Supervision and Regulation: 2nd Report of Session 2008–09, Vol. 2: Evidence* (The Stationery Office 2009).

Housing and Community Development Act of 1992 HR 5334.

Husisian, G. 'What Standard of Care Should Govern the World's Shortest Editorials? An Analysis of Bond Rating Agency Liability' [1989–90] 75 *Cornell Law Review* 410.

Iannotta, G. *Investment Banking: A Guide to Underwriting and Advisory Services* (Springer Science & Business Media 2010).

Investment Company Act of 1940 Pub. L. 76-768 2(a)(51)(A).

Isidore, C. '35 bankers were sent to prison for financial crisis crimes' [2016] CNN (28 April). http://money.cnn.com/2016/04/28/news/companies/bankers-prison/ [accessed 7/5/16]

Jackson, H.E. 'The Role of Credit Rating Agencies in the Establishment of Capital Standards for Financial Institutions in a Global Economy' in Ferran, E. and Goodhart, C.A.E. (eds) *Regulating Financial Services and Markets in the 21st Century* (Hart Publishing 2001).

James R. Koren 'CalPERS settles with Moody's for $130 million in ratings case' [2016] *LA Times* (9 March). www.latimes.com/business/la-fi-calpers-moodys-settlement-20160309-story.html [accessed 18/2/18].

Jo, T. 'A Heterodox Microfoundation of Business Cycles' in Leclaire, J.L., Jo, T. and Knodell, J. (eds) *Heterodox Analysis of Financial Crisis and Reform: History, Politics and Economics* (Edward Elgar Publishing 2011).

Jones, H. 'EU watchdog imposes its first fine on rating agency DBRS' [2015] Reuters (29 June). www.reuters.com/article/2015/06/29/eu-dbrs-fine-idUSL5N0ZF2C32015 0629#jJ0YOYCKBWYvbGY3.97 [accessed 10/09/15].

Kasler, D. 'CalPERS cleared to sue ratings agencies' [2014] *Sacramento Bee* (15 September). www.sacbee.com/news/business/article2609814.html [accessed 3/1/16].

King County, Washington and Iowa Student Loan Liquidity Corporation v IKB Deutsche Industriebank AG, Moody's Investors Service, Inc., The McGraw Hill Companies, Inc., Fitch, Inc. and Morgan Stanley & Co. Incorporated [2012] 863 FSupp2d 288 (4 May).

King v Patterson (1887) 49 New Jersey Law Reports 417, 9 A. 705.

Klein, A. 'Credit Raters' Power Leads to Abuses, Some Borrowers Say' [2004] *Washington Post* 24 November [accessed 18/2/18].

Kolb, R.W. *The Financial Crisis of Our Time* (Oxford University Press 2010).

Kolko, G. *The Triumph of Conservatism* (Quadrangle Books 1963).

Koren, J.R. 'CalPERS settles with Moody's for $130 million in ratings case' [2016] *LA Times* (9 March). www.latimes.com/business/la-fi-calpers-moodys-settlement-20160309-story.html [accessed 17/2/18].

Kraakman, R., Armour, J., Davies, P., Enriques, L., Hansmann, H.B., Hertig, G. and Hopt, K.J. *The Anatomy of Corporate Law: A Comparative and Functional Approach* (Oxford University Press 2009).

Kroszner, R.S. and Rajan, R.G. 'Is the Glass-Steagall Act Justified? A Study of the U.S. Experience with Universal Banking Before 1933' [1994] 84 *The American Economic Review* 4.

Krugman, P. 'Evil > Stupid' [2011] *The New York Times* blog (15 July). http://krugman.blogs.nytimes.com/2011/07/15/evil-stupid/?_r=0 [accessed 3/5/14].

Kumar, A., Chuppe, T.M. and Perttunen, P. *The Regulation of Non-bank Financial Institutions: The United States, the European Union and Other Countries, Parts 63–362* (World Bank Publications 1997).

Langley, P. *Liquidity Lost: The Governance of the Global Financial Crisis* (Oxford University Press 2015).

Langohr, H.P. and Langohr, P.T. *The Rating Agencies and Their Credit Ratings: What They Are, How They Work and Why They are Relevant* (John Wiley & Sons 2010).

Leonard, B. *Summary Report of Issues Identified in the Security and Exchange Commission Staff's Examinations of Select Credit Rating Agencies* (DIANE Publishing 2009).

Levine, M.E. and Forrence, J.L. 'Regulatory Capture, Public Interest and the Public Agenda: Towards a Synthesis' [1990] 6 *Journal of Law, Economics and Organisation*.

Levitin, A.J. 'The Politics of Financial Regulation and the Regulation of Financial Politics: A Review Essay' [2014] 127 *Harvard Law Review* 1991.

Linarelli, J. 'Luck, Justice and Systemic Financial Risk' [2015] *Journal of Applied Philosophy* 331.

Lindblom, C.E. *Politics and Markets: The World's Political-Economic Systems* (Basic Books 1977).

Lipton, R. and Labaton, S. 'Deregulator looks back, unswayed' [2008] *The New York Times* (16 November). www.nytimes.com/2008/11/17/business/economy/17gramm. html?pagewanted=all&_r=0 [accessed 10/4/15].

Listokin, Y. and Taibleson, B. 'If You Misrate, Then You Lose: Improving Credit Rating Accuracy through Incentive Compensation' [2010] 27 *Yale Journal on Regulation* 91.

Lowi, T.J. *The End of Liberalism* (WW Norton & Company 1979).

Lucy, W.N.R. and Mitchell, C. 'Replacing Private Property: The Case for Stewardship' [1996] 55 *The Cambridge Law Journal* 3.

Mackenzie, D. *What's Happening in the Mathematical Sciences, Vol. 8* (American Mathematical Society 2010).

Maruthappu, M., Watkins, J., Noor, A.M., Williams, C., Ali, R., Sullivan, R., Zeltner, T. and Atun, R. 'Economic Downturns, Universal Health Coverage and Cancer Mortality in High-income and Middle-income Countries, 1990–2010: a longitudinal analysis' [2016] *The Lancet* (online, 25 May).

Mattarocci, G. *The Independence of Credit Rating Agencies: How Business Models and Regulators Interact* (Academic Press 2014).

McDonald, O. *Fannie Mae and Freddie Mac: Turning the American Dream into a Nightmare* (A&C Black 2013).

Morelli, M. 'These 3 Companies Have Debt Rated "AAA" But Not All Are Buys' [2015] Seekingalpha.com. http://seekingalpha.com/article/3418446-these-3-companies-have-debt-rated-aaa-but-not-all-are-buys [accessed 3/4/16].

Neuman, N.B. 'A Sarbanes-Oxley for Credit Rating Agencies? A Comparison of the Roles Auditors' and Credit Rating Agencies' Conflicts of Interests Played in Recent Financial Crises' [2010] 12 University of Pennsylvania Journal of Business Law 921.

Neumann, J. 'Cost of Ratings Suit: $225 Million' [2013] *The Wall Street Journal*. www. wsj.com/articles/SB10001424127887323528404578453292918428224 [accessed 18/2/18].

Nolan, A. *Economic and Social Rights after the Global Financial Crisis* (Cambridge University Press 2014).

Nolan, B., Salverda, W., Checchi, D., Marx, I., McKnight, A., Tóth, I.G. and Van de Werfhorst, H. *Changing Inequalities and Social Impacts in Rich Countries: Thirty Countries' Experiences* (Oxford University Press 2014).

OECD *OECD Employment Outlook 2015* (OECD 2015).

Olson, M. *The Logic of Collective Action: Public Goods and the Theory of Groups* (Schocken Books 1968).

Partnoy, F. 'How and Why Credit Rating Agencies Are Not Like Other Gatekeepers' in Fuchita, Y. and Litan, R.E. (eds) *Financial Gatekeepers: Can They Protect Investors?* (Brookings Institution Press 2007).

Partnoy, F. 'The Siskel and Ebert of Financial Markets? Two Thumbs Down for the Credit Rating Agencies' [1999] 77 *Washington University Law Quarterly* 3.

Partnoy, F. *The Match King: Ivar Kreuger and the Financial Scandal of the Century* (Profile Books 2010).

Peltzman, S. 'Toward a More General Theory of Regulation' [1976] 19 *Journal of Law and Economics* 211.

Phalon, R. *Forbes Greatest Investing Stories* (John Wiley & Sons 2004).

Pinto, E.J. 'Government Housing Policies in the Lead-up to the Financial Crisis: A Forensic Study' [2011] American Enterprise Institute.

Reeves, A., McKee, M. and Stuckler, D. 'Economic Suicides in the Great Recession in Europe and North America' [2014] *The British Journal of Psychiatry* 246.

Riegle-Neal Interstate Banking and Branching Efficiency Act of 1994 Pub. L. 103–328.

Rothbard, M.N. 'The Federal Reserve as a Cartelisation Device: The Early Years 1913–1930' in Siegel, B.N. (ed.) *Money in Crisis* (Ballinger 1984).

Rousseau, S. 'Enhancing the Accountability of Credit Rating Agencies: The Case for a Disclosure-based Approach' [2005] Capital Markets Institute.

Ryder, N. *The Financial Crisis and White Collar Crime: The Perfect Storm?* (Edward Elgar Publishing 2014).

Ryder, N., Turksen, U. and Hassler, S. *Fighting Financial Crime in the Global Economic Crisis* (Routledge 2014).

Sagoff, M. *Price, Principle and the Environment* (Cambridge University Press 2004).

Saks, M. *Professions and the Public Interest: Medical Power, Altruism and Alternative Medicine* (Routledge 2005).

Schneeman, A. *Law of Corporations and Other Business Organisation* (Cengage Learning 2009).

Securities Act of 1933 Pub. L. 73–22, 48 Stat 74 Rule 144A.

Securities and Exchange Commission 'Egan-Jones Rating Co. and Sean Egan charged with making material misrepresentations to SEC' [2012] Press Release (2012–75).

Securities and Exchange Commission *Order Instituting Administrative and Cease-and-Desist Proceedings, Pursuant to Section 8A of the Securities Act of 1933 and Sections 15E (d) and 21C of the Securities Exchange Act of 1934, Making Findings and Imposing Remedial Sanctions and a Cease-and-Desist Order* [2015] Release No 9705; 74104, File No 3–16348.

Sergakis, K. 'Proxy Advisory Firms under ESMA's Microscope: A Perfectible Regulatory Approach?' [2014] 25 *International Company and Commercial Law Review* 4.

Shefrin, H. and Statman, M. 'Behavioural Finance in the Financial Crisis: Market Efficiency, Minsky and Keynes' in Blinder, A.S., Loh, A.W. and Solow, R.M. (eds) *Rethinking the Financial Crisis* (Russell Sage Foundation 2013).

Siddaiah, T. *Financial Services* (Pearson Education India 2011).

Silvers, D. 'Deregulation and the New Financial Architecture' in Wolfson, M.H. and Epstein, G.A. (eds) *The Handbook of the Political Economy of Financial Crises* (Oxford University Press USA 2013).

Sjostrom, W.K. 'The Birth of Rule 144A Equity Offerings' [2008] 56 *UCLA Law Review* 409.

Sriramesh, K. 'Power, Distance and Public Relations: An Ethnographic Study of Southern Indian Organisations' in Culbertson, H.M. and Chen, N. (eds) *International Public Relations: A Comparative Analysis* (Routledge 2013).

Stigler, G.J. 'The Theory of Economic Regulation' [1971] 2 *Bell Journal of Economics and Management Science* 3.

Sunstein, C. *Free Markets and Social Justice* (Oxford University Press 1999).

Swan, P.L. 'The Global Crisis and Its Origins' in Kolb, R.W. (ed.) *Lessons from the Financial Crisis: Causes, Consequences and Our Economic Future* (John Wiley & Sons 2010).

Tabarrok, A. 'The Separation of Commercial and Investment Banking: The Morgans vs. The Rockefellers' [1998] 1 *The Quarterly Journal of Austrian Economics* 1.

Tilson, W. and Tongue, G. *More Mortgage Meltdown: 6 Ways to Profit in These Bad Times* (John Wiley & Sons 2009).

Tymoigne, E. and Wray, L.R. *The Rise and Fall of Money Manager Capitalism: Minsky's Half Century from World War Two to the Great Recession* (Routledge 2013).

Ülgen, F. 'Financial Liberalism and New Institutional Environment: the 2007–08 Financial Crisis as a (De)Regulatory Deadlock' in O'Sullivan, P., Allington, N.F.B. and Esposito, M. (eds) *The Philosophy, Politics and Economics of Finance in the 21st Century: From Hubris to Disgrace* (Routledge 2015).

Underhill, G. 'The Public Good Versus Private Interests and the Global Financial and Monetary System' in Drache, D. (ed.) *The Market or the Public Domain: Redrawing the Line* (Routledge 2005).

United Nations *The Global Economic and Financial Crisis: Regional Impacts, Responses and Solutions* (United Nations Publications 2009).

United States Department of Justice *Justice Department and State Partners Secure Nearly $864 Million Settlement With Moody's Arising from Conduct in the Lead up to the Financial Crisis* [2017]. www.justice.gov/opa/pr/justice-department-and-state-partners-secure-nearly-864-million-settlement-moody-s-arising [accessed 17/2/18].

United States Department of Justice 'Fraud Section (FRD)' [2015] (15 November). www.justice.gov/criminal-fraud [accessed 15/11/15].

United States Department of Justice '*Justice Department and State Partners Secure $1.375 Billion Settlement with S&P for Defrauding Investors in the Lead Up to the Financial Crisis*' [2015]. www.justice.gov/opa/pr/justice-department-and-state-partners-secure-1375-billion-settlement-sp-defrauding-investors [accessed 14/12/15].

United States Department of the Treasury *Remarks of Treasury Secretary Lawrence H Summers to the Securities Industry Association* (Treasury Press Centre 9 November 2000).

United States Senate, Committee on Banking, Housing and Urban Affairs *The Role and Impact of Credit Rating Agencies on the Subprime Credit Markets* (GPO 2009).

United States Senate, Permanent Subcommittee on Investigations *Wall Street and the Financial Crisis: Anatomy of a Financial Collapse* (GPO 2011).

Veljanovski, C. 'Economic Approaches to Regulation' in Baldwin, R., Cave, M. and Lodge, M. (eds) *The Oxford Handbook of Regulation* (Oxford University Press 2012).

Wall Street Journal 'A Poor Standard of Justice' [2015] (8 February). www.wsj.com/articles/a-poor-standard-of-justice-1423180955 [accessed 14/12/15].

Wallison, P.J. 'Dissenting Statement' in Angelides, P. *Financial Crisis Inquiry Report* (DIANE Publishing 2011).

Watson, M. *Uneconomic Economics and the Crisis of the Model World* (Palgrave Macmillan 2014).

Weisburd, D. and Waring, E. *White-collar Crime and Criminal Careers* (Cambridge University Press 2001).

White, L.J. 'The Credit-rating Agencies and the Subprime Debacle' in Friedman, J. (ed.) *What Caused the Financial Crisis?* (University of Pennsylvania Press 2011).

3 Why the agencies transgress and what allows them to do it

Introduction

In the conclusion of the last chapter, it was declared that only by acknowledging the *actual* can we make truly impactful reforms. The divergence between the *actual* and the *desired* is such that predominantly focusing on the *desired* results only in an increase of that divergence. So, to attempt to understand the divergence more, so that we can begin to position a reform proposal as effectively as possible, it will now be important to examine what allows the agencies to transgress in the way that they do and why they do so. To do that, this chapter will focus on three major elements of the credit rating industry: its oligopolistic structure; its issuer-pays remuneration system (adopted widely within the industry); and finally the reliance on the agencies exhibited by regulators.

These three elements are all crucial components of the divergence. What is also important to note is that they operate interdependently; one cannot survive on its own in the long term. Yet, these elements are not 'explanations' for the divergence; they are, in fact, 'components' that allow for the agencies to transgress and therefore create the divergence that was established in the previous chapter. The three elements are all predicated upon the existence of a self-interested ethos and as such are all manifestations of that ethos. Although it may seem obvious that a private company would have a self-interested ethos, it is the gatekeeping position that the agencies exploit which dictates that a *wholly* self-interested ethos is undesirable. This self-interested ethos essentially dictates the conduct of the agencies and the actions that they take, so assessing their adoption of the issuer-pays model or the manoeuvres that the agencies make to preserve their oligopolistic industry structure (i.e. buying out new competitors) can only be truly understood when one considers their underlying ethos.

However, perhaps the most obvious issue here is that it is extremely difficult to *prove* an entity's ethos indefinitely, so, with that in mind, the only option available is to conduct a lengthy historical assessment to reveal patterns in the industry's conduct. A research project that would present a genealogical review of the actions of the leading agencies from their origination to the present day would be beneficial for the field, but for now, such an assessment is beyond the scope of this work. Nevertheless, the literature concerned with the history of the industry reveals an ethos that, up until the late 1960s, was solely concerned with surviving via defence. This manifested itself in smear campaigns against those the agencies had wronged and in concerted legal campaigns to absolutely deny any liability.[1]

The chapter will begin by assessing one of the key components that allow the agencies to transgress: the oligopolistic structure of their industry. Oligopolies vary by way of the norms that form their parameters, so depending on the product that is being sold, the members of the oligopoly may choose to compete against each other in a seemingly open (but actually constrained) market (i.e. airline companies) or may choose to form a cartel or monopolistic structure because their product is finite and linked to external factors like national position (i.e. OPEC).[2] The external factors that affect the rating oligopoly, the perceived need for their output and the effect it has (e.g. upon society) results in a unique situation (although it is rare that two oligopolistic structures are alike).

Even though the ratings industry has fallen within the confines of an oligopolistic structure since 1851 and has experienced times when it was legitimately facing extinction,[3] we will see that the structure is a 'natural oligopoly' in that the end-users – investors – would be disadvantaged by increased competition. In light of this we shall also see how many alternatives that have been advanced, ranging from the complete removal of the agencies[4] to a non-profit-based supplementation, are rarely practical given the *actual* dynamics of the ratings arena;

1 The legal campaigns adopted by the agencies were discussed earlier, see Rhinebridge (and Cheyne Finance) SIVs (n 93). In addition to this, see Scott Sandage's excellent account of the appalling treatment of John Beardsley, Scott A. Sandage *Born Losers: A History of Failure in America* (Harvard University Press 2006).

2 William A. McEachern *Economics: A Contemporary Introduction* (Cengage Learning 2011) 236

> At one extreme, oligopolists may try to coordinate their behaviour so they act collectively as a single monopolist, forming a cartel, such as OPEC. At the other extreme, oligopolists may compete so fiercely that price wars erupt, such as those that break out among airlines …

3 Partnoy notes that 'the rating agencies were struggling when John Moody died in 1958. By the 1960s, the rating agencies employed only half-a-dozen analysts each and generated revenues primarily from the sale of published research reports' see Frank Partnoy 'The Paradox of Credit Ratings' in Richard M. Levich, Giovanni Majnoni and Carmen Reinhart (eds) *Ratings, Rating Agencies and the Global Financial System* (Kluwer 2002) 70. Wilson and Fabozzi note that in relation to Standard & Poor's, Paul Babson gained control and removed Poor's from Bankruptcy. In 1940, it sold its manual subscription list to Moody's Investors Service. However, still having a difficult time, it merged with Standard Statistics in 1941, see Richard S. Wilson and Frank J. Fabozzi *Corporate Bonds: Structures & Analysis* (Frank J. Fabozzi Associates 1996) 211. Abdelal succinctly puts this period of hardship down to the economic health of the period: 'the late 1940s, 1950s and 1960s were happier to both issuers and holders of securities, but for the rating agencies the times were perhaps too good: no one seemed to default', Rawi Abdelal *Capital Rules: The Construction of Global Finance* (Harvard University Press 2007) 167.

4 An example of a proposal that calls for the removal of the rating agencies, at least as they exist now, is in Emilios Avgouleas *Governance of Global Financial Markets: The Law, The Economics, The Politics* (Cambridge University Press 2012) 394–447. An example of transferring the role of producing financial indicators to market-based measures (i.e. credit spreads) can be found in Frank Partnoy 'How and Why Credit Rating Agencies Are Not Like Other Gatekeepers' in Yasuyuki Fuchita and Robert E. Litan (eds) *Financial Gatekeepers: Can They Protect Investors?* (Brookings Institution Press 2007).

the ultimate conclusion will be that the success or failure of the arena is solely dictated by the investors, which is an important point to consider when formulating reform proposals.

The oligopolistic structure of the ratings industry

In *The Industry: Who They Are* there were a number of references to the ratings industry as being a 'de facto' oligopoly or perhaps even a 'partner-monopoly'.[5] The connotations attached to such structures require more analysis than would be appropriate within the 'primer' section, but it is important to examine them because, if Suarez-Villa is correct in stating that 'the relations of power that oligopolies represent are largely ignored by the public today',[6] then providing a clear examination of the power structures within oligopolies and within the rating oligopoly in particular, will be very important. Suarez-Villa qualifies this statement by confirming that the reason for this public ignorance is because the information that is needed to educate people to the potentially destructive power of these structures is lost in numerous pro-corporate reports that view corporate interests as 'beneficial to [almost] everyone'.[7]

An *oligopoly*, a Greek word meaning 'few sellers', describes an industry that has a small number of firms with incredible power.[8] Perhaps the defining feature of an oligopoly is the interdependence between its members, something we will see over and over again in our assessment of the ratings industry. This notion of the members being interdependent makes analysing an oligopoly within generalised parameters difficult, mostly because each oligopoly will have different norms which influence the actions of its members. For example, OPEC,[9] is an almost monopolistic oligopoly, because its dynamics differ from the airlines. OPEC members have their national position to consider and also have a product that is finite, whereas the airlines operate for the benefit of their shareholders (for the most part) and offer a service to the public that has no defined end-date, which arguably results in a competitive nature not seen between the OPEC members who concentrate upon maximising the *collective* return from their position as opposed to *individual* return.

However, while they are difficult to examine in general terms, there are aspects that (almost) all oligopolies share. The issue of competition is an inherent issue within any oligopoly, but is an issue that manifests itself in different forms. Every oligopoly contains inefficiencies because of competition,[10] which often stems from the decrease in competitive pressures and usually leads to a reduction in quality

---

5 See *The Industry: Who They Are* (n 9); (n 10); (n 11).
6 Luis Suarez-Villa *Corporate Power, Oligopolies and the Crisis of the State* (SUNY Press 2014) 10.
7 ibid.
8 McEachern (n 1) 233.
9 (n 1).
10 James A. Caporaso and David P. Levine *Theories of Political Economy* (Cambridge University Press 1992) 96.

(owing to the protected nature of each member's position), with the difference between each oligopoly perhaps being the conditions discussed earlier (i.e. the differences based upon the products being sold (e.g. airline vs oil); the competitive pressures at work in the rating oligopoly result in a lax approach that reduces quality while the openly competitive nature of the airline industry, albeit amongst a small number of providers (but not as concentrated as the ratings industry), results in a 'race-to-the-bottom' that incorporates price as well as quality (the price of ratings has not decreased as a result of the competitive dynamic within the rating oligopoly).

The dynamics within an oligopoly vary, but all are technically constrained by anti-competitive laws that a given jurisdiction has in place (e.g. anti-trust laws in the US). So, to further understand these dynamics within an oligopoly, the economic theory known as 'Game Theory'[11] can be particularly useful. The seminal work in this field, *Theory of Games and Economic Behavior*, written by John Von Neumann and Oskar Morgenstern in 1947,[12] created a theory that provides an insight into the dynamics of oligopolistic interdependence (it was not until the 1970s that the field of Game Theory began to take shape).[13] The theory views oligopolistic behaviour as a series of moves amongst rival firms within an oligopoly, with each move and countermove searching for a possible equilibrium; as Stroux describes, 'everything revolves around the search for a possible equilibrium or equilibria, i.e. a combination of the strategies that represent the best strategy for every competitor or player, who is presumed to make "rational" decisions in order to maximise profits'.[14]

While these elements are admittedly generalisations of the dynamics within an oligopoly, they are extraordinarily accurate when applied to the ratings industry. Speaking in general terms, Sabnavis notes that, with regard to the rating oligopoly, 'there are the classic elements of game theory here, where each agency does not know the stance taken by the other'.[15] Drawing conclusions from this, he suggests that the result is that the perceived penalty for a firm taking a 'strict' stance – whether economically, ethically or something else – is that business will move towards any competitor who has not taken such a strict stance; the obvious result is an incentive to increase the levels of liberality within the particular industry. Such liberal undertakings are rarely the precursor to sensible or ethically based economic actions.

The dynamics within the rating oligopoly can be seen to be the most demonstrable 'cause' of the divergence between what is desired of the agencies and

---

11 For a representative coverage of the literature on 'Game Theory' see James Friedman *Oligopoly Theory* (Cambridge University Press Archive 1983) Ch. 9; Michael Waterson *Economic Theory of the Industry* (Cambridge University Press Archive 1984) Ch. 3; Graham Romp *Game Theory: Introduction and Applications* (Oxford University Press 1997) Ch. 4.

12 John Von Neumann and Oskar Morgenstern *Theory of Games and Economic Behavior* (Princeton University Press 1947).

13 Sigrid Stroux *US and EC Oligopoly Control* (Kluwer Law International 2004) 13.

14 ibid.

15 Madan Sabnavis *Macroeconomics Demystified* (Tata McGraw-Hill Education 2008) 104.

what they actually deliver. However, it is important to pause for a moment to consider the *strength* of the oligopoly, so that the analysis that follows is properly contextualised. The strength of an oligopoly can be measured or at least understood, in a variety of ways. To begin with it is probably best to focus on the dominance of the Big Three and in particular the Big Two within the industry. Tennant and Tracey note that across the world, between the 1970s and 2000s, only 68 new rating agencies were created, with only four in existence before 1970. Additionally, the vast majority of these 'new' agencies tend to offer specialised services, which naturally prohibits them from ever posing a threat to the leaders in the field. In adding to some of the figures assessed in *The Industry: Who They Are*, Tennant and Tracey state that the Big Three capture more than 90 per cent of the value of all issues rated worldwide and that Moody's and S&P have a combined global market share of 80 per cent (with the Big Three having more than 95 per cent of the market).[16] While the figures regarding market capitalisation tend to differ ever so slightly between analyses, the sentiment is always the same: the Big Three and the Big Two in particular, dominate the rating industry and therefore the industry is 'characterised by incomplete competition and an oligopolistic structure'.[17] There are a number of other indicators to provide support for this understanding of outright dominance of the industry by the Big Three.[18]

The oligopolistic structure conveys a power that is rarely seen within other industry structures. Darbellay makes the point that while rating announcements clearly have an important impact upon the financial markets, it is the presence of a rating oligopoly that makes those announcements particularly powerful, 'especially if the three leading CRAs – even coincidentally – coordinate their rating practices'.[19] It is worth remembering that according to Game Theory, the likelihood is that the oligopolistic structure *dictates* that the rating practices of the leading agencies will be aligned, which is a particularly important issue to consider.

Darbellay continues by stating that the Big Three have continuously been accused of abusing their market power and that the dominance of the rating market 'may have detrimental effects on the proper functioning of competitive forces in the rating industry'.[20] Darbellay is correct, but it is safe to go further and state that the oligopolistic structure *has* had a detrimental effect upon the proper functioning of competitive forces in the industry, rather than it *may*, while the oligopolistic structure is not the sole factor in this regard, as this chapter will

---

16 David F. Tennant and Marlon R. Tracey *Sovereign Debt and Credit Rating Bias* (Palgrave Macmillan 2015) 53.

17 ibid.

18 See Ahmed Naciri *Credit Rating Governance: Global Credit Gatekeepers* (Routledge 2015) 55–60 for his analysis of indicators such as the amount of ratings issued, the amount of analysts employed and the revenue trends of each of the major rating agencies.

19 Aline Darbellay *Regulating Credit Rating Agencies* (Edward Elgar 2013) 165.

20 ibid.

ultimately demonstrate, it is an important factor. It has this detrimental effect because of certain elements that protect and advance the oligopoly, some of which are more obvious than others.

Perhaps the most prevalent argument regarding the protection of the oligopoly is that the oligopoly is a 'natural oligopoly'. Tennant and Tracey discuss studies that have concluded that the rating market is natural oligopoly, based upon the realisation that the nature of the market makes it extraordinarily difficult for new agencies to succeed. The scholars focus upon the large economies of scale that come with being the leading members of an oligopoly, which translate to the ability to hire more staff and be able to invest in better IT systems. It is correct, as Tennant and Tracey state, that 'new entrants have high start-up costs related to acquiring the requisite staffing, analytical tools and information technology systems and few resources with which to meet these costs'.[21] The Big Three employ over 3,000 credit analysts combined, which represents approximately 90 per cent of the total number of analysts working for all of the NRSROs.[22] Therefore, it is easy to see why an influential issuer would not want to purchase the services of a smaller agency, simply due to the lower capacity the agency would have to deal with a complex issue. This leads to the understanding that the concentration of resources allows the Big Three to systematically dismantle any perceived threats through a coordinated campaign of acquisitions. The ability to acquire newer agencies is a particularly useful weapon for the established agencies; a weapon that is continually wielded[23] (hence the prevalence for start-ups to focus on specialised sectors or local communities rather than a widespread coverage of their ratings, which would take them into the firing line of the Big Three).

Another issue that protects the oligopoly sees us revisit the notion of competition. While in an industry such as the airline industry, competition may be expected to lead to a decrease in price for the consumer, the ratings industry operates within different parameters. The argument of those that claim the ratings industry is a natural oligopoly is that for the users of ratings, the investors, increased competition is simply not desired. The theoretical purpose of using ratings, from the perspective of the investor at least, is to *assist* with the deciphering of a issuing firm's financial position *while* keeping costs at a level which makes investing in a given firm's debt economically viable; if an investor had to survey a multitude of agencies' ratings then the use of ratings would become a hindrance rather than an aid, which would defeat the purpose. Andenas and Chiu, citing a paper by Lawrence J. White, explain that users' 'desire for consistency of ratings across investments products helps to sustain reliance on the few incumbents in the credit rating market. The multiplication of rating providers may decrease

21 Tennant and Tracey (n 16) 54.

22 ibid.

23 See Herwig P. Langohr and Patricia T. Langohr *The Rating Agencies and Their Credit Ratings: What They Are, How They Work and Why They Are Relevant* (John Wiley & Sons 2010) 386–410 for a representative analysis of the Big Three's acquisition strategies over the last decade (up unto 2010).

comparability and fuel race-to-the-bottom tendencies'.[24] We have seen in *A Snapshot of the Regulatory Framework*,[25] and will continue to see in Chapter 4 (*Tried and Failed*), that the stated purposes of regulatory reforms have been to *increase* competition within the ratings market; with what we know now this is clearly a demonstration of the divergence between what is required and what is delivered – not considering the *actual* is a constant and important issue it seems.

This position of the 'user' or more precisely the 'investor' and their requirements is a particularly important aspect to consider when it comes to assessing the justification for the oligopolistic structure within the rating industry. Schroeter, in sharing the views of White, argues that financial markets are 'frequented by investors with a limited capacity to assimilate and process information ... therefore always result[ing] in an investor-driven natural oligopoly of rating suppliers, making attempts to increase the number of relevant credit rating agencies futile'.[26] While this assertion does not take into account the position of institutional investors, who have the capability to assimilate and process information, the sentiment is indeed correct; the oligopoly is driven by the investors. However, there is an incredible situation that appears when we come to look at the qualities that these 'incapable' investors require. The main barrier to entry, which maintains the oligopoly, is widely accepted as being the issue of reputation. Schroeter continues:

> The prevailing opinion in the literature points to the high barriers of entry that new entrants to the credit rating business face, namely the challenge of having to develop and demonstrate a sufficient track record in order to acquire credibility with investors, which again is necessary to persuade issuers to buy their rating service.

Schroeter goes further by stating that it is precisely the oligopolistic structure, when understood in terms of the members each having over 100 years of experience, that maintains its existence; 'new credit rating agencies therefore find themselves in a Catch-22 situation because they need a sufficient number of rating contracts to develop a reputation, which they fail to receive for lack of said reputation'.[27]

However, while this understanding is true, it is arguably obsolete; as we shall see in much greater detail in *Regulatory Reliance*, the concept of reputational capital was obliterated in 1973 with the incorporation of credit ratings into the burgeoning capital markets, the forced usage of ratings produced by an NRSRO, a term which both solidified the existence of the oligopoly and removed any reputational concerns the Big Three (in particular the Big Two) may have had. In reality, however, the NRSRO designation served to ratify the position of the

24 Mads Andenas and Iris H.Y. Chiu *The Foundations and Future of Financial Regulation: Governance for Responsibility* (Routledge 2013) 197.
25 *A Snapshot of the Regulatory Framework* (n 108).
26 Ulrich G. Schroeter 'Credit Ratings and Credit Rating Agencies' in Gerard Caprio (ed.) *Handbook of Key Global Financial Markets, Institutions and Infrastructure* (2013) 387.
27 ibid 386.

Big Two, because the historical dominance of Moody's and S&P is seemingly the most important factor in the eyes of the investor. This is, however, an overly simplistic deduction), although there are questions to be asked regarding the issue of perceived penalties for issuers who do not choose the Big Two.[28] It is worth noting that before the incorporation of the agencies' ratings the agencies were almost out of business,[29] which leads us to conclude that reputation alone is not the reason for their successes.

The oligopolistic structure, therefore, is based upon this superficial notion of 'reputation', although in keeping with the analysis of the divergence between the *desired* and the *actual*, it is clear that any value users (and therefore issuers) place in the reputational capital of the agencies is not shared by the agencies; their abhorrent practices that contributed to the financial crisis are the clearest of indicators that losing reputational capital is just not a concern for the agencies, despite their protests (after the fact) to the contrary. Perhaps a subsequent question that could be asked is why do investors continue to use the ratings of these agencies when the reputation that the investors value is simply not a concern for them? One answer to this question lies in the notion of there not being a viable alternative or 'substitute'.[30]

Proposed alternatives to the rating oligopoly

The first alternatives that are worth examining, to show the extremes that exist if nothing else, are from Frank Partnoy and Emilios Avgouleas. Partnoy suggests that the rating agencies' informational value is so low that replacing their credit ratings as signifiers of market performance with market-based measures such as 'credit spreads' would be much more appropriate and efficient[31] (credit spreads are the difference in yield between any type of bond and a US treasury bond of the same maturity [that are considered to carry no risk of default]). Partnoy counters the arguments against the use of market-based measures by stating that although the measures may be volatile (because of the attachment to the volatility of the market), it is infinitely better if the regulators could make transparent choices about this volatility rather than leaving it to the agencies who do not consider systemic consequences. The volatility in rating downgrades, which may be just as *subjective* as the rating process seen before the crisis, is obviously a counterbalance to the criticisms against the use of market-based measures. There is, however, a different criticism which is harder to argue against, as we shall see shortly.

Avgouleas also argues for the removal of the rating agencies. However, his arguments with regard to the rating agencies are part of systemic transformation,

---

28 See Rhinebridge (and Cheyne Finance) SIVs (n 93) for the discussion regarding potential threats for selecting a competitor to the Big Two.

29 Partnoy (n 2) 72.

30 Tennant and Tracey (n 16) 53: 'The elasticity of demand is, however, affected not only by the nature of the product/service, but also by the availability of substitutes'.

31 Partnoy (n 3). Partnoy also suggests that credit default swaps would be a better method than using ratings.

which separates it from Partnoy's proposals. He argues for a recalibration of accepted governance models and centres the new framework on a redeveloped OECD (Organisation for Economic Co-operation and Development) which incorporates research expertise from the Bank of International Settlements (BIS).[32] The issue with this 'big-bang' approach is that it requires so much political appetite, the likes of which have arguably never been seen, that considering it can only be an academic exercise. Although Avgouleas and Partnoy should be praised for offering alternatives, because as Avgouleas rightly states, such exercises being academic should not stop people from advancing them,[33] examining the potential for application is also an important exercise. In doing this, it quickly becomes clear that there is little appetite for the complete removal of the agencies, for a variety of reasons.

In a similar vein to calling for an alternative that effectively seeks to eliminate the rating agencies, there are a growing number of proposals that argue for the public provision of credit ratings. The argument is based upon the notion that the provision of credit ratings is a 'public good' and, as such, 'the public should be responsible for financing the production of this information'.[34] There are clear benefits attached to this approach as some scholars have claimed: 'a public rating agency would not just be financially independent from issuers but it would be open to a level of public scrutiny that even heavily regulated private companies are not submitted to'.[35] However, there are a multitude of issues with the public agency approach.

If the state provides the funding for this agency, a new conflict of interest arises, as Listokin and Taibleson note: 'if money comes from the public fisc, then all taxpayers must pay for a product that directly benefits only a narrow class of investors'.[36] If the answer is to force investors to pay the costs, then deciding which class of investors must meet this obligation is just as problematic.[37] The fact that private institutions usually pump considerably more resources into research than does the state is another element that needs to be considered; would the research conducted by the public agency be extensive enough to meet the demands that are placed upon the current agencies? Also, if the state were to set up a rating agency, it would theoretically lose the authority it requires based on the notion that rating agencies have their authority based on their independence

32 Avgouleas (n 3) 450. For the proposal itself see 394–447.
33 ibid 431.
34 Viktar Fedaseyeu 'Economics of Information' in Rhona C. Free (ed.) *21st Century Economics: A Reference Handbook* (SAGE Publications 2010) 736.
35 Akos Rona-Tas and Stefanie Hiss 'The Role of Ratings in the Subprime Mortgage Crisis: The Art of Corporate and the Science of Consumer Rating' in Michael Lounsbury and Paul M. Hirsch (eds) *Markets on Trial: The Economic Sociology of the US Financial Crisis, Part 1* (Emerald Group Publishing 2010) 149.
36 Yair Listokin and Benjamin Taibleson 'If You Misrate, Then You Lose: Improving Credit Rating Accuracy Through Incentive Compensation' [2010] 27 *Yale Journal on Regulation* 96 102.
37 ibid.

(it would also do no favours for the US-centric allegations aimed at the current industry structure[38]).

Therefore it is not reasonable to suggest that the state would sanction enough resources to meet the requirements that are on the current agencies.[39] In addition, if issuers now court the ratings of two agencies (at least) and investors tend to take into account two ratings, then does that mean the state will have to create two separate agencies? This would double the cost and make no impact on the differential independence. Lastly, the legal problems that would emerge from claims by investors that they lost money by using information that was directly produced by the state would make the whole endeavour counterproductive. Overall, the proposal is simply not practicable

Supplementation

There are some proposals, however, that do not seek to remove the agencies, but challenge their dominance. The preface to these approaches is the 'public utility' model, whereby the state would set up and manage an agency that would produce ratings which would be used by investors to check the validity of the rating agencies.[40] The problem with this approach, of course, is that governmental intervention in no way guarantees the accuracy of the rating. The idea is useful, but only if a rating agency that could demonstrate a high enough level of independence and also develop a reputation for its accuracy, would take on the role of 'bench-marker'. At first glance there is an issue here: who would take on such a role when there was no financial reward to be gained from it?

This is where, potentially, non-profit offerings start to make more sense. There are two non-profit credit rating agency proposals that are worth considering. First there is the 'Credit Rating Initiative' that was developed by Jin-Chuan Duan as part of the National University of Singapore's Risk Management Institute.[41] The project aims to develop an organic 'selective-Wikipedia-style' database of credit rating assessments on hundreds of thousands of firms, covering 'macroeconomic, financial and default related information'.[42] By publishing daily PDs (Probability of Default), the Initiative aims to provide a purely public good. The project's initial cost was $5 million, with the proposed model going forward being to apply for grants to meet the operational costs.

The other version is the International Non-profit Credit Rating Agency (INCRA), developed by the Bertelsmann Foundation. INCRA aims to provide sovereign ratings that incorporate not only economic and short-term

---

38 Kenneth Dyson *States, Debt and Power: 'Saints' and 'Sinners' in European History and Integration* (Oxford University Press 2014) 390.

39 Fedaseyeu (n 34).

40 Raquel G. Alcubilla and Javier R. del Pozo *Credit Rating Agencies on the Watch List: Analysis of European Regulation* (Oxford University Press 2012) 249.

41 Jin-Chuan Duan and Elisabeth Van Laere 'A *Public Good* Approach to Credit Rating – from Concept to Reality' [2012] 36 *Journal of Banking & Finance* 3240.

42 ibid 3243.

socio-political factors, but also long-term socio-political factors.[43] The agency proposes to develop transparent and accountable governance structures which it hopes will stimulate funding. However, the issue of funding is again an issue, with the agency predicting that $400 million would be required to begin and maintain operations. The Foundation's target for funding is the G20, which it argues should fund INCRA to reduce costs that will occur later through CRA failures.

These two endeavours unfortunately share a common problem: they are both offering an addendum to the current credit rating system, therefore it is proving difficult to generate funding. However, there is a massive issue here: this facility already exists, arguably, with the smaller nationally recognised statistical ratings organisation (NRSROs) who operate on an 'investor-pays' basis (mostly just Egan-Jones in this respect, although smaller agencies are often used for this purpose irrespective of their remuneration model). Their ratings are considered independent from any issuer influence and are commonly used by the larger investors to gain perspective and check conformity with the Big Three on the more obvious credit ratings. The level of independence and, therefore, perceived accuracy is arguably less than the smaller NRSROs should the two endeavours obtain the public funding they are hoping for. I have argued elsewhere that the two entities should perhaps combine to cover all aspects of the provision of credit ratings and that they should also seek funding from private philanthropic sources, to increase their all-important perceived independence. Were they to combine, there is also a role that seems perfectly suited for the agencies within current SEC regulations, which closely resembles the public utility model discussed earlier.[44]

The conclusion that must be drawn from this analysis of alternatives to the existing system is that they are not particularly viable in their current form. Not because overhauling the system as we know it is incorrect, but it is particularly impracticable given the dynamics that exist; one can imagine that the Big Three would spend everything they had lobbying against their removal. The dynamics of the rating oligopoly are, perhaps, unique. We have seen that the structure is determined by the requirements of the end-users, the investors, who fundamentally prescribe the actions of every participant within the ratings market. It has been noted that issuers, who actually pay for the ratings, are only concerned with the agency that enjoys the most market reliance;[45] if this is the case, then reducing the influence of the Big Two will be particularly difficult, but not impossible. While large impactful reforms may be interesting to consider, it is arguable that they can never be realised. What can be realized, however, are incremental reform proposals that incorporate the *actual* dynamics of the industry, rather than what is *desired*.

---

43 Bertelsmann Stiftung *Blueprint for INCRA – An International Non-profit Credit Rating Industry: Executive Summary* (2012). www.bertelsmann-stiftung.de/en/press/press-releases/press-release/pid/blueprint-for-an-international-non-profit-credit-rating-agency-incra/

44 Daniel Cash 'The International Non-profit Credit Rating Agency: The Viability of a Response' [2016] 37 *The Company Lawyer* 6.

45 Darbellay (n 19) 169.

The issuer-pays remuneration model

The issuer-pays remuneration model was first adopted in 1969. It operates on a simple basis: credit ratings are initiated by issuers, rather than investors, who approach the agency and order a creditworthiness assessment; payment for this service can range from $1,500 to $2,500,000, depending upon the size and issue of the given security.[46] Schroeter suggests that agencies operating under this model determine 99 per cent of the total outstanding credit ratings in the United States,[47] which demonstrates the importance of assessing this model and revealing both its advantages and disadvantages. The vast majority of the literature, including this contribution, focuses upon the negative aspects of this model. However, there are arguments *for* the model that must be included before we continue. Probably the most obvious and rational argument is that without it, the agencies simply could not meet the demand that they are faced with. Alcubilla and del Pozo note that 'new markets required more specialisation, more qualified and higher paid analysts, lawyers and compliance officers, the opening of offices in regional areas and so on. And the increased costs associated with the production of ratings of quality could not be funded just by subscribers';[48] the reason why this cost cannot be met by subscribers is because advances in technology have created the ability for subscribers to share the rating information with non-subscribers (this will be discussed more in *The Impact of Technological Advancement*).

In addition to this practical 'advantage', there is a theoretical advantage created by the issuer-pays model, in that the agency must liaise with the issuer (their client) and this 'provides the rating analysts with a better understanding of the issuer's financial situation and business prospects';[49] this affirms what was discussed earlier with regard to 'Signalling Theory'.[50] In what is arguably the only other argument *for* the model, rating agencies themselves vehemently argue that the perceived ills of the issuer-pays model would also be witnessed in the subscriber-pays model. Their argument is based upon the idea that the paying party naturally wants the situation to be geared towards their advancement over the opposing party; the suggestion being that 'investors would prefer lower ratings (since they will then receive higher yields), as would the short sellers of any other security of the issuing company'.[51] Yet, there is much that these simplistic understandings of the model do not consider.

---

46 Schroeter (n 26) 383.
47 ibid.
48 Alcubilla and del Pozo (n 40) 248.
49 Schroeter (n 26) 383.
50 See *The Desired Situation for Issuers*.
51 Matthew Richardson and Lawrence J. White 'The Rating Agencies: Is Regulation the Answer?' in Viral V. Acharya and Matthew Richardson (eds) *Restoring Financial Stability: How to Repair a Failed System* (John Wiley & Sons 2009) 107.

Hypotheses for the adoption of the issuer-pays model

A definitive explanation for the adoption of the issuer-pays model would reveal the mentality of the industry at that time, which would go a long way to confirming the existence of an underlying approach taken by the industry (as will be advanced in the last section to this chapter). However, 'the reasons for this change have never been established definitively'.[52] In light of this fact, what follows is an assessment of the two commonly accepted reasons for this change in policy: as a response to the collapse of Penn Central; and as a response to technological advances witnessed in the late 1960s.

The collapse of Penn Central hypothesis

That the rating agencies altered their remuneration models as a reaction to the changing market dynamics after the collapse of Penn Central in 1970 is by far and away the most common hypothesis. The hypothesis intimates that the increased nervousness felt by investors after the collapse altered the market dynamics in that investors no longer trusted in 'household names', with the result being that they required some third-party verification to calm their nerves when investing.[53] Yet, this version of events paints a picture of a passive industry being given the opportunity to play a central role by pure chance; nothing that has been discussed so far should lead one to accept that the ratings industry has developed by chance alone.

The proponents of this hypothesis are wide and varied, with Partnoy,[54] Geisst[55] and a whole host of others subscribing.[56] The clarity with which these proponents make the statement is such that it suggests that no other alternative explanation exists. For example, Hudson, Colley and Largan are emphatic in their statement that 'at that time, investors relied on name recognition as the principal criterion for issuer selection'.[57] If this was the case, that would mean that the *industry* was almost non-existent or at least extremely ineffectual; this tallies with previous statements made by other proponents[58] regarding the health of the *rating*

---

52 Lawrence J. White 'Financial Regulation and the Current Crisis: A Guide for Antitrust' in American Bar Association *Competition as Public Policy* (American Bar Association 2010) 90 (footnote 90).

53 Larry Allen *The Encyclopedia of Money* (ABC-CLIO 2009) 94.

54 Partnoy (n 2) 72.

55 Charles R. Geisst *Encyclopedia of American Business History* (Facts on File 2006) 112.

56 Just some of the many works that are representative of this view include Enrica Detragiache 'Rational Liquidity Crises in the Sovereign Debt Market: In Search of Theory' [1996] 43 *International Monetary Fund: Staff Papers* 3 565; Daniel Immergluck *Foreclosed: High-risk Lending, Deregulation and the Undermining of America's Mortgage Market* (Cornell University Press 2011) 111; Benjamin Taupin 'Perpetuating the Regulatory Order in the Credit Rating Industry' in Isabelle Hault and Chrystelle Richard (eds) *Finance: The Discreet Regulator – How Financial Activities Shape and Transform the World* (Palgrave Macmillan 2012) 86; Allen (n 53) 94.

57 Robert Hudson, Alan Colley and Mark Largan *The Capital Markets and Financial Management in Banking* (Routledge 2013) 175.

58 Partnoy (n 2).

industry prior to 1970. However, there is a reason why the words 'industry' and 'rating' were emphasised in the preceding sentence; there is an oversight made by many when they differentiate between the pathways of the reporting agencies, like Dun & Bradstreet and the rating agencies like Moody's and Standard & Poor's. Although it will form the central component of the last section of this chapter, it is worth noting here that up until 2000, Moody's was owned by Dun & Bradstreet, who had purchased the company in 1962 upon John Moody's death.[59] Moody's was the first rating agency to initiate the issuer-pays model on an extensive scale in 1970[60] and it is clearly unwise to overlook the position of the parent company at that time.

So, in what represents a wildly different take on the conditions in the economy before the collapse of Penn Central, the SEC in its Staff Report confirmed that the 'National Credit Office' (NCO) was 'the only national rating service of commercial paper'.[61] Combined with the importance of the commercial paper market to the American economy in the late 1960s (and early 1970s), this demonstrates the importance and centrality of Dun & Bradstreet's National Credit Office.[62] The NCO was a part of Dun & Bradstreet in the same way that Moody's Investment Services was and was acquired through a merger with Arthur D. Whiteside in 1931.[63] The SEC noted that 'customers relied heavily on the NCO prime rating as an independent opinion of the creditworthiness of commercial paper issuers',[64] which clearly flies in the face of the claims of those mentioned earlier with regard to investors simply 'trusting' in issuers' abilities to pay back their debts (arguably a ludicrous suggestion given the 170 years of experience exhibited by the rating/reporting industry).

In presenting the NCO we simultaneously debunk two common misconceptions: first that investors simply relied upon the reputation of issuers when determining creditworthiness; and second that 'the late 1940s, 1950s and 1960s were happier to both issuers and holders of securities, but for the rating agencies the times were perhaps too good: no one seemed to default'.[65] The first misconception is debunked by the SEC's Staff Report. The second can be set straight by understanding that the 'prime rating' awarded by the NCO was the equivalent of today's AAA rating. Fight confirms that the NCO had more

---

59 Geisst (n 55) 111.
60 Moody's began using the issuer-pays model in 1970 after Standard & Poor's had begun using it in its Municipal Bond rating service in 1969, see Naciri (n 18) 16.
61 Securities and Exchange Commission *The Financial Collapse of the Penn Central Company: Staff Report of the SEC to the Special Subcommittee on Investigations* (GPO 1972) 10.
62 Markham notes that 'Corporations in America were borrowing large amounts of money in May of 1970 through the commercial paper market. Outstanding commercial paper rose from $17.5 billion to $38 billion between April of 1968 and April of 1970'; see Jerry W. Markham *A Financial History of the United States: From Enron-era Scandals to the Great Recession* (Routledge 2015) 5.
63 Whiteside would bring the National Credit Office with him when he joined Dun & Bradstreet, two years before his company would eventually merge with D&B, see 'Your Credit Good? Dun & Bradstreet Knows' [1947] Kiplinger's Magazine September edition 28.
64 Securities and Exchange Commission (n 61).
65 Abdelal (n 2) 167.

than 600 commercial paper ratings outstanding at the time of Penn Central's collapse and that all of them were 'prime', which should not only strike a chord with respect to our understanding of the events of 2007/8, but also reveals that the availability of 'prime' ratings, that investors 'relied' upon, ultimately meant that the malaise experienced by rating agencies was solely due to the liberality of their reporting partners. As Fight affirms: 'Who would want to run the risk of a lower credit rating when the National Credit Office was certain to award a Prime rating?'.[66]

So, the hypothesis that rating agencies began charging issuers for ratings because the collapse of Penn Central made investors nervous about investing can be dismissed; as we have seen, it was not the case that some implicit trust was shattered by the shock collapse of a major national company. However, that is not the end of the story. In understanding further the collapse of Penn Central and the involvement of the NCO in that collapse, we shall identify two things: first, that rather than it being the case that some implicit trust was broken, investors were actually betrayed by the NCO; and second, that comparisons with the recent financial crisis are very strong indeed. Again, the words of Machiavelli are appropriate here, as is the commonly misattributed line from Mark Twain: 'History never repeats itself but it rhymes'.[67]

To understand the collapse of Penn Central we must first understand the commercial paper market and what it represented in the late 1960s/early 1970s. Commercial paper usually takes the form of 'short-term unsecured promissory notes', which at the time provided a very attractive alternative to bank financing for short-term borrowing. It was a particularly inexpensive mode of financing, which was easy to use and viewed by investors 'as almost entirely without risk'.[68] As we now know, this belief was not due to an implicit belief in the creditworthiness of commercial paper issues, but the widespread coverage of the NCO's prime ratings.

It is because of this widespread belief in the safety of commercial paper that the collapse of Penn Central caused such a shock to the economy. Penn Central was a subsidiary of a larger holding company, the Penn Central Transportation Company, which was the largest non-financial company in the United States; at one point the company held over $200 million in commercial paper[69] (the US Government would go onto transform the remnants of Penn Central into Amtrak in 1971). Yet, despite its size and dominance of the market place, the company

---

66 Andrew Fight *Understanding International Bank Risk* (John Wiley & Sons 2004) 48.

67 The usage here was initially based upon Richard Sylla's usage of the quote from Mark Twain in Richard Sylla 'An Historical Primer on the Business of Credit Ratings' in Richard M. Levich, Giovanni Majnoni and Carmen Reinhart (eds) *Ratings, Rating Agencies and the Global Financial System* (Kluwer 2002) 34. However, further research confirms that the quote has been mistakenly attributed to Twain but in fact stems from John R. Colombo *Neo Poems* (Sono Nis Press 1970) in which a poem contains the line '"History never repeats itself but it rhymes", said Mark Twain'.

68 J.W. Hicks 'Commercial Paper: An Exempted Security Under Section 3(a)(3) of the Securities Act of 1933' [1976] 24 *UCLA Law Review* 227.

69 Markham (n 62) 5.

was heavily criticised for a number of things including its structure, its operations and widespread mismanagement.[70] This adds further weight to the claim made here that rather than relying on the reputation of these large companies (which was not exactly pristine), the investors relied upon a third party to verify the creditworthiness of these large companies.

The company would go on to file for bankruptcy on 21 June 1970, after running into financial difficulties. In essence, it had over-leveraged itself: it struggled to integrate an extensive transportation network that stretched from St Louis to Boston to Canada; it was being constrained by governmental regulation (owing to their providing a 'public good'); it was running money-losing passenger trains; and was suffering from endemic mismanagement.[71] At the time of bankruptcy it defaulted on $80 million (or $82 million dependent upon the source[72]) worth of commercial paper, making it the largest bankruptcy in US history at that point.

So, in the investigations that followed this enormous collapse, a number of telling aspects were revealed that implicated the NCO, but also revealed a familiar pattern within the economy that is particularly disheartening. First, the SEC noted that as opposed to the usual practice for commercial paper, Penn Central had been using it as if it were long-term financing, which alludes to Penn Central over-leveraging itself. In addition to the multiple instances of insider trading amongst executives, the firm was also operating against its investors for the benefit of investment banks, Goldman Sachs in particular, by way of providing Goldman Sachs with advance warning of financial troubles in the firm *while* concealing all negative information from the investing public. During this whole period, the NCO never once removed its prime rating. Goldman Sachs acted upon this information and purposefully, but covertly, reduced its holding in the company while maintaining the appearance of holding a significant stake. As a result, investors were fraudulently soothed by the presence of Goldman Sachs – but at the time of the bankruptcy the bank held no commercial paper issued by the railroad company.[73]

Although legal action was brought against Goldman Sachs (and the NCO as a part of that action), the individual nature of that particular case resulted in the court finding that the plaintiff was not in a position to have relied upon the NCO's prime ratings (the plaintiff was not a subscriber to the NCO, but had received the information regarding the prime rating, allegedly from a Goldman Sachs employee).[74] So, even though the reporting agency was complicit in the

---

70 For a sample of the general discussion and criticism of Penn Central see Joseph R. Daughen and Peter Binzen *The Wreck of the Penn Central* (Beard Books 1999); Michael Bezilla and Jack Rudnicki *Rails to Penn State: The Story of the Bellefonte Central* (Stackpole Books 2007); Clifton Wilcox *Groupthink: An Impediment to Success* (Xlibris Corporation 2010) 43–5.
71 Bezilla and Rudnicki (n 70) 247.
72 Markham (n 62) 5 states $80 million, while Partnoy (n 2) 72 states $82 million.
73 Securities and Exchange Commission (n 61) 10.
74 *Mallinckrodt Chemical Works v Goldman, Sachs & Co*, 420 F Supp 231 (SDNY 1976).

largest bankruptcy in US history (which we know with hindsight would not be the last time), there were very few consequences for their actions.

Before we conclude this section it is worthwhile understanding the NCO a little more. The NCO, which had been rating commercial paper since 1920 and was in effect the only national rater in that market, was never registered with the SEC as an investment advisor; it was only after the collapse of Penn Central that Dun & Bradstreet transferred the NCO to Moody's Investors Service, which at that point was a registered investment advisor. The SEC stated in their report that the NCO grew concomitantly with the commercial paper market in the late 1960s and that 'most of the data contained in the NCO releases [was] a mere reprint of Penn Central press releases or excerpts from annual reports'; the similarities with the modern rating agencies are incredible and suggest that differentiating between the path taken by the reporting agencies and rating agencies is a potentially serious oversight; furthermore, dealers were utilising NCO ratings as a marketing tool because many customers 'were required by statute or resolutions of their boards of directors or trustees, to purchase only that commercial paper which was rated prime by NCO'.[75]

The impact of technological advancement

So, if it was not the case that the rating agencies adopted the issuer-pays model because of an overwhelming desire from investors to have a third-party verify a firm's creditworthiness, then what were the reasons for its adoption? The answer to that question is that technological advancement in the late 1960s essentially forced the agencies into a corner, forcing them to act. While it is the case that the fall of the Bretton Woods monetary system facilitated the explosion of the capital markets,[76] which in turn empowered the agencies given the centrality of their service to the requirements of the burgeoning capital markets,[77] the fall of the system represented the *opportunity* to take advantage of their position not to implement the issuer-pays model, because quite simply the agencies had already incorporated the model (to differing levels initially) a few years before the collapse of Bretton Woods.

Simply put, technological advancements were a real threat to the agencies as their ability to charge investors (or any consumer) for the service of published credit ratings was obliterated because of the 'free rider' problem. A simplified explanation of the 'free-riding' concept would be when an entity cannot capture

---

75 Securities and Exchange Commission (n 61) 294.
76 For a representative analysis of the Bretton Woods monetary system see Michael D. Bordo and Barry Eichengreen *A Retrospective on the Bretton Woods System: Lessons for International Monetary Reform* (University of Chicago Press 2007); Benn Steil *The Battle of Bretton Woods: John Maynard Keynes, Harry Dexter White and the Making of a New World Order* (Princeton University Press 2013); Eric Helleiner *Forgotten Foundations of Bretton Woods: International Development and the Making of the Postwar Order* (Cornell University Press 2014). For a specific discussion of the expansion of the capital markets as a result of the collapse of Bretton Woods see Alcubilla and del Pozo (n 40) 6.
77 Cormac Butler *Accounting for Financial Instruments* (John Wiley & Sons 2009) 58.

the benefits of producing a product because that product can be duplicated or shared easily, which results in its undersupply (if those conditions that prompted free-riding persist). Though this concept is part of a larger theoretical discipline known as public choice theory (part of the study of regulation), which in itself can be an important theoretical framework with which one can examine the ratings industry,[78] for now this simplified description will suffice because the impact of this concept upon the agencies in the 1960s and 1970s is straightforward. As just one analysis that is representative of the literature states:

> Starting at this time, the major rating agencies began to charge issuers for ratings assessments. One reason was the diminishing viability of investor subscriptions as a source of financing ratings. Technological changes in the dissemination of information, including the spreading use of photocopying, had made it increasingly difficult to restrict the beneficial use of ratings assessments only to paying subscribers. Since ratings information quickly became available to most market participants, the free-rider problem intensified and the value of subscribing to a rating service was diminished.[79]

This succinct understanding is universally accepted across the literature.[80] The threat itself came from the new product released by the Xerox Corporation, the Xerox 914, which was advertised on television in 1959 and subsequently became a vital part of Xerox's revenue (thus highlighting its popularity).[81] The

---

78 The public choice field is extensive and concerns itself with a number of issues regarding the use of economic tools to study political issues. For our analysis this relates to the claims that rating agencies are providing a 'public good' by way of the method in which credit ratings are provided (i.e. they are free to all [non-excludable] and the consumption of the rating does not affect the consumption by another [non-rival]). As usual, however, this narrative does not detail the *actual* version of events, as Langohr and Langohr explain when they reveal that the most relevant and user-friendly information is secluded behind pay walls, see Langohr and Langohr (n 23) 173. For a sample of the literature that position the agencies as a provider of a public good see Jeffrey Manns 'Rating Risk after the Subprime Mortgage Crisis: A User Fee Approach for Rating Agency Accountability' [2007–08] 87 *North Carolina Law Review* 1060; Mohammed Hemraj *Credit Rating Agencies: Self-regulation, Statutory Regulation and Case Law Regulation in the United States and European Union* (Springer 2015) 1. For just a very small sample of the seminal works in the public choice field see Arthur C. Pigou *The Economics of Welfare* (Macmillan and Company 1920); Paul A. Samuelson 'The Pure Theory of Public Expenditure' [1954] 36 *The Review of Economics and Statistics* 4; James M. Buchanan and Robert D. Tollison *The Theory of Public Choice* (University of Michigan Press 1962); John G. Head 'Public Goods and Public Policy' [1962] 17 *Public Finance* 3; Mancur Olson *The Logic of Collective Action: Public Goods and the Theory of Groups* (Schocken Books 1968); Ronald H. Coase 'The Lighthouse in Economics' [1974] 17 *Journal of Law and Economics* 2.

79 Andrew Crockett *Conflicts of Interest in the Financial Services Industry: What Should We Do About Them?* (Centre for Economic Policy Research 2003) 45.

80 Robert M. Hardaway *Great American Housing Bubble: The Road to Collapse* (ABC-CLIO 2011) 146; Gianluca Mattarocci *The Independence of Credit Rating Agencies: How Business Models and Regulators Interact* (Academic Press 2014) 72; White (n 52).

81 Eva H. Wirten *No Trespassing: Authorship, Intellectual Property Rights and the Boundaries of Globalization* (The University of Toronto Press 2004) 61.

popularity of the model therefore dictated that the agencies simply could not garner any financial recompense from subscribers, which was in addition to the paucity of subscribers anyway because of their preference for believing the 'prime' assessments of the NCO. What was becoming apparent to the ratings industry is that without an event that would change the dynamics of the economy, they would most likely go out of business.

That this threat was clearly understood by the agencies is not surprising, but it is at this point that we must apply what we know about them and how they operate to an analysis of that particular era. In the 1960s the agencies were dominated by the NCO, primarily because the NCO was the only national assessor within the commercial paper market, which was the driver for economic activity. Furthermore, they were faced with a real threat of extinction because whatever revenue they could garner from subscribers would likely be lost because of free-riders utilising the technology that was available in the 1960s. So, the official story goes from this chain of events to the issuer-pays model being adopted in 1970; it is clear to see that there is a part missing. The fall of the Bretton Woods monetary system in the late 1960s had the effect of escalating the capital markets. This created the need for third-party verification (even after the failings of the NCO). However, this narrative means that the potential to change the remuneration model, based upon the issuer needing to signify their creditworthiness to the now-global markets (a new market which had different requirements), happened *just by chance*. It is this understanding of events that leads to a possible line of future research: what was the level of direct involvement by the agencies in bringing about the fall of Bretton Woods? It is documented that large and influential companies lobbied heavily to promote a freer market during the 1960s,[82] which cumulated in the demise of Bretton Woods. However, we do not know the differentiation within this concerted lobbying campaign, which in an era of limited publicly available information would be admittedly difficult to source. What can be said, given our analysis of the rating industry so far, it that it is just too coincidental that the capital markets, which naturally rely upon the presence of a third party to verify creditworthiness, would open up just at the time the industry was facing extinction; it may be a stretch to suggest that the rating agencies played a significant role in destroying an international monetary system, but to rule out any involvement in light of what we know would surely be imprudent.

The effects of the issuer-pays remuneration model

Schroeter's analysis of the advantages and disadvantages that are inherent within the issuer-pays model is a good place to start this section. In describing the advantages, Schroeter advances the notion that the increased exposure to issuers, as opposed to under the subscriber-pays model, results in a more open relationship that has the theoretical potential to increase the amount of information within

---

82 Benjamin C. Waterhouse *Lobbying America: The Politics of Business from Nixon to NAFTA* (Princeton University Press 2013) 34.

the system as a whole (i.e. ratings analysts will have more information which should therefore result in a more accurate rating; this was discussed earlier with regard to the concept of Signalling Theory).[83] In describing the disadvantages, Schroeter states that the primary disadvantage is the obvious conflict that arises out of the arrangement:

> since it is in every issuer's economic interest to receive as high a rating as possible, there is an incentive for the credit rating agency not to displease the paying issuers, lest he may take his future rating business elsewhere.[84]

Yet, as Schroeter understands, the situation regarding competitive pressures differs between the corporate bond and structured product markets (investors and therefore issuers, usually only require one rating for a structured product, which increases the competitive pressure within the oligopoly, as opposed to the corporate bond market where two ratings are usually mandated). Not giving a favourable structured product rating will result in lost business, which may result in further lost business because that issuer, who may well also have corporate bond ratings outstanding, may choose to use the third member of the oligopoly, Fitch Ratings, to discipline the offending agency[85] (this does not take into account the revenues that may be withdrawn from the ancillary service business as well, but that discussion is best saved for Chapter 5).

So, the issuer-pays model transformed the ethos of the rating agencies; their fortunes are inextricably linked to the will of the issuers. This tying of the agencies' ethos to the will of the issuer is demonstrated when we consider that an investor needs to have the rating constantly reviewed so that their information is accurate and up-to-date. However, because the agency is only concerned with the will of its client, who as an issuer will only be concerned with the *initial* rating (so that the debt can be traded), the lack of incentive created by the issuer-pays model to review ratings has the potential of being an extremely important consequence of this particular conflict of interest. This also relates to the nature of the oligopoly when, as Dombalagian states, 'the highly concentrated nature of the credit-rating industry may reduce the incentive for established credit-rating agencies to compete on the basis of better methodologies or diligence'.[86] As we saw in the methodological race-to-the-bottom witnessed before and after the recent financial crisis,[87] the incentive to be diligent is arguably non-existent.

This transformation in ethos manifested itself almost immediately after the issuer-pays model was incorporated. As Moody's was the first to incorporate it on an extensive basis, researchers have endeavoured to gauge their ratings

---

83 (n 49).

84 Schroeter (n 26) 384.

85 Han Xia 'Can Investor-paid Credit Rating Agencies Improve the Information Quality of Issuer-paid Rating Agencies? [2014] 111 *Journal of Financial Economics* 451.

86 Onnig H. Dombalagian *Chasing the Tape: Information Law and Policy in Capital Markets* (MIT Press 2015) 82.

87 See the discussion on the Copula Formula in *Where Loyalties Lie – The Relationship Between the Investor and the Agency* for just one example.

against that of Standard & Poor's who incorporated the model in the same manner almost four years later. If, as the agencies suggest, the 'Issuer-pays' model does not affect the operations of the agencies, then the expected result of such studies would be that there would be very little noticeable difference between Moody's' ratings from 1970 onwards when compared to Standard & Poor's' (given their similarities in a wide range of areas, i.e. market capital-isation, resources and rating models etc). Jiang, Stanford and Xie conducted this research under the title of 'Does it Matter who Pays for Bond Ratings?' and the results are spectacularly revealing. Using a sample of 797 corporate bonds issued between 1971 and 1978 that were rated by both Moody's and Standard & Poor's, the scholars find that between 1971 and June 1974, when Moody's charged issuers for bond ratings and Standard & Poor's charged investors, Moody's ratings were, on average, '*higher* than S&P's ratings for the same bond'. During the period in which both Standard & Poor's and Moody's both charged issuers for the bond ratings – July 1974 to 1978 – the researchers find that 'Moody's ratings are *no longer* higher than those of S&P'. The scholars finish by determining that the change in the difference between the two agencies' ratings derives 'from an increase in S&P's ratings around 1974, rather than from any change in Moody's ratings'. The natural conclusion to this empirical research is that 'this finding supports the view that the issuer-pay model leads to higher bond ratings'.[88]

This incredible empirical research provides evidence for assertions of the same nature within the literature: the OECD states in a report that 'the ratings inflation was attributable not to the valuation models used by the agencies, but rather to systematic upward adjustments in ratings in efforts to retain or capture business, a direct consequence of the issuer-pays business model'.[89] Although Jiang et al.'s research was based on a small sample of the agencies' history, it was the only avail-able time period in which there was a divergence between the two leaders of the oligopoly; any claims that suggest that the issuer-pays model is not a conflict of interest or can be managed, can be dismissed.

Finally, one issue that stems from this understanding that the issuer-pays model inherently results in rating inflation is the systemic effect that the system will inev-itably produce. Bar-Isaac and Shapiro state that several economic fundamentals suggest that 'ratings quality is lower in booms and improves in recessions'. This systemic understanding displays for us the realisation that agencies are, in effect, the facilitators of economic expansion in that they primarily serve to create bubbles; their output is weaker during a time when the public interest needs it to be stronger and their output is stronger when there is less need for their product at all (owing to reduced investment after a burst bubble). This also has the effect of prolonging the damage that their weak output contributed to in the first place. The reason why this dynamic exists is rather simple: 'The CRA can earn more in a

---

88 John (Xuefeng) Jiang, Mary H. Stanford and Yuan Xie 'Does it Matter who Pays for Bond Ratings? Historical Evidence' [2012] 105 *Journal of Financial Economics* 2.

89 Organisation for Economic Cooperation and Development *Bank Competition and Financial Stability* (OECD Publishing 2011) 26.

boom and so may be tempted to capitalise on the opportunity to earn the higher revenues available'.[90] It is safe to say that at this point we can discount the word 'may' from Bar-Isaac and Shapiro's statement.

Now that we understand the effects of the issuer-pays model, we will look at the last commonly understood facilitator of the divergence: the concept of 'regulatory reliance'. In the 1970s, the SEC purposefully integrated the agencies into the regulatory framework, which sought to give authority to the practices that were already in place within the economy (as we saw earlier, large investors were already dependent upon the NCO ratings prior to the 1970s[91]). With competitive pressures resulting in the eradication of ratings quality, particularly in light of the incorporation of the issuer-pays model which promised huge returns for doing so,[92] the SEC created the NRSRO position which essentially ring-fenced the ratings industry from any new competitors from that point on. What effect would this ratification have upon the divergence? The answer to this question lies in the understanding that whatever effect it had could not be reversed; a fact which is proven by the continued growth of the industry even after the references to rating agencies were removed from every governmental regulation as mandated by the Dodd-Frank Act of 2010.

Regulatory reliance

The third and final commonly advanced facilitator of the divergence is that a campaign by the SEC in the 1970s to incorporate the ratings of the agencies into a number of regulations was a prime cause of the agencies' shortcomings 30 years later. The period of incorporation, which saw the agencies being granted recognised status, is often cited as being the most important aspect in the development of the ratings industry, as Barth et al. claim:

> How did these agencies become so pivotal? Until the 1970s credit-rating agencies were comparatively insignificant institutions that sold their assessments of credit risk to subscribers ... the answer lies with the Guardians of Finance, especially the SEC, which created a climate in which it is virtually impossible for a firm to issue a security without first purchasing a rating.[93]

Yet, as our analysis so far has revealed, to attribute the rapid growth of the industry to just one element is misleading; is it really true that the SEC created the fertile environment for the ratings industry? Alternatively, the appropriate way forward is to consider a number of aspects as part of a 'causal web'. The benefits

90 Heski Bar-Isaac and Joel Shapiro 'Ratings Quality over the Business Cycle' [2013] 108 *Journal of Financial Economics* 62.

91 (n 75).

92 Bo Becker and Todd Milbourn 'How did Increased Competition Affect Credit Ratings?' [2011] 101 *Journal of Financial Economics* 494; Jonathan R. Macey *The Death of Corporate Reputation: How Integrity Has Been Destroyed on Wall Street* (Pearson Education 2013) 171.

93 James R. Barth, Gerard Caprio and Ross Levine *Guardians of Finance: Making Regulators Work For Us* (MIT Press 2012) 106.

of doing so revolve around the push to be open-minded when considering the *reasons* for the divergence identified in this work.

This assessment will be helpful because many analyses seem to direct absolute blame towards the SEC,[94] but understanding whether or not this is deserved is important because these claims simultaneously divert blame away from the agencies, which is particularly distasteful given their actions. Yet, the SEC did – and continues to – play a vital role in the continuation of the rating oligopoly so, on the basis of moving forward within that open-minded mentality, their role must be examined thoroughly. However, with the agencies' history pre-dating that of the SEC, a more wide-ranging analysis is required.

Regulatory reliance: the blame game

Flandreau and Sławatyniec attempt to dispel the myth that before the 1970s the ratings industry was of limited importance.[95] This myth is a prime example of the effect that misguided information can have, because the reality is that the agencies were extremely important, in the context of that era and were relied upon heavily by a number of parties. Ultimately, this goes against the narrative of the SEC incorporating the agencies unexpectedly and the damage caused after this therefore being the fault of regulators. It seems as if assessments of the industry's importance stems from their involvement with the globalised capital markets, but when we understand that between 1900 and 1940 the US judiciary *overwhelmingly* relied upon the rating agencies in commercially concerned cases because

> both banks who originated the products and those who distributed them were, *already in the 1920s*, highly dependent on the decisions of rating agencies for they benefited from the ratings being generous (as they would be able to sell more products without facing liability risks),[96]

then the relevance of understanding someone's meaning of the term 'importance' is all too apparent. So, in opposition to the claims that that revolutions occurred in the usage of ratings in the 1930s[97] or the 1970s,[98] it is actually the case that they were *relied upon* by financial institutions and investors long before this.

As a result of this understanding it is clear that a switch in emphasis needs to occur, based upon the *actual* version of events. While the common assertion is

---

94 Barth, Caprio, Levine (n 93); Fight (n 66) 54; Jonathan R. Macey *Corporate Governance: Promises Kept, Promises Broken* (Princeton University Press 2010) 115; Thierry Paulais *Financing Africa's Cities: The Imperative of Local Investment* (International Bank for Reconstruction and Development/The World Bank 2012) 49.

95 Partnoy (n 2) 70.

96 Marc Flandreau and Joanna K. Sławatyniec 'Understanding Rating Addiction: US Courts and the Origins of Rating Agencies' Regulatory Licence (1900–1940)' [2013] 20 *Financial History Review* 3 240.

97 Gilbert Harold is recognised as being the originator of this view. See Gilbert Harold *Bond Ratings as an Investment Guide* (Ronald Press 1938).

98 Partnoy, in general, but particularly in (n 2) is a key component of this scholarly view.

that the regulatory incorporation of the 1970s created an 'artificial demand',[99] and that essentially the industry was forced upon the marketplace, it is actually the case that the market relied upon the agencies' output long before an institution representing the state sought to ratify their output.

This sentiment is confirmed by Flandreau and Sławatyniec's research which found that the courts refused to technically endorse the rating agencies, but rather confirmed their acceptance of the understanding that the ratings had become a conventionally accepted benchmark in the banking and securities trading professions.[100] It is on this basis that it is contested here that the focus on the SEC when it comes to apportioning blame is not entirely justified because, just like the SEC in 1975 and the judiciary before the 1930s, it was actually the market that was dictating the acceptance of the agencies, not the regulatory bodies (who can be seen to be retroactive in this light). In evaluating Partnoy's well-known but contentious principle of the SEC granting 'regulatory licences',[101] Flandreau and Sławatyniec are correct in noting that the judiciary's understanding of the agencies' systemic importance, which was merely transferred to regulatory bodies (the OCC in 1931 and the SEC in 1975), represents a 'legal' rather than a 'regulatory' licence.

What this does, then, is shift our attention to the market. It has been stated that 'regulatory use occurred because rating agencies already were providing a well-known and valuable product to market participants'[102] which, of course, is true when we consider that in 1931, when the OCC incorporated technical elements of the agencies' products into their regulations, they did not have to supplement this with any explanation; the market was well aware of the agencies' products because they had been using them for over 50 years (in some cases even longer). This calls into question the wisdom of championing the removal of references to the agencies within the regulations in the Dodd-Frank Act of 2010 because, as Darbellay and Partnoy note, 'behavioural reliance on ratings has been deeply anchored in the financial markets'.[103] The scholars go on to ask whether behavioural reliance is the key factor driving the Big Three's market share. The answer has to be a resounding 'yes'.

Ultimately this understanding of the *actual* version of events can help us to prepare reform proposals that are more appropriate. If it is the case that the market dictates that the Big Three remain in power, then what use is removing references within the regulations –the investors will continue to use the agencies regardless. The actual effect, which we shall see in the Chapter 4, is that now the state has removed itself from the equation, superficially, investors have no

99 Macey (n 94) 115.
100 Flandreau and Sławatyniec (n 96) 246.
101 Partnoy develops this theory, predominantly, in two works: Frank Partnoy 'The Siskel and Ebert of Financial Markets? Two Thumbs Down for the Credit Rating Agencies' [1999] 77 *Washington University Law Quarterly* 3; Frank Partnoy (n 2).
102 House of Lords *Banking Supervision and Regulation: 2nd Report of Session 2008–09. Vol. 2: Evidence* (The Stationery Office 2009) 77.
103 Aline Darbellay and Frank Partnoy 'Credit Rating Agencies and Regulatory Reform' in Claire A. Hill, James L. Krusemark, Brett H. McDonnell and Solly Robbins (eds) *Research Handbook on the Economics of Corporate Law* (Edward Elgar Publishing 2012) 290.

recourse to complain that they were forced to use the agencies. What is important for our analysis is that a correct account of the history of the ratings industry is consistently advanced, because an account that focuses on the 1970s as the real turning point neglects over 130 years of actions that can reveal the true characteristics of the target for reform.

The effects of SEC incorporation

It is important here to reaffirm that we must understand the following 'effects' of regulatory reliance in conjunction with the effects of the oligopolistic structure and the issuer-pays remuneration model, because they all form part of a six-year campaign that has come to define the modern rating industry. This is perhaps better emphasised when we assess the effect that regulatory incorporation had upon competition within the industry. It has been noted that the incorporation in 1975 essentially made competition within the industry 'almost impossible',[104] but as we now know, the oligopolistic structure and the requirements of those in the corporate bond market are the actual reason why competition is 'almost impossible'; at most, the SEC rules served to officially ratify what was already occurring. Fight suggests that assigning NRSRO status actually allowed the US Government the opportunity to insert itself into this area that is dominated by the market to protect its own hegemonic interests: '… the defining criteria (of NRSRO status) have never been articulated by the SEC (advantageous if the goal is to block the road to foreign rating agencies!)'.[105]

The NRSRO status altered the dynamics within the industry, because now rather than operating under the façade of being constrained by competitive and reputational pressures, they were purely bound by regulatory pressures. As Freidman suggests:

> their financial success did not depend on the ability of these techniques to produce accurate ratings. Instead, their profitability depended on government protection. If the rating agencies used inaccurate rating procedures, they would not suffer for it financially – let alone would they go out of business.[106]

From 1975 onwards the only real concern for a NRSRO was not losing its status. With regulatory pressure being the only true pressure that serves to constrain the agencies, it has been argued that agencies' outputs tend to be homogenised so that no one agency steps away from the crowd;[107] this makes sense because before the financial crisis the SEC would never had removed all of the NRSRO designations as a punishment (Congress did with the Dodd-Frank

---

104 Paulais (n 94) 49.
105 Fight (n 66) 54.
106 Jeffrey Freidman 'Capitalism and the Crisis: Bankers, Bonuses, Ideology and Ignorance' in Jeffrey Freidman (ed.) *What Caused the Financial Crisis?* (University of Pennsylvania Press 2011) 13.
107 House of Lords (n 102) 78.

Act but that is another matter). This homogenisation has a systemic effect in that the uniformity in opinion increases the degree and spread of procyclicality. A downgrade for a firm is more likely to result in multiple downgrades which would devastate their position and if the agencies all respond to an event in exactly the same manner (i.e. the response to the collapse of Lehman Brothers) then the spread of downgrades and losses is almost instantaneous.[108]

Part of the reason for this uniformity, other than not wanting to draw undue attention to a given agency, is because the agencies began to construct their ratings so that they achieved a regulatory purpose rather than representing the underlying creditworthiness of the given entity; this is particularly relevant to the structured finance market.[109] For example, the CDOs and SIVs that came to define the pre-crisis era were all designed so that they had just enough attributes to be rated as AAA, but not enough that they reduced the profits available for the entities that created them; as a result, when the first products began to default it quickly became apparent that all of the products that had the same rating were of a similar nature, which is the reason why we saw mass downgrades in 2007 and 2008. This notion of being able to construct an offering so that it just passed the regulatory threshold for what was required was a direct result of the incorporation in the 1970s (although subsequent additions to the SEC rules affected SIVs and CDOs).

The effects of regulatory incorporation – procyclicality, an official termination of competitive and reputational pressures and an emphasis on meeting regulation standards rather than quality standards – are indeed incredible. However, one can only gauge just how incredible they are by understanding that before the CRA Duopoly Relief Act of 2005, the CRA Reform Act of 2006 and the Dodd-Frank Act of 2010, the SEC received very little information from the agencies. Miller notes that the SEC often received their information on the operations of the agencies *through business publications or from competing rating agencies*. 'For example, the (SEC) learned about McGraw-Hill Inc.'s (S&P's parent company) acquisition of J.J. Kenny Co., a bankers' broker, from a *Wall Street Journal* article'.[110] Paired with the fact that no formal training, educational qualification or professional qualification is required to become a rating analyst,[111] this arguably leads to the conclusion that, until 2006, the ratings industry was, in essence, unregulated.

The regulation of the credit rating industry is a particularly complex area to assess and admittedly many aspects have been deferred to the next chapter, which examines in greater detail the regulatory response to the crisis and incorporates an analysis of the regulatory failings that the Dodd-Frank Act attempted to rectify. What is abundantly clear from this analysis, however, is that the regulatory incorporation that took place in the 1970s was an important factor in the development of the industry we see today, but it was not the decisive factor; it is

108 Stijn Claessens and Kirsten Forbes *International Financial Contagion* (Springer Science & Business Media 2013) 443.
109 Douglas D. Evanoff *The First Credit Market Turmoil of the 21st Century* (World Scientific 2009) 177.
110 Gerald J. Miller (ed.) *Handbook of Debt Management* (CRC Press 1996) 518.
111 Fight (n 66) 54.

simply not appropriate to consider just one of the 'causes' of the failings of the industry in isolation.

Conclusion

Though there are many instances that illustrate that the idealised position of the parties that surround the agencies – the state, investors and issuers – is nothing more than a fallacy, the fact still remains that reforms have been consistently founded upon the realisation of the requirements of these idealised positions. We shall see in the next chapter that the once-in-a-generation opportunity to enact meaningful change that the Dodd-Frank Act represented was squandered because it focused on the *desired* rather than the *actual*. The next chapter is framed within that understanding, so for that analysis to be effective, we first had to understand the reasons for the divergence and how they contribute to the perpetuation of it.

Upon learning that the ratings industry represents an oligopolistic structure at work and that this structure prevents any competition-based reforms, it is easy to see that attempting to do so can only have one consequence: failure. The rating agencies, however, fully understand the parameters of their industry and operate accordingly, which is demonstrated by the lack of regard for the reputational damage that was the obvious result of their collusion with the issuers of structured finance products. Yet, for many reasons, the agencies have navigated many economic cycles and have positioned themselves in such a way that the threats of the past, in terms of their position, will not be repeated. By developing a remuneration system that fundamentally favours their position and by acknowledging that it is the marketplace that dictates their continuation, not the regulators, the agencies have developed into a stage of their progression whereby they are, ostensibly, immune to failure.

It is on this understanding that the reform proposal that will be established in Chapter 6 operates; the ability of the rating agencies to take advantage of their position must be constrained. While it is very difficult to foresee a chain of events that would result in their actual position being fundamentally altered, it is far more reasonable to suggest that by constraining their ability to take advantage of that position, by way of excessive profits from activities that are not important for the actual act of rating (i.e. ancillary services) the financial penalties that are seemingly the only threat *may* have more of an impact then they do now. We will see in the next chapter that this focus on the *actual* version of events was simply not considered in the wake of the financial crisis. In order to provide weight to the reform proposal examined in Chapters 5 and 6, we will have to understand where the current regulatory sentiment lies and, ultimately, where it has failed.

Bibliography

'Your Credit Good? Dun & Bradstreet Knows' [1947] *Kiplinger's Magazine* September edition 28.
Abdelal, R. *Capital Rules: The Construction of Global Finance* (Harvard University Press 2007).

Alcubilla, R.G. and del Pozo, J.R. *Credit Rating Agencies on the Watch List: Analysis of European Regulation* (Oxford University Press 2012).

Allen, L. *The Encyclopedia of Money* (ABC-CLIO 2009).

Andenas, M. and Chiu, I.H.Y. *The Foundations and Future of Financial Regulation: Governance for Responsibility* (Routledge 2013).

Avgouleas, E. *Governance of Global Financial Markets: The Law, The Economics, The Politics* (Cambridge University Press 2012).

Bar-Isaac, H. and Shapiro, J. 'Ratings Quality over the Business Cycle' [2013] 108 *Journal of Financial Economics* 62.

Barth, J.R., Caprio, G. and Levine, R. *Guardians of Finance: Making Regulators Work for Us* (MIT Press 2012).

Becker, B. and Milbourn, T. 'How Did Increased Competition Affect Credit Ratings?' [2011] 101 *Journal of Financial Economics* 493.

Bertelsmann Stiftung *Blueprint for INCRA – An International Non-profit Credit Rating Industry: Executive Summary* (2012).

Bezilla, M. and Rudnicki, J. *Rails to Penn State: The Story of the Bellefonte Central* (Stackpole Books 2007).

Bordo, M.D. and Eichengreen, B. *A Retrospective on the Bretton Woods System: Lessons for International Monetary Reform* (University of Chicago Press 2007).

Buchanan, J.M. and Tollison, R.D. *The Theory of Public Choice* (University of Michigan Press 1962).

Butler, C. *Accounting for Financial Instruments* (John Wiley & Sons 2009).

Caporaso, J.A. and Levine, D.P. *Theories of Political Economy* (Cambridge University Press 1992).

Cash, D. 'The International Non-profit Credit Rating Agency: The Viability of a Response' [2016] 37 The Company Lawyer 6.

Claessens, S. and Forbes, K. *International Financial Contagion* (Springer Science & Business Media 2013).

Coase, R.H. 'The Lighthouse in Economics' [1974] 17 *Journal of Law and Economics* 2.

Colombo, J.R. *Neo Poems* (Sono Nis Press 1970).

Crockett, A. *Conflicts of Interest in the Financial Services Industry: What Should We Do About Them?* (Centre for Economic Policy Research 2003).

Darbellay, A. *Regulating Credit Rating Agencies* (Edward Elgar 2013).

Darbellay, A. and Partnoy, F. 'Credit Rating Agencies and Regulatory Reform' in Hill, C.A., Krusemark, J.L., McDonnell, B.H. and Robbins, S. (eds) *Research Handbook on the Economics of Corporate Law* (Edward Elgar Publishing 2012).

Daughen, J.R. and Binzen, P. *The Wreck of the Penn Central* (Beard Books 1999).

Detragiache, E. 'Rational Liquidity Crises in the Sovereign Debt Market: In Search of Theory' [1996] 43 International Monetary Fund: Staff Papers 3.

Dombalagian, O.H. *Chasing the Tape: Information Law and Policy in Capital Markets* (MIT Press 2015).

Duan, J.-C. and Van Laere, E. 'A *Public Good* Approach to Credit Rating – From Concept to Reality' [2012] 36 *Journal of Banking & Finance* 3239.

Dyson, K. *States, Debt and Power: 'Saints' and 'Sinners' in European History and Integration* (Oxford University Press 2014).

Evanoff, D.D. *The First Credit Market Turmoil of the 21st Century* (World Scientific 2009).

Fedaseyeu, V. 'Economics of Information' in Free, R.C. (ed.) *21st Century Economics: A Reference Handbook* (SAGE Publications 2010).

Fight, A. *Understanding International Bank Risk* (John Wiley & Sons 2004).

Flandreau, M. and Sławatyniec, J.K. 'Understanding Rating Addiction: US Courts and the Origins of Rating Agencies' Regulatory License (1900–1940)' [2013] 20 *Financial History Review* 3.

Freidman, J. 'Capitalism and the Crisis: Bankers, Bonuses, Ideology and Ignorance' in Freidman, J. (ed.) *What Caused the Financial Crisis?* (University of Pennsylvania Press 2011).

Friedman, J. *Oligopoly Theory* (Cambridge University Press Archive 1983).

Geisst, C.R. *Encyclopaedia of American Business History* (Facts on File 2006).

Hardaway, R.M. *Great American Housing Bubble: The Road to Collapse* (ABC-CLIO 2011).

Harold, G. *Bond Ratings as an Investment Guide* (Ronald Press 1938).

Head, J.G. 'Public Goods and Public Policy' [1962] 17 Public Finance 3.

Helleiner, E. *Forgotten Foundations of Bretton Woods: International Development and the Making of the Postwar Order* (Cornell University Press 2014).

Hemraj, M. *Credit Rating Agencies: Self-regulation, Statutory Regulation and Case Law Regulation in the United States and European Union* (Springer 2015).

Hicks, J.W. 'Commercial Paper: An Exempted Security Under Section 3(a)(3) of the Securities Act of 1933' [1976] 24 *UCLA Law Review* 227.

House of Lords *Banking Supervision and Regulation: 2nd Report of Session 2008–09, Vol 2: Evidence* (The Stationery Office 2009).

Hudson, R., Colley, A. and Largan, M. *The Capital Markets and Financial Management in Banking* (Routledge 2013).

Immergluck, D. *Foreclosed: High-risk Lending, Deregulation and the Undermining of America's Mortgage Market* (Cornell University Press 2011).

Jiang, J.(X.), Stanford, M.H. and Xie, Y. 'Does it Matter who Pays for Bond Ratings? Historical Evidence' [2012] 105 *Journal of Financial Economics* 3.

Langohr, H.P. and Langohr, P.T. *The Rating Agencies and Their Credit Ratings: What They Are, How They Work and Why They are Relevant* (John Wiley & Sons 2010).

Listokin, Y. and Taibleson, B. 'If You Misrate, Then You Lose: Improving Credit Rating Accuracy Through Incentive Compensation' [2010] 27 *Yale Journal on Regulation* 91.

Macey, J.R. *Corporate Governance: Promises Kept, Promises Broken* (Princeton University Press 2010).

Macey, J.R. *The Death of Corporate Reputation: How Integrity Has Been Destroyed on Wall Street* (Pearson Education 2013).

Mallinckrodt Chemical Works v Goldman, Sachs & Co., 420 F Supp 231 (SDNY 1976).

Manns, J. 'Rating Risk after the Subprime Mortgage Crisis: A User Fee Approach for Rating Agency Accountability' [2007–08] 87 *North Carolina Law Review* 87.

Markham, J.W. *A Financial History of the United States: From Enron-era Scandals to the Great Recession* (Routledge 2015).

Mattarocci, G. *The Independence of Credit Rating Agencies: How Business Models and Regulators Interact* (Academic Press 2014).

McEachern, W.A. *Economics: A Contemporary Introduction* (Cengage Learning 2011).

Miller, G.J. (ed.) *Handbook of Debt Management* (CRC Press 1996).

Naciri, A. *Credit Rating Governance: Global Credit Gatekeepers* (Routledge 2015).

Olson, M. *The Logic of Collective Action: Public Goods and the Theory of Groups* (Schocken Books 1968).

Organisation for Economic Cooperation and Development *Bank Competition and Financial Stability* (OECD Publishing 2011).

Partnoy, F. 'How and Why Credit Rating Agencies Are Not Like Other Gatekeepers' in Fuchita, Y. and Litan, R.E. (eds) *Financial Gatekeepers: Can They Protect Investors?* (Brookings Institution Press 2007).

Partnoy, F. 'The Paradox of Credit Ratings' in Levich, R.M., Majnoni, G. and Reinhart, C. (eds) *Ratings, Rating Agencies and the Global Financial System* (Kluwer 2002).

Partnoy, F. 'The Siskel and Ebert of Financial Markets? Two Thumbs Down for the Credit Rating Agencies' [1999] 77 *Washington University Law Quarterly* 3.

Paulais, T. *Financing Africa's Cities: The Imperative of Local Investment* (International Bank for Reconstruction and Development/The World Bank 2012).

Pigou, A.C. *The Economics of Welfare* (Macmillan and Company 1920).

Richardson, M. and White, L.J. 'The Rating Agencies: Is Regulation the Answer?' in Acharya, V.A. and Richardson, M. (eds) *Restoring Financial Stability: How to Repair a Failed System* (John Wiley & Sons 2009).

Romp, G. *Game Theory: Introduction and Applications* (Oxford University Press 1997).

Rona-Tas, A. and Hiss, S. 'The Art of Corporate and The Science of Consumer Credit Rating' in Lounsbury, M. and Hirsch, P.M. (eds) *Markets on Trial: The Economic Sociology of the U.S. Financial Crisis, Part 1* (Emerald Group Publishing 2010).

Sabnavis, M. *Macroeconomics Demystified* (Tata McGraw-Hill Education 2008).

Samuelson, P.A. 'The Pure Theory of Public Expenditure' [1954] 36 *The Review of Economics and Statistics* 4.

Sandage, S.A. *Born Losers: A History of Failure in America* (Harvard University Press 2006).

Schroeter, U.G. 'Credit Ratings and Credit Rating Agencies' in Caprio, G. (ed.) *Handbook of Key Global Financial Markets, Institutions and Infrastructure* (Academic Press 2013).

Securities and Exchange Commission *The Financial Collapse of the Penn Central Company: Staff Report of the SEC to the Special Subcommittee on Investigations* (GPO 1972).

Steil, B. *The Battle of Bretton Woods: John Maynard Keynes, Harry Dexter White and the Making of a New World Order* (Princeton University Press 2013).

Stroux, S. *US and EC Oligopoly Control* (Kluwer Law International 2004).

Suarez-Villa, L. *Corporate Power, Oligopolies and the Crisis of the State* (SUNY Press 2014).

Sylla, R. 'An Historical Primer on the Business of Credit Ratings' in Levich, R.M., Majnoni, G. and Reinhart, C. (eds) *Ratings, Rating Agencies and the Global Financial System* (Kluwer 2002).

Taupin, B. 'Perpetuating the Regulatory Order in the Credit Rating Industry' in Hault, I. and Richard, C. (eds) *Finance: The Discreet Regulator – How Financial Activities Shape and Transform the World* (Palgrave Macmillan 2012).

Tennant, D.F. and Tracey, M.R. *Sovereign Debt and Credit Rating Bias* (Palgrave Macmillan 2015).

Von Neumann, J. and Morgenstern, O. *Theory of Games and Economic Behavior* (Princeton University Press 1947).

Waterhouse, B.C. *Lobbying America: The Politics of Business from Nixon to NAFTA* (Princeton University Press 2013).

Waterson, M. *Economic Theory of the Industry* (Cambridge University Press Archive 1984).

White, L.J. 'Financial Regulation and the Current Crisis: A Guide for Antitrust' in American Bar Association *Competition as Public Policy* (American Bar Association 2010).

Wilcox, C. *Groupthink: An Impediment to Success* (Xlibris Corporation 2010).

Wilson, R.S. and Fabozzi, F.J. *Corporate Bonds: Structures & Analysis* (Frank J. Fabozzi Associates 1996).

Wirten, E.H. *No Trespassing: Authorship, Intellectual Property Rights and the Boundaries of Globalization* (The University of Toronto Press 2004).

Xia, H. 'Can Investor-paid Credit Rating Agencies Improve the Information Quality of Issuer-paid Rating Agencies? [2014] 111 *Journal of Financial Economics* 2.

4 Tried and failed

Introduction

It should be obvious that the United States was not the only country to enact major reforms in the wake of the crisis. With regard to the ratings industry, the European Union (EU) enacted particularly extensive pieces of legislation after the collapse, the first to be established anywhere in the wake of the crisis.[1] However, for our analysis it will be important to remain focused on the United States for a number of reasons. Perhaps the most important reason is that the agencies were created and continue to be headquartered, in the United States. While the financial crisis spread around the globe (mostly in the West but there was naturally a knock-on effect for the rest of the World), it originated in the US with US-based institutions selling products that were primarily based upon US housing mortgages; this resulted in the US being seen as having to take the lead with regard to regulation. Also, the nature of the EU means that different factors are important in comparison with the US, which may alter its focus when regulating the ratings industry. One clear example of this would be the rating agencies' involvement in the sovereign debt crisis that still has the EU in a state of flux.[2]

So, we will start by assessing the relevant sections of the US's legislative response (The Dodd-Frank Act of 2010). It will then be important to detail some of the issues that have arisen from this, particularly with regard to the administering of its rules and guidance, which is a real issue with this piece of legislation. The chapter will then use these analyses to judge the effect the Dodd-Frank Act has had in relation to the *desired v actual* framework. The consequences of this are important for the projection of potential validity for the reforms proposed later on.

1 Niamh Moloney *EU Securities and Financial Markets Regulation* (Oxford University Press 2014). For the actual Acts see Regulation (EU) No 1060/2009 [2009] OJ L302/1; Regulation (EU) No 513/2011 [2011] OJ L145/30; Regulation (EU) No 462/2013 [2013] OJ L146/1. There was also a significant directive which contributed to the direction of CRA related regulation in the EU: Directive 2013/14/EU [2013] OJ L145/1.
2 For more on the EU sovereign debt crisis and the agencies' role in it see Lucia Quaglia *The European Union and Global Financial Regulation* (Oxford University Press 2014).

The Dodd-Frank Act of 2010 – what were its aims?

As we have heard throughout, the US responded to the financial crisis by enacting the Dodd-Frank Wall Street Reform and Consumer Protection Act of 2010. In its preamble the Act states that its aim is to

> promote the financial stability of the United States by improving account-ability and transparency in the financial system, to end 'too big to fail', to protect the American taxpayer by ending bailouts, to protect consumers from abusive financial services practices and for other purposes.[3]

For our analysis the most important section of the Act is Title IX 'Investor Protections and Improvements to the Regulation of Securities' – Subtitle C 'Improvements to the Regulation of Credit Rating Agencies'. This expansive section aims to readdress certain elements and ultimately build upon both the Securities and Exchange Act of 1934 and the Credit Rating Agency Reform Act of 2006 with respect to rating agencies.

It has been noted by various onlookers that the Act covers nine particular areas with respect to the ratings industry. It aims to legislate in the areas of: SEC oversight; governance and compliance; conflict of interest management; account-ability for ratings procedures; transparency of ratings procedures and methodolo-gies; the use of ratings within statutes and regulations; SEC-provided penalties; Securities Act registration; and the private right of action.[4] Before we continue, it is appropriate to note that, from this cursory review, the Act appears to be chal-lenging the constructs that make up the *actual* to bring about the *desired* as much as possible. Does this understanding hold up under closer inspection?

Congress was of the opinion that the SEC required more power in this area than it had been granted in the CRA Duopoly Relief Act of 2005 and the CRA Reform Act of 2006. While it is to be expected that Congress appointed the SEC as the state's representative in such matters, given its position within the regu-latory framework since its inception in 1934, it is apparent that a lot of the Act leaves the *making* and *enforcing* of those rules to the SEC; the Act simply dictates on a number of occasions that the SEC takes action.[5]

All of the elements of the Act are important, although some are crucial to deciding the course for the industry and the effects that that may have. With regard to the *actual*, in theory a number of the stated aims of the Act aim to change or restrict it. Perhaps the most noteworthy attempt comes in the form of Congress attempting to remove the systemic reliance upon the agencies by removing references to them within statutory and regulatory documents. Again,

3 *The Dodd-Frank Wall Street Reform and Consumer Protection Act of 2010* 124 Stat 1376.
4 Claire A. Hill 'Limits of Dodd-Frank's Rating Agency Reform' [2011] 15 *Chapman Law Review* 1; Jeffrey Haas *Corporate Finance* (West Academic 2014).
5 Aline Darbellay and Frank Partnoy 'Credit Rating Agencies and Regulatory Reform' in Claire A. Hill, James L. Krusemark, Brett H. McDonnell and Solly Robbins (eds) *Research Handbook on the Economics of Corporate Law* (Edward Elgar Publishing 2012) 280.

in deferring the particular details to the respective agencies, the Act instructs those governmental agencies that have historically used the ratings as a standard measure of creditworthiness to 'remove any reference to or requirement of reliance on credit ratings and to substitute in such regulations such standard of credit-worthiness as each respective agency shall determine as appropriate for such regulations'.[6] Macey has noted that, in theory, this act of removing statutory reliance forces investors (particularly institutional investment managers) to analyse investments by taking into account a variety of information and not to lean upon the agencies, which leads to the reduction of systemic risk by 'decreasing the tendency of mutual funds to have investments that are highly correlated with (i.e. the same as) the investments of other mutual funds'.[7] To avoid any confusion, it is worth noting that the Act merely states that ratings cannot be the *only* declared source of investment guidance used by investment managers. The effect of this is negligible as we shall see; we already know that the larger investors incorporate ratings *into* their analysis rather than relying upon it; what it does change, however, is the dynamics of the agency problems we have discussed as shareholders cannot use the ratings as the only benchmark by which to constrain the decisions of managers.

Another aim of this particular order is to reduce the availability of the state-induced crutch for investors, by forcing the agencies to compete 'on the basis of the quality of their ratings as the artificial demand for their services created by regulation subsides'.[8] This concept raises all of sorts of problems as it brings into the equation the notion of 'competition', which due to the dynamics of the industry is very difficult to realistically induce. Macey also suggests that this move will lead to the ironic situation of the agencies' quality improving just as their relevancy decreases,[9] although this notion is particularly representative of an attempt to move the situation into the realm of the *desired* while not taking into account the *actual*; as we shall see, the agencies have lost none of their 'relevancy'.

The other crucial part of Subtitle C was that Congress made the agencies liable for their ratings. This went against vast amounts of judicial precedent and established practice. Congress deemed the agencies' operations to be commercial in nature, thus they were to be held to the same professional levels of accountability as registered public accounting firms or securities analysts under the securities laws.[10] The Act states that in order to make a claim for damages emanating from a credit rating the plaintiff must be able to prove that the credit rating agency 'knowingly or recklessly failed … to conduct a reasonable investigation of the rated security with respect to the factual elements … (and/or) to obtain reasonable verification of such factual elements'.[11] It is for exactly this reason that

---

6 *The Dodd-Frank Act of 2010* (n 3) § 939A (b).

7 Jonathan R. Macey 'The Nature and Futility of "Regulation by Assimilation"' in Greg Urban (ed.) *Corporations and Citizenship* (University of Pennsylvania Press 2014) 217.

8 ibid.

9 ibid.

10 *The Dodd-Frank Act of 2010* (n 3) §933 (a)(m)(1).

11 ibid (B).

CalPERS settled with Fitch for important and incriminatory documents rather than money; the documents allowed CalPERS to *prove* the 'state of mind' of Standard & Poor's and Moody's.[12]

These are indeed the key elements, although it will be useful to briefly go through the other elements when we look at the potential issues with the Act. There are a number of references to the internal organisation of the agencies and the responsibilities which must be met. For example, half of the Board members at an NRSRO must now be independent (at least half but a minimum of two). The agencies must now also publish the methodologies that have been used to formulate a rating; that methodology must have be used across the entire class of ratings or the rating agency must publish the reasons for not doing so. The agencies are also prohibited from using universal rating symbols to avoid the confusion over the structured finance ratings as discussed earlier,[13] while they are also forced to prove they have considered more information to produce their ratings than that provided by the issuer. Also, they are now obliged to inform law enforcement authorities when they become aware that the issuing company is acting (or has acted) in a manner that is deemed illegal; this alters their role within the framework because, as we saw, the agencies are adamant that they are not in the business of detecting fraud.[14] In terms of their capability to enforce the rules of the Act, the SEC has now been given the power to suspend or revoke an NRSRO's licence or suspend it from a certain area of ratings (which it has done with relation to S&P and Egan-Jones as we have already seen). The SEC was also instructed to create an 'Office of Credit Ratings' that was to be at the epicentre of its relations with the agencies.

On paper, these steps are admittedly a positive step in countering the distasteful practices of the agencies and the issuers with whom they were in cahoots (the Dodd-Frank Act covers almost every aspect of the pre-crisis system). It appears that the Act has managed to focus on the *actual* more than the state ever has, at least since the New Deal era, to achieve the *desired*. However, if this was the case there would be very little criticism, as the *desired* is seemingly widely coveted. Yet, it has been claimed that the reforms are directed at the *symptoms* rather than the *cause*, which has had the effect of altering the façade rather than the structure.[15] If the Act was successful in its mission, then the oligopoly would have been dismantled, the rate of profit and revenue would have decreased and the financial sector would have been weaned off of its 'addiction to ratings';[16] this has simply not been the case. To understand why, it is important that we turn our attention to the many criticisms of that Act and the way in which its legislative rulings have been administered.

---

12 *The Case of CalPERS.*
13 *A Snapshot of the Regulatory Framework* (n 127).
14 *The Industry: What It Does* (n 60).
15 Darbellay and Partnoy (n 5) 286.
16 Daniel Cash 'Sustainable Finance Ratings as the Latest Symptom of "Rating Addiction"' [2018] 3 *Journal of Sustainable Finance & Investment* 1.

A reality check

The Dodd-Frank Act has been widely criticised from a number of different perspectives,[17] which is to be expected when such extensive reforms are enacted (e.g. the New Deal reforms were also criticised in the wake of their enactment).[18] However, for our analysis it is important to look at two particular aspects. First, we need to establish what the effects of the rules have been in reality and second, we need to understand the complexities involved in transferring those rules from the pages of the statute to the everyday running of the financial sector. If the intended effects are different to the effects of the *actual*, then there are two potential explanations for this: either the legislators have mistakenly interpreted the *actual* dynamics of the ratings industry and all that comes with that or they have mistakenly interpreted the dynamics of the regulatory framework that governs the ratings industry.

To begin with the issues surrounding the interpretation of the industry itself, one commentator has noted that in aiming to remove the reliance upon NRSROs and making them more accountable, the Dodd-Frank Act has actually served to empower the Big Three and disadvantage its 'competitors'. Pierce argues that the requirements relating to organisational structures and internal governance are disproportionately burdensome for the smaller agencies.[19] Pierce does acknowledge, however, that the SEC has been granted powers by the Dodd-Frank Act to exempt smaller agencies in the name of reducing the burden that comes with adhering to the Act, although he does have reservations about whether the SEC will use these powers. Since 2013, when Pierce's work was published, the SEC has granted exemptions to four NRSROs where it concerned being excluded from the marketplace as a result of adhering to the new requirements,[20] although

---

17 The criticisms of the Act come from literally every affected aspect of the financial system, whether it is rating agencies, banks, insurers or a number of other financial sectors. For just some of the resources that are representative of the sentiment aimed at the failings of the Act, see Christian Evans 'The Dodd-Frank Wall Street and Consumer Protection Act: A Missed Opportunity to Rein in Too-Big-to-Fail Banks' [2011] 13 *Duquesne Business Law Journal* 43; Hill (n 4); Edward J. Kane 'Missing Elements in US Financial Reform: A Kübler-Ross Interpretation of the Inadequacy of the Dodd-Frank Act' [2012] 36 *Journal of Banking & Finance* 654.

18 Burton W. Folsom *New Deal or Raw Deal?: How FDR's Economic Legacy Has Damaged America* (Simon and Schuster 2009) 219.

19 Hester Pierce 'A Title-by-title Look at Dodd-Frank: Title IX – Securities and Exchange Commission' in Hester Pierce and James Broughel (eds) *Dodd-Frank: What It Does and Why It's Flawed* (Mercatus Center at George Mason University 2013) 102.

20 The SEC granted temporary exemption to MorningStar, LACE Financial Corporation and Kroll Bond Rating Services. MorningStar applied for an exemption as their planned switch to the issuer-pays system would have seen them violate certain aspects of the Act. Kroll applied so they could expand their operations into CMBS markets. LACE applied because they had ratings outstanding on a client who provided more than the permitted 10 per cent of total revenue (which is clearly more of a concern to smaller agencies than the Big Three). The SEC also granted an exemption to the Japan Credit Rating Agency, although this was to ensure that they complied with regulatory requirements regarding board structure in the US as well as Japan, see the following for the respective SEC Releases: Securities and Exchange Commission *Release Nos 34-71219; 34-71220; 34-57301; 34-75747.*

one agency did relinquish its NRSRO status in the wake of the Dodd-Frank Act being implemented.[21]

While the concept of disproportionality seems to have been negated by the Act with regard to the potential burdens for the smaller agencies, what it has not countered is the disproportionate effect the opening of liability may have on the smaller agencies. Pierce makes the valid argument that the larger NRSROs (the Big Three) have specialised legal departments *devoted* to repelling legal actions, whereas the smaller agencies are less able to defend themselves;[22] it is certainly true that the Big Three have much more experience of repelling legal action against their conduct. Also, the larger agencies have the capacity to absorb any fines levied against them, mostly because of their vast size and compartmentalised sources of revenue (yet another of the major issues with ancillary service provision).

If we look more closely at what the Act is asking the agencies to do, then Hill's perception that 'Dodd-Frank does not ask rating agencies to guarantee results, only processes'[23] is particularly astute. This adds weight to the notion that the legislators have failed to learn from, what we now understand because of the analysis in Chapter 2, the actual conduct and processes of the credit rating agencies because, as Hill argues, 'the essential conflict, that the issuer is the client, remains, no matter what formal separations of duties and outside monitoring is mandated'.[24] If we accept this understanding then Hill's argument that the Act will serve to perfect concealment rather than quality is logical, given that the core of the agencies' business is to cater for their clients, which as we know are the issuers of the securities they rate. It is fathomable to suggest that the agencies will now invest heavily in working out how to navigate their way through the restrictions imposed by the Act so that they can enable the issuers to take profitable securities to the marketplace; or perhaps they and the issuers, will bide their time before collective amnesia takes hold once again and deregulation becomes acceptable.

In the same vein as Hill, Pagliari argues that the Act has only sought to intervene in the façade and has avoided altering the *actual*. Pagliari has a particular concern regarding allowing the agencies to dictate their methods and only having to declare their practices in the name of transparency. Although the sentiment for us is slightly different, it is similar to Pagliari in that it is placing trust in the agencies to perform in the correct manner, which is at the heart of the divergence. For Pagliari, the real issue lies in the regulators' reluctance to intervene in determining the models to be used by the agencies despite their obvious shortcomings.[25] He suggests that the reason for not doing so is that regulators and the state in general, are reluctant to be seen as validating the operation of

---

21 Rating and Investment Information, Inc. (R&I) withdrew on 13 October 2011, stating that the withdrawal was 'based on its own business judgment' see Rating and Investment Information, Inc 'R&I to withdraw from NRSRO registration with USSEC' [2011] R&I News Release.

22 Pierce (n 19) 103.

23 Hill (n 4) 145.

24 ibid 146.

25 Stefano Pagliari 'Who Governs Finance? The Shifting Public–Private Divide in the Regulation of Derivatives, Rating Agencies and Hedge Funds' [2012] 18 *European Law Journal* 56. See also

the agencies as this would be seen to be 'creating moral hazard and exacerbating over-reliance on ratings'.[26] This is obviously a valid concern and a positive stance to take, although while they may not intervene for these reasons, is it actually the case that the Act has managed to avoid such negative consequences?

In reality, the Act has created a wonderfully confusing dynamic that is not helpful to society whatsoever. It removes all reliance on the agencies for a number of reasons, but some are more obvious than others. Yes it removes the ability of investors to rely on the ratings and claim that they were forced to use them when times turn bad. However, Pierce argues that giving the SEC the ability to suspend or revoke registration sends the message that the ratings industry and its outputs have a 'government imprimatur'.[27]. This is obviously in direct contradiction to the stated aims of the Act.

This process is an important one and has been reviewed by two scholars who label it the 'Emperor's equivocation'[28]. Scalet and Kelly claim that the ability to 'pass the buck' was institutionalised in the system that preceded the crisis, in that the state forced investors towards the agencies who expressly denied responsibility for their actions.[29] However, this notion of the institutionalisation of the ability to 'pass the buck' has arguably been reinforced by the Dodd-Frank Act, in that the state has now removed itself, on the face of it at least, from the ratings process, while the agencies can argue that investors are not forced to rely upon their ratings. The issue with this is that it does not take into account that the state has been systematically embedding the agencies into the fibre of the economy for over 35 years prior to the enactment of the Dodd-Frank Act[30] (even longer when we consider the early stages of the credit reporting and credit rating industries[31]). This alludes to the existence of a regulatory 'sleight of hand' which is just one worrying aspect; the criticisms reviewed in this section all point to the notion of the state only chipping away at the façade of the *actual* in the name of chasing the *desired*, when in reality they have strengthened the *actual* and distorted the reality of the ratings realm even further. Before we conclude, however, it is important to ask how this has been done. Every Act must be enforced, so whether or not the intentions of the legislators are honourable is irrelevant if there are issues with the administering of their decisions. As we shall see, there a number of concerns regarding the vehicle for administering the rules under the Dodd-Frank Act: the SEC.

Nicholas Ryder *The Financial Crisis and White Collar Crime: The Perfect Storm?* (Edward Elgar Publishing 2014) 65.

26 ibid.

27 Pierce (n 19) 103.

28 Steven Scalet and Thomas F. Kelly 'The Ethics of Credit Rating Agencies: What Happened and the Way Forward' [2012] 111 *Journal of Business Ethics* 477.

29 ibid 488.

30 Manns agrees with this sentiment in that the escalation of the reliance on the agencies by governmental bodies has 'survived the abolition of these requirements'; see Jeffrey Manns 'The Sovereign Rating Regulatory Dilemma' in Nigel Finch (ed.) *Emerging Markets and Sovereign Risk* (Palgrave Macmillan 2014) 132.

31 Flandreau and Sławatyniec (n 16).

It would be misleading to suggest that the legislative process ends with the signing of an Act of Congress into law. Arguably, this represents just half of the whole process because, as the post-Act dynamics develop, affected parties will seek to minimise the effect that the democratically created legislation will have on their organisation. Kane suggests that 'during and after the extended post-Act rulemaking process, decision makers will be opportunistically lobbied to scale back consumer benefits and to sustain opportunities for extracting safety-net subsidies'.[32] Macey agrees, stating that 'the rating agencies have begun a guerrilla campaign of behind-the-scenes lobbying to weaken the Commission's efforts to carry out other parts of Dodd-Frank'.[33] Concerned onlookers have endeavoured to chart the amount and extent of lobbying within the United States and have found that the financial sector lobbies more than any other sector and that rating agencies are key members of that movement.[34] This is the expected first stage of the post-Act response. However, the important question is has this pressure from the financial sector paid dividends? Some evidence regarding the SEC's administering of the Dodd-Frank Act paints a particularly damning picture.

Macey asks the question: 'Is the SEC simply "captured" or is it suffering from "Stockholm Syndrome" too?'[35] He asks this question because one act of the SEC diluted the Dodd-Frank Act's aims almost immediately. Barnett describes how on 21 July 2010, President Obama signed the Act into law; the very same day S&P, Moody's and Fitch, all asked that their ratings not be used in any new bond sales,[36] in direct response to the increased exposure in liability. To digress for one moment, this chain of events is indicative of not focusing on the *actual*, because this act by the agencies was their obvious 'joker in the pack' and they did not hesitate to use it. This understanding will be important for us later because it is becoming apparent that when making (or attempting to make) changes to the ratings industry, one must attempt to anticipate the reactionary moves the agencies will make and attempt to counter them first; this is, admittedly, not a simple task.

To continue, this removal of their ratings had the effect of bringing the entire market for asset-backed securities to a standstill. In response, the SEC established another of their infamous 'no-action letters'[37] in which issuers were informed that

---

32 Edward J. Kane 'The Expanding Financial Safety Net: The Dodd-Frank Act as an Exercise in Denial and Cover-up' in Susan M. Wachter and Marvin M. Smith (eds) *The American Mortgage System: Crisis and Reform* (University of Pennsylvania Press 2011) 274.

33 Jonathan R. Macey *The Death of Corporate Reputation: How Integrity Has Been Destroyed on Wall Street* (FT Press 2013) 232. See also Michael Lounsbury and Paul M. Hirsch (eds) *Markets on Trial: The Economic Sociology of the US Financial Crisis: Part A* (Emerald Group Publishing 2010) 91 for more on the financial sector's lobbying efforts after the Dodd-Frank Act.

34 The highest spending lobbying client in the US between 1998 and 2015 has been the US Chamber of Commerce. It spent $1.16 billion, two-thirds more than the next closest client, the American Medical Association. For more on the lobbying statistics, see the Centre for Responsive Politics.

35 Macey (n 33).

36 Harold C. Barnett 'Risk and Mortgage-backed Securities in a Time of Transition' in H.K. Baker and Greg Filbeck (eds) *Investment Risk Management* (Oxford University Press 2015) 418.

37 See *A Snapshot of the Regulatory Framework* (n 105) for the use of this method in creating the reliance upon agencies in 1975.

the SEC would not bring enforcement actions against the agencies if they did not disclose ratings in the prospectuses. The result was that the expert liability that the Dodd-Frank Act had sought to establish for the agencies was immediately obliterated because the ratings were no longer attached overtly to the securities on offer (although they were available from a number of other sources, of course). This was consolidated when the SEC 'subsequently extended this non-enforcement stance indefinitely'.[38]

The issue here is that the legislators behind the Dodd-Frank Act made a crucial mistake when formulating the Act. A number of important issues were not dealt with robustly and allowed for a lot of autonomy on the part of the SEC. While we understand that the SEC has been chastised for its part in the pre-crisis era,[39] it is a very questionable strategy to trust that same organisation to administer such a crucial Act (what the alternative is, however, is hard to say). It has been noted that the Act prescribes that the SEC had to adopt a number of rules to govern various aspects of the rating agencies' operations without detailing how it was to obtain the necessary expertise to carry out this mandate effectively[40] and that ultimately 'the Act provides regulators with significant room for interpretation and implementation'.[41] Subjectivity in this domain is a particularly dangerous concept.

As Macey suggests, the SEC is particularly vulnerable to being 'captured'. Earlier we spoke of the 'revolving door' theory[42] and this is particularly relevant when talking about the relationship between the SEC and the rating agencies. First, the Dodd-Frank Act has (probably unwittingly) increased the potential for this to happen by the forced establishment of the Office of Credit Ratings. If we accept Macey's perception that 'the major credit rating agencies are a significant source of support and employment for SEC alumni',[43] then forcing a dedicated number of SEC staffers to be the focal point for SEC–CRA relations is obviously not ideal. The SEC's nonchalant attitude towards to the Office of Credit Ratings in the wake of the Dodd-Frank Act (the Office remained unstaffed for 12 months[44]) also paints a worrying picture of its approach to fulfilling its mandate.

Before this section concludes it will be useful to analyse just one example of the SEC's favourable approach to the Big Three, an example which also throws further light on events first described in Chapter 2. Earlier, we heard how the Egan-Jones Rating Company had been punished by the SEC for making misrepresentations

---

38 Barnett (n 36).
39 Thomas J. Schoenbaum *The Age of Austerity: The Global Financial Crisis and the Return to Economic Growth* (Edward Elgar Publishing 2012) 166; Mehmet Odekon *Booms and Busts: An Encyclopedia of Economic History from the First Stock Market Crash of 1792 to the Current Global Crisis* (Routledge 2015) 734.
40 Markham (n 386) 729.
41 Darbellay and Partnoy (n 5) 286.
42 See *Mechanistic Importance* (n 170).
43 Macey (n 33).
44 Darbellay and Partnoy (n 5) 280.

in its application to become a NRSRO.[45] However, with what has been alleged against the SEC, with regard to its potentially favourable approach to the Big Three, this needs to be reassessed. Macey is a strong critic of the SEC and he pulls no punches in admonishing it in this instance. He tells us that the story between Egan-Jones and the SEC began in 2008 when, under pressure from Congress to increase competition within the ratings industry, the SEC 'grudgingly' allowed Egan-Jones to receive the NRSRO designation. However, in 2012, the SEC announced that it was suing Egan-Jones and would be attempting to remove its NRSRO status. Macey argues that in suing this relatively small agency (it had, at the time, just 20 employees) the SEC demonstrated its 'pure maliciousness' towards any competitor to the Big Three.[46] It is worth noting at this juncture that Egan-Jones is the only NRSRO that does not use the issuer-pays compensation model and is forthright in promoting the understanding that it is more accurate and timely in administering its ratings than any other agency as a result; this is an important factor.

Macey continues by alleging that Egan-Jones' problems began in July 2011 when the company had downgraded the US' sovereign debt rating by one notch; the SEC contacted the agency immediately to ask for explanation for its decision. Three months later the SEC notified the firm that it was the target of an investigation and, in April 2012, began legal proceedings against the agency and its co-founder Sean Egan. However, the content of this legal action is where the true nature of the SEC begins to appear. The action was not concerned with its ratings, methodologies or professional conduct (as they should have been with the Big Three), but instead with a technical element of the firm's NRSRO registration. The main issue was whether the agency met the SEC requirement that the ratings be 'disseminated publicly', which as we know now is a laughable idea because the Big Three put their full and easy-to-use ratings and ratings decisions behind pay-walls.[47] The obvious issue here is that Egan-Jones *cannot* publicly disseminate their ratings because not doing so is how they make money; it is inherent within the subscriber-pays model that people must pay to view the ratings. In essence then, Egan-Jones was punished predominantly because it had not incorporated the conflict-of-interest inducing system of issuer-pays, which is an extraordinary understanding. For daring to do this, Egan-Jones was banned for 18 months from rating any asset-backed securities.

Conclusion

Before this analysis started it was always clear where the regulatory response would fall with regard to this framework simply by analysing the trajectory of the ratings industry post crisis. That the Big Three have resumed their pre-crisis rates

45 *The Actual Situation* (n 42).

46 Macey (n 33) 232–35.

47 See *The Impact of Technological Advancement* (n 78) for Langohr and Langohr's assessment of the availability of credit ratings.

of growth both in terms of revenue and profit, that their position as an oligopoly has been strengthened and also that the major threats to their existence that were advanced post-crisis have been circumvented (liability concerns), all contributes to the realisation that the regulatory response did not take aim at the *actual* state of affairs. In essence, the legislators sought to move the industry towards the *desired* by aiming for the middle ground, which inevitably has resulted in failure and the widening of divergence. In addition, we now see that the state has managed to exonerate itself from any future blame even though the system that it was responsible for creating has not changed; this is a worrying development within the financial sector.

One of the main sentiments established here is that *effective* regulation must first seek to focus on the *actual* to accurately describe what the *desired* can be and then whether that situation can be achieved. The regulatory response to the crisis has not done this; instead it has placed the onus (and future blame) on investors, while also absolving issuers. It has paid lip service to holding the agencies accountable for their actions, as the administering of the legislative rules have gone on to confirm (almost immediately after the Act was enacted).

Admittedly, this chapter leaves a sour taste. It is contested here that the once-in-a-generation opportunity to enact socially impactful reforms has been scuppered by the presence of captured administrators, which results in the understanding that proposing any sort of socially beneficial reforms *and have them come to fruition* is a difficult concept in itself. However, while accepting defeat in this endeavour may be rational, it is important to advance proposals that may educate people about the *reality* of the situation, however unlikely it may be to see it realised. In proposing that the rating agencies be forced to choose between ratings provision and ancillary service provision, our aim is to present both a socially beneficial solution to the exploitative nature of the ratings industry and its ability to absorb any punishment *while also* developing the narrative that this reality exists; this is perhaps the key point to reform proposals regarding such seemingly immoveable objects. This narrative has now been established; what is important is that the reform proposal is introduced. However, to do so we will need to know much more about the division that is the target for that proposed reform and precisely why it needs to be removed.

Bibliography

Barnett, H.C. 'Risk and Mortgage-backed Securities in a Time of Transition' in Baker, H.K. and Filbeck, G. (eds) *Investment Risk Management* (Oxford University Press 2015).

Centre for Responsive Politics. www.opensecrets.org [accessed 2/1/16].

Daniel Cash 'Sustainable Finance Ratings as the Latest Symptom of "Rating Addiction"' [2018] 3 *Journal of Sustainable Finance & Investment* 1.

Darbellay, A. and Partnoy, F. 'Credit Rating Agencies and Regulatory Reform' in Hill, C.A., Krusemark, J.L., McDonnell, B.H. and Robbins, S. (eds) *Research Handbook on the Economics of Corporate Law* (Edward Elgar Publishing 2012).

Directive 2013/14/EU [2013] OJ L145/1.

Dodd-Frank Wall Street Reform and Consumer Protection Act of 2010 124 Stat. 1376.

Evans, C. 'The Dodd-Frank Wall Street and Consumer Protection Act: A Missed Opportunity to Rein in Too-Big-To-Fail Banks' [2011] 13 *Duquesne Business Law Journal* 43.

Folsom, B.W. *New Deal or Raw Deal?: How FDR's Economic Legacy Has Damaged America* (Simon and Schuster 2009).

Haas, J. *Corporate Finance* (West Academic 2014).

Hill, C.A. 'Limits of Dodd-Frank's Rating Agency Reform' [2011] 15 *Chapman Law Review* 1.

Kane, E.J. 'Missing Elements in US Financial Reform: A Kübler-Ross Interpretation of the Inadequacy of the Dodd-Frank Act' [2012] 36 *Journal of Banking & Finance* 654.

Kane, E.J. 'The Expanding Financial Safety Net: The Dodd-Frank Act as an Exercise in Denial and Cover-up' in Wachter, S.M. and Smith. M.M. (eds) *The American Mortgage System: Crisis and Reform* (University of Pennsylvania Press 2011).

Lounsbury, M. and Hirsch, P.M. (eds) *Markets on Trial: The Economic Sociology of the U.S. Financial Crisis: Part A* (Emerald Group Publishing 2010).

Macey, J.R. 'The Nature and Futility of "Regulation by Assimilation"' in Urban, G. (ed.) *Corporations and Citizenship* (University of Pennsylvania Press 2014).

Macey, J.R. *The Death of Corporate Reputation: How Integrity Has Been Destroyed on Wall Street* (Pearson Education 2013).

Manns, J. 'The Sovereign Rating Regulatory Dilemma' in Finch, N. (ed.) *Emerging Markets and Sovereign Risk* (Palgrave Macmillan 2014).

Markham, J.W. *A Financial History of the United States: From Enron-era Scandals to the Great Recession* (Routledge 2015).

Moloney, N. *EU Securities and Financial Markets Regulation* (Oxford University Press 2014).

Odekon, M. *Booms and Busts: An Encyclopedia of Economic History from the First Stock Market Crash of 1792 to the Current Global Crisis* (Routledge 2015).

Pagliari, S. 'Who Governs Finance? The Shifting Public–Private Divide in the Regulation of Derivatives, Rating Agencies and Hedge Funds' [2012] 18 *European Law Journal* 1.

Pierce, H. 'A Title-by-title Look at Dodd-Frank: Title IX – Securities and Exchange Commission' in Pierce, H. and Broughel, J. (eds) *Dodd-Frank: What It Does and Why It's Flawed* (Mercatus Center at George Mason University 2013).

Quaglia, L. *The European Union and Global Financial Regulation* (Oxford University Press 2014).

Rating and Investment Information, Inc. 'R&I to withdraw from NRSRO registration with USSEC' [2011] R&I News Release. www.r-i.co.jp/eng/body/regulatory_affair/ info/2011/10/info_20111014_557626781_01.pdf [accessed 4/3/16].

Regulation (EU) No 462/2013 [2013] OJ L146/1.

Regulation (EU) No 513/2011 [2011] OJ L145/30.

Regulation (EU) No 1060/2009 [2009] OJ L302/1.

Ryder, N. *The Financial Crisis and White Collar Crime: The Perfect Storm?* (Edward Elgar Publishing 2014).

Scalet, S. and Kelly, T.F. 'The Ethics of Credit Rating Agencies: What Happened and the Way Forward' [2012] 111 *Journal of Business Ethics* 477.

Schoenbaum, T.J. *The Age of Austerity: The Global Financial Crisis and the Return to Economic Growth* (Edward Elgar Publishing 2012).

Securities and Exchange Commission *Release Nos 34-71219; 34-71220; 34-57301; 34-75747.*

5 The issue of ancillary service provision

Introduction

'Ancillary services' is a term used loosely to describe services that credit rating agencies offer in addition to their rating services. While the actual definition of what these services are has not been definitively established,[1] Moody's has defined their offering as including services such as: 'Cashflow Models; Credit Models; Pool, Loan and Performance Data; and Valuation & Advisory Services'.[2] Yet, while the definition of what ancillary services actually consist of may be undecided, what is very clear is that the revenue from ancillary service provision represents a significant portion of the agencies' overall revenue, while it is also recognised that the provision of additional services within such a systemically important sector is extremely controversial.[3] This controversial, yet substantial, growth of a business that is not important to the development of accurate credit ratings is at the heart of this chapter's analysis.

Essentially, no nationally recognised statistical rating organisation (NRSRO) is prohibited from providing 'ancillary services', which is more accurately represented by Moody's when they affirm that 'Moody's Investor Services (MIS) does not *currently* offer ancillary services *but may do so in the future*'.[4] What they are prohibited from offering is pre-rating advice to an issuer, as detailed by the SEC: 'Paragraph (c)(5) of Rule 17g-5 prohibits an NRSRO from issuing or maintaining a credit rating with respect to an obligor or security where the NRSRO or person associated with the NRSRO *made recommendations to the obligor or the issuer, underwriter or sponsor of the security about the corporate or legal structure, assets, liabilities or activities of the obligor*

1 Raquel G. Alcubilla and Javier R. del Pozo *Credit Rating Agencies on the Watch List: Analysis of European Regulation* (Oxford University Press 2012) 145.
2 Moody's Analytics *How Do You Transform Risk into High Performance? An Overview of Moody's Analytics* (2015). https://www.economy.com/getlocal?app=eccafile&q=24c8c19b-6ace-4979-9374-d3960332669f
3 Aline Darbellay *Regulating Credit Rating Agencies* (Edward Elgar Publishing Limited 2013) 122.
4 Moody's *Policy for Ancillary and Other Permissible Services: Compliance* (Moody's 2013) (emphasis added). www.moodys.com/uploadpage/Mco%20Documents/Policy_for_Ancillary_and_Other_Permissible_Services.pdf

or issuer of the security.[5] The aim of this regulation was to stop the process detailed earlier where agencies were involved in the construction of SIVs;[6] just one example of what is commonly referred to as the agencies 'rating their own work'. While Moody's do not offer 'ancillary services', they do offer more than 17 services described as 'other permissible activities'.[7] So, while pre-rating services are prohibited, the provision of ancillary services contributes greatly to the Big Three (and the Big Two in particular).

The term 'ancillary services' is used here to mean any service offered by a credit rating agency (CRA) which is not expressly attached to their service of credit rating provision and is not available to issuers before the credit rating of a particular security has been disseminated, should that entity require an issuance to be rated (as that practice has now been prohibited). The second aspect that needs to be established is that there will be a noticeable favouritism in analysing Moody's Analytics over S&P Capital IQ; this is solely because the data for Moody's Analytics is readily available with Moody's being a publicly traded company, as opposed to S&P which is part of the McGraw-Hill company (the same applies to Fitch Ratings).

In terms of the aims of this chapter, the analysis begins with an examination of the vehicles that deliver ancillary services, namely Moody's Analytics and S&P Capital IQ. Rather than examining what the ancillary services actually are and how they are utilised by the market, which is an issue that will be raised in *Avenues for Future Research*, it is more appropriate here to assess these subsidiary components and their contribution to the parent company's financial position overall. One of the key contentions here is that the agencies understood intently the environment that surrounded them in the early 2000s and took a conscious decision to *take advantage* of their unique position that was protected by the state and was central to the burgeoning securitised issuance market. To test this hypothesis the chapter will make use of figures that chart the rise of securitised product issuances, the acquisition trends of the Big Two and the growth of Moody's Analytics in comparison to the economic fluctuations that took place in the 2000s (because financial performance figures for Moody's Analytics are available throughout the period); what we will see is that the Big Two (S&P predominantly, although the duopolistic nature of the industry means the other companies would surely follow suit, which Moody's did) took notice of the demise of the consultancy operations of the leading public accounting firms in the wake of the Enron and WorldCom affairs and sought to merge the same exploitative ideal with their unique position – while Arthur Andersen would fail and PwC, Deloitte and others would have to divest

---

5 Securities and Exchange Commission *Final Rule Analysis – Securities and Exchange Commission Release No 34-72936; File No S7-18-11* (2014) footnote 70 (emphasis added). This sentiment is also the one adopted by European regulatory authorities, see Alcubilla and del Pozo (n 1) 147.

6 See *Collusion* and the analyses of the SIVs that the CRAs were a part of.

7 Moody's makes clear that it does not offer consultancy or advisory services to rated entities (in addition to 'Ancillary Services'), but does offer 'Credit Rating Services and "Other Permissible Services"', which include, but are not limited to: Bond Fund Ratings; Common Representative Quality Assessments; Equity Fund Assessments; Indicative Ratings; and Rating Assessment Services. See Moody's *Rating Symbols and Definitions* (Moody's 2016) for further details.

their consultancy operations, the credit rating agencies would create more havoc than was witnessed during the Enron scandal *while* instituting an ancillary business that has become widely accepted by regulators as just being part of the service.

Essentially, the proposal here is to prohibit the provision of ancillary services (presented, in detail, in Chapter 6) and it is acknowledged that there are not many, if any, direct calls for the prohibition of ancillary services anywhere else;[8] in fact, some, rather incredibly, suggest that ancillary services are a 'nonissue'.[9] Yet, by joining the criticisms of the ancillary service provision with the economic theory of 'economic rent' and the concept of there being a divergence between the *actual* and the *desired*, the resulting analysis has the capacity to induce a wider understanding of the real effect of ancillary service provision upon the role of the rating agencies, upon which the reform proposal will be presented.

S&P Capital IQ and Moody's Analytics: vehicles of profit

The growth of the asset-backed securities market is an important component of this story and reveals to us the concerted and deliberate nature of the agencies' decisions. The Securities Industry and Financial Markets Association

---

8 With regard to the prohibition of ancillary service provision by rating agencies, there are very few proposals. In addition to any fleeting musings that appear within analyses, perhaps the only distinct call in the literature comes from a General Counsel in his testimony to the US House of Representatives (which demonstrates the scarcity of this viewpoint in the literature). See Testimony of Gregory W. Smith, General Counsel, Colorado Public Employees' Retirement Association in US House of Representatives: Committee on Financial Services *Hearing Before the Subcommittee on Capital Markets, Insurance and Government Sponsored Enterprises: Approaches to Improving Credit Rating Agency Regulation* (GPO 2009) 22.

9 Nicole Neuman asserts that

> unlike the auditing industry, the credit rating industry does not need formal governmental regulation to solve the problems it faces ... credit rating agencies have actually maintained their independence. The 'client-pays' model does not tempt credit rating agencies to inflate ratings ... furthermore, ancillary services are a non-issue because they contribute an insignificant fraction of the credit rating agencies' total revenue. Finally, credit rating agencies have firewalls and self-regulation in place to prevent any conflict of interests from negatively impacting the integrity of their rating processes.

The SEC, in utilising Neuman's research as a counterbalance to criticisms of ancillary service provision, explained that for these conclusions, the author 'relies upon the (SEC) 2003 Report'. There are some very important issues here: first, Neuman's is the only research to downplay the effects of the issuer-pays system and the provision of ancillary services, which then serves to single out the research; secondly, Neuman does not refer to the 2003 report when making these statements in the article, which suggests that it was not based upon the report at all. Even if Neuman used the 2003 report, to make such statements based on data that is over seven years old is extremely misleading. We know from our own analysis that the issuer-pays system *does* result in ratings inflation and that when the article was published ancillary service revenue for Moody's accounted for *a quarter* of their entire revenue. For Neuman's article see Nicole B. Neuman 'A Sarbanes-Oxley for Credit Rating Agencies? A Comparison of the Roles Auditors' and Credit Rating Agencies' Conflicts of Interests Played in Recent Financial Crises' [2010] 12 *University of Pennsylvania Journal of Business Law* 921. For the SEC Report that cites Neuman's work, see Securities and Exchange Commission *Report to Congress: Credit Rating Agency Independence Study* (2013) 45.

(SIFMA) has published figures that detail the growth of the sector in the US and the results make for a very interesting read when one considers the actions of the agencies. In 1985, when the SIFMA's analysis begins, the total issuance of ABS, which for their analysis includes automobile, credit cards, equipment, housing-related, student loans and other securities, was just $1.2 billion. When student loan securities were first registered in 1993 the total issuance stood at $51 billion. Most interestingly for our analysis, when 'housing-related' securities were first registered in 2003, the total issuance stood at $228 billion, with the housing-related securities making up just $55 million of that total. The next year that contribution rose to $270 million of $222 billion which demonstrates the relative explosion of the RMBS market that is so crucial to our analysis. Between 2003 and 2007 when the financial crisis took hold, the issuance of housing-related securities had surpassed $900 million, with the total ABS issuance for the same period coming in at just under $1 trillion. While the housing-related securities segment made up just 9 or 10 per cent of the total ABS issuance, the rapid growth of that particular market had an effect on other markets too, with the general fervour in the marketplace also producing significant increases within the markets for automobile and student loan securities.[10]

These figures from SIFMA serve to demonstrate the rapid growth of the RMBS market that came to dominate the headlines surrounding the financial crisis. The figures will provide us with a statistical basis that will be required as a foundation for the following analyses concerning the evolution of the rating agencies' ancillary service offerings. It is worth noting before we continue that the aim of the agencies' creation of these divisions was not just to capitalise upon a market that would last for four years, but was also to cement itself within the securitisation process because, as we know from earlier, the housing-related market went on to develop at an unprecedented pace just a year or two after the height of the crisis[11] (a fact which is confirmed by SIFMA when it shows that housing-related ABS issuances rose to $2.6 billion after a two-year hiatus during the crisis[12]). The agencies' cementation of their position in advance of such an incredible rate of growth in this particular market, not including the other sectors within which the agencies have a role to play once the securities have been bundled together, is our focus here.

S&P Capital IQ

As was stated earlier in the introduction, any analysis of S&P's ancillary service division, S&P Capital IQ, will be naturally limited because of the private structure of S&P's parent company McGraw-Hill. While the company has revealed the

---

10 The Securities Industry and Financial Markets Authority *Statistics: US ABS Issuance and Outstanding (1985 to 2016)* (SIFMA 2016).
11 See *The SEC's 'Cease and Desist' Order against S&P* (n 99).
12 The Securities Industry and Financial Markets Authority (n 10).

performance figures for its ancillary division on occasion, it is not consistent (and in some instances simply not available), which makes building a complete picture almost impossible. The most detail that is available on S&P and its divisions is contained within McGraw-Hill's yearly financial reports (Form 10-K) to the SEC. While McGraw-Hill conceal the performance figures of S&P and its divisions before 2011 (the figures are all combined in 'segments' rather than individual companies and divisions), we can see the acquisitions that took place and chart them against the evolution of the structured finance market *and* the financial performance of Moody's during the same period because, even though S&P is a larger agency, the presence of the duopoly dictates that the performance between the two has always been comparable.

In the next subsection we will see that within Moody's corporation lies two entities: Moody's Investors Services and Moody's Analytics, so one can easily chart the financial performance of the ancillary service division and then compare that to the performance of the investors service which is Moody's traditional base. However, McGraw-Hill differentiates itself into two divisions: McGraw-Hill Financial and McGraw-Hill Education. Within McGraw-Hill Financial there are a number of businesses including: S&P Ratings Services; S&P Capital IQ, which is adjoined to SNL which was acquired in 2015; S&P Dow Jones Indices; Platts and JD Power.

The issue with assessing the impact of S&P Capital IQ upon the rating agency is that S&P Capital IQ's figures have only been reported in isolation by McGraw-Hill from 2011 to 2013. Although we will look at the acquisitions made by McGraw-Hill in much more detail shortly, it is worth noting here that McGraw-Hill acquired Capital IQ in 2004, but it was not until 2010 that the company merged with S&P to become S&P Capital IQ and it would be another year until the company moved from being a standalone subsidiary to a McGraw-Hill financial company (with it being safe to assume that this was in response to the enactment of the Dodd-Frank Act). So, before 2011 the financial performance of the ancillary divisions of S&P are simply not reported, which is in addition to the lack of information on S&P itself; McGraw-Hill provides financial information for the 'financial services' segment which includes S&P Dow Jones Indices as well as S&P Ratings Services, which is a very important market actor in its own right.

So, while we may not be able to demonstrate the financial impact that the provision of ancillary services had upon Standard & Poor's as it navigated its way through the extraordinarily lucrative pre-crisis era, we can see how a number of acquisitions present the picture of a company preparing to take full advantage of its position. S&P's relationship with ancillary services began in the wreckage of the Enron affair when they acquired the consultancy arm of PriceWaterhouseCoopers, who had been essentially forced by the Sarbanes-Oxley Act to divest from the consultancy business after its appalling conduct, like many of the other top public accounting firms. Interestingly, but admittedly a victim of hindsight, Ellen Haley who in 2003 was the Vice President of Development and Research at McGraw-Hill states in the Form 10-K submission that 'It's been said that the genius of capitalism is to pacify greed into benign self-interest. In the boom years, greed often went unchecked. Too many took advantage of a financial system that is based on trust and integrity. But now we're seeing changes …'.[13] Unfortunately for society, rather than the change being that 'auditors are now doing a better job' as Haley went on to suggest, the rating industry was evolving a practice that decimated both the accounting industry and the marketplace.

The pressure created by the Sarbanes-Oxley Act had resulted in a mass selling of highly focused advisory services.[14] The timing of S&P's purchase of the consulting arm of PwC in 2001 could not have been better because in 2003/4 two important aspects emerged. First, structured finance issuances began what turned out to be an unprecedented rise (as demonstrated by SIFMA earlier and Moody's' financial disclosures that will be assessed next) and second, on 28 April 2003, ten large investment banks settled with the SEC (and others) regarding conflicts of interest relating to equity research, with one important component of the settlement being that the firms spend $432.5 million over a five-year period to provide a minimum of three sources of independent equity research to their clients. Standard & Poor's almost jubilantly stated in their 2003 annual report: 'as a leading provider of independent equity research, Standard & Poor's believes that it is uniquely positioned to capitalise on this opportunity'.[15] This turn of events also allowed the agency to peddle their newly acquired ancillary services to the investment banks that, through their own fraudulent behaviour, were now being funnelled through the credit-rating machine.

Building on this fortuitous turn of events, the agency then began a rapid phase of growth in relation to the securitisation process that was growing at an unprecedented rate. The lack of publicly available information in the process meant that the rating industry was central to both issuers and investors: S&P made sure that they would have the tools to facilitate the business of its most important clients, the issuers. In 2004, when the rate of securitised issuances rose significantly, S&P purchased Capital IQ, a firm that specialised in offering 'high-impact information solutions to the global investment and financial services communities'.[16] S&P boasted that the newly acquired company allowed it to 'empower clients with workflow solutions and idea-generation tools', which was important because there was a noted increase in the issuance of US CDOs which S&P stated were due to 'an improving economy, strong consumer spending, increasing investor confidence and the *quality of the underlying transaction collateral in CDOs*'.

We now know that this was not true at all. However, the aftermath of the crisis has revealed the urgency with which the rating agencies sought to provide its clients with the ratings that were necessary to keep the process going; we saw earlier how the agencies adopted the Gaussian Copula formula to facilitate the ever-increasing number of structured products that were being peddled.

13 McGraw-Hill Education, Inc. *Form 10-K* (SEC 2003).
14 Kathryn Cearns 'Auditors and International Financial Reporting' in Carien van Mourik and Peter Walton (eds) *The Routledge Companion to Accounting, Reporting and Regulation* (Routledge 2013) 386.
15 McGraw-Hill Education, Inc (n 13).
16 McGraw-Hill Education, Inc *Form 10-K* (SEC 2005).

To compliment this approach, the agency began adding a number of elements that would assist with this aim and encourage supplemental business through the ancillary division, so in 2005 the company acquired Vista Research, Inc and CRISIL Ltd, which increased the agency's capacity to deliver equity research on a global scale. They also introduced what is referred to as 'S&P Compustat', an improved database of financial, statistical and market data.[17] Superficially, these moves all paint a picture of efficiency which would have contributed to a greater understanding of risk within the marketplace, which is, in essence, the fundamental concern of a rating agency. But, through all of our analysis, we know that this was not the case. S&P did not have a good understanding of the underlying collateral in CDOs and other securitised products and they certainly did not seek to pass on this increased knowledge to investors who were devastated by the unprecedented number of mass downgrades in 2008. What can be seen then is not a company that is seeking to provide for its clients and end-users but one that is purposefully positioning itself within the financial information market *based upon* its 'reputation' garnered through its rating business – a highly contestable notion in itself – to extract the maximum amount of money from the system.

S&P would go onto acquire a number of other companies to consolidate its position.[18] What is clear, when assessing the company and its decisions, is that the financial crisis did not represent the end of any strategy; in reality it was just the beginning. The foresight is evident when we consider that in adjoining the research elements with the rating brand, at a time when all securitised products *had to be rated by an NRSRO*, the agencies had developed a consulting arm that would dwarf that of the accounting industry some years before. Furthermore, it was a business that would be developed in such a way that those in power would consider the provision of ancillary services to be beneficial to the marketplace, even when this was already provided by such an integral sector of the financial system. In essence, in just seven years, Standard & Poor's created a division that would record annual revenues almost equivalent to the unprecedented record fine it had received from the US Justice Department; the effect of that punishment was therefore negligible at best.

Moody's Analytics

While assessing S&P Capital IQ's performance and its effect on the fortunes of the rating agency was difficult given the nature of McGraw-Hill's disclosure practices, we have no such issue with the assessment of Moody's ancillary service division Moody's Analytics. Moody's corporation, a public company, includes within its annual statements detailed performance information. As a result, this section will examine the many acquisitions undertaken by Moody's, but crucially we can then attach this examination to an assessment of the financial performance of Moody's

---

17 ibid (SEC 2006).
18 Assirt; TheMarket.com; and Pipal Research Corporation have all been added to the ancillary service
   division since 2005.

Analytics. What is revealed is that during the same upsurge in securitised issuances around 2004 as detailed in the previous section, Moody's began an incredibly concerted operation to build an ancillary service division that would take advantage of the environment and the parent company's place within it. The result of this concerted effort was that, today, Moody's Analytics generates only a few hundred million dollars fewer than the revenue received from the rating of corporate bonds, which has been the cornerstone of its operations since the company was founded. This incredible fact lends credence to the contention presented here that the issues surrounding the ancillary service division must be addressed because its impact on the fortunes of the rating agency is highly significant.

Unlike S&P, which had started in the ancillary field by acquiring the consulting division of PwC, Moody's took a different path. Initially, while S&P was profiting from the Sarbanes-Oxley rules, Moody's was being transformed into public company by Warren Buffett in 2000 as discussed earlier. This may be a reason why the company did not partake in the purchasing of accountancy-related consulting divisions in the wake of the Enron scandal. However, it did enter the ancillary marketplace with the acquisition of KMV in 2002, which was already a leader in the provision of qualitative credit analysis for lenders, investors and corporations.[19] This acquisition was to be the cornerstone of Moody's Ancillary operations and would be the brand by which Moody's ancillary services would be recognised until the adoption of Moody's Analytics in 2007 (prior to Moody's Analytics, the division was known as Moody's KMV).

The significance of these acquisitions only becomes apparent when one considers the environment before the crisis in 2007/8. The rapid growth of the structured-finance market, which as discussed earlier was based upon (predominantly) non-public information, led to a duality which the rating agencies capitalised upon. After the acquisition of KMV, Moody's acquired Economy.com in 2005 and Wall St Analytics in 2006; these companies would all be merged into Moody's Analytics in 2007. KMV was a pioneer in creating commercially available credit loss prediction models, like the 'Loss Given Default' (LGD) model and the 'Expected Default Frequency' (EDF) model. Once connected to Moody's, KMV created the Moody's KMV RiskCalc and LossCalc models, which became significant tools for banks and other market actors trading in the structured finance markets. So, rating agencies made these models available to issuers and investors. Any structured product had to have been rated by a leading NRSRO to be considered worthy of investment in the capital markets, because the investors were regulatory constrained to invest in products that carried certain ratings (i.e. AAA for banks).

This incredible consideration, that the agencies' were effectively creating an additional business for something they were already doing but just packaging it

---

19 Moody's Analytics *History of KMV* (2016). This was not the first acquisition by Moody's in this field, but it was certainly the first significant acquisition. The first acquisition was that of the Crowe Chizek Products Group.

to be used before the rating phase, is further demonstrated by understanding the purpose of Wall St Analytics. In hindsight, the company's acquisition in 2006 represents a clear conflict of interest when we consider that Wall St Analytics was 'a leading provider of specialised software and data tools for the structuring, analysis, management and servicing of structured debt instruments'. Furthermore, 'the addition of Wall St Analytics enhanced Moody's Analytics' current Collateralised Debt Obligations product suite and immediately added mortgage-backed securities and asset-backed securities analytic software capabilities'.[20] It is clear from this description that Moody's sought to provide the consultancy for the preparation and maintenance of structured products that it would most likely have to rate (given that the Big Two were the overwhelming choice) for the products to enter the capital markets.

So, Moody's had positioned itself as the gatekeeper to the capital markets (with the assistance of the SEC). Not only did it provide the information needed to efficiently structure and service structured products, it also provided the information regarding the risk involved with the process. Moody's would go onto acquire six more companies in this quest to cover all the bases regarding the securitisation process.[21] A cursory analysis of the financial rewards for doing so reveal that, for the agency, it was very much worth it.

A simple collation of the figures declared in Moody's annual statements reveals the actual impact of the adoption of ancillary services at the turn of the century. Table 5.1 shows us that, in just 15 years, the corporation had gone from recording revenues of $796 million in 2001 to $3.4 billion in 2015, an incredible achievement given the turbulent events of that short space of time. For our analysis of the ancillary services that the agency began to provide from 2002 onwards, we can clearly see that the revenues from ancillary services experienced a sharp rise in line with the sharp rise in structured product issuance around 2004 but, more importantly, kept rising even when structured and corporate finance issuances fell sharply during the crisis in 2007 and 2008. In fact, there was a point in 2009 when ancillary services were generating more for the corporation than any other revenue stream, which is extraordinary in itself. In 2013/14 this passed the $1 billion mark for the first time, confirming its increasing importance to the health of the company.

These aspects of the financial figures are clear. What is also clear is that the data presented above would seem to confirm the hypothesis, established earlier, that the agencies (it is safe to assume that S&P Capital IQ had a similar trajectory) established these divisions in the knowledge that the position of the industry within the financial sector would mean that when the structured product boom (inevitably) collapsed, the division that was created to assist the boom would continue. The real question is why would it continue when the market for structured

---

20 Moody's Analytics *History of Wall Street Analytics* (2016).
21 After creating Moody's Analytics as a 'separate' entity it would acquire Fermat and ENB consulting in 2008; CSI Global Education, Inc in 2010; Copal Partners and Barrie & Hibbert Limited in 2011; and finally Lewtan and WebEquity Solutions in 2014.

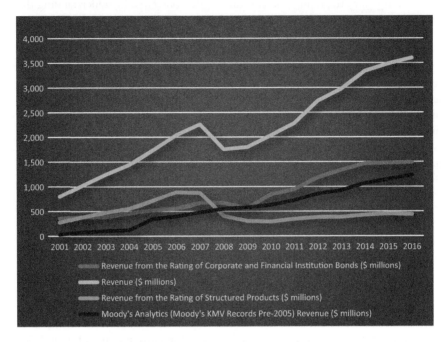

Figure 5.1 Financial data collected from Moody's Corporation annual statements
2001–2016

finance issuances collapsed and has yet to recover to pre-crisis rates? The data above suggests that the market for corporate bond issuances recovered after one or two years. We know from our earlier assessments that there is less need for the services that the ancillary service divisions offer (i.e. structured product risk indicators and assessments of non-public information, when one is concerned with corporate bonds) this is, therefore, hard to explain.

One explanation is that the agencies focused more on the analytical side of corporate bond finance to fall in line with the dramatic drop in structured finance product issuance. However, we have already seen that this is not necessarily the case, because the agencies have continued to acquire components that enhance the structured-finance packages that they offer. Put simply, there is very little that the agencies can offer prospective clients when it comes to corporate bond issuances; the reason why the ancillary service divisions flourished with the expansion of the structured finance market and not before, is because there is no real need for in-depth assessments of corporate bonds, owing to the publicly available nature of the underlying information and the data that is contained within the ratings provided by the rating agencies (as well as the specialised in-house analytical capabilities of sophisticated investors).

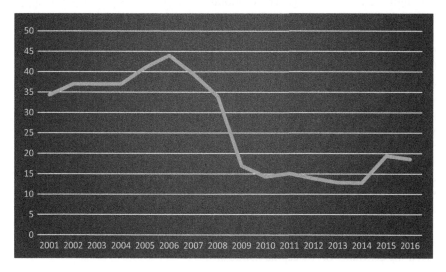

Figure 5.2 Data collected from Moody's Corporation annual statements – percentage of revenue from the rating of structured finance products

Figure 5.2 reveals that the structured finance market did indeed drop significantly between 2006 and 2008 and has yet to recover. The fact that the ancillary service division of Moody's has gone from strength to strength despite this obvious issue leads to a very important inference. It is important for the development of this aspect of the discipline that we understand exactly what it is that clients find beneficial when subscribing to these services; more will be said on this point in the concluding chapter, because whether through qualitative or quantitative research there is a need to understand further the rationale of the division's clientele. The real reason why this is an important endeavour is because without any data regarding the benefits of usage of the ancillary services the only inference that can be made is that clients purchase the services to gain favour or protect their position, which is a conflict which is particularly venomous. We shall see in the next section that many onlookers have realised this facet that is hard to explain and have come to the same inference.

The inherent issues with ancillary service provision – the view from the literature

Though the practice of providing ancillary services continues unabated, there is a wide acceptance of the conflicts that come with the provision within the literature. In this section we shall assess some of the more obvious conflicts discussed before looking closely at the concept of 'economic rent'; this is important because although the concept is a general economic concept that may or may not apply to each individual industry, we shall see that the general principle of a company extracting more resources than its input dictates is very much attributable to the ratings industry. The appalling performance of the industry over the past 15 years (and arguably longer still) simply does not tally with the incredible rate of growth and profitability we witnessed earlier in – the growth of a billion-dollar sub-division like Moody's Analytics (and S&P Capital IQ), based upon the unique position of the ratings industry, is a classic example of economic rent. This section will ultimately show that while we are aware of the issues surrounding ancillary service provision, the bigger picture regarding the industry and its position within society is overlooked. The aim is to show that the ancillary services are not just an attempt to garner some extra revenue, but in fact represent a conscious decision to both embed the agencies further into the modern economy and protect against financial penalties that aim to stifle the fraudulent and criminal actions that have made the agencies multi-billion dollar institutions. Removing this capacity has the potential to avert or lessen the impact of the next financial crisis given the centrality of the capital markets.

Pressure

The most obvious conflict that comes with ancillary service provision is based upon the notion of 'pressure'. With respect to the rating industry this can take one of two forms: either the agency exerts pressure upon its rating clients to purchase additional services, with the lure of potentially receiving or maintaining a higher rating; or, alternatively, the rating client could threaten to stop purchasing the additional services (which we know are incredibly lucrative) unless a high or at least required rating is given. We shall begin by assessing the first of these two forms which is referred to as 'tying'.

'Tying' occurs when an agency 'forces' a rated company to purchase other services,[22] although there are other examples of agency-dictated pressure that also represent the manifestation of conflicts. For example, it has been noted that agencies have requested payment for unsolicited ratings,[23] have issued lower-than-warranted ratings to punish a firm for purchasing rating services from a competitor[24] and have also reduced or refused to rate a pool of assets (e.g. in a CDO) unless a substantial proportion of the pool's individual securities were also rated by the same agency.[25] This is referred to as 'notching'.

---

22 Herwig P. Langohr and Patricia T. Langohr *The Rating Agencies and Their Credit Ratings: What They Are, How They Work and Why They are Relevant* (John Wiley & Sons 2010) 423.

23 Mark J. Flannery 'Supervising Bank Safety and Soundness: Some Open Issues' [2007] 92 *Economic Review* 1 & 2 88.

24 See Rhinebridge (and Cheyne Finance) SIVs (n 93) for information on the case of Hannover Re where Moody's downgraded the company in an unsolicited rating because the firm had chosen a competitor.

25 Flannery (n 23).

The common word within the literature with regard to 'tying' is the word 'fear'. As Rousseau states: 'issuers may feel the need to subscribe to such services simply "out of fear that their failure to do so could adversely impact their credit rating (or, conversely, with the expectation that purchasing these services could help their credit ratings)"'.[26] The SEC and other authorities were aware of this practice and sought to prohibit it in the CRA Reform Act of 2006[27] after hearing testimonies from witnesses confirming their suffering at the hands of the agencies.[28] We will cover the regulatory response to these conflicts in greater detail below, but for now it is enough to state the SEC's position on such offences:

> Rule 17g-6 prohibits, among other things, an NRSRO from: (1) conditioning or threatening to condition the issuance of a credit rating on the purchase by an obligor or issuer or an affiliate of the obligor, of any other services or products, including pre-credit rating assessments products, of the NRSRO or any person associated with the NRSRO; (2) issuing or offering or threatening to issue, a credit rating that is not determined in accordance with the NRSRO's established procedures and methodologies for determining credit ratings, based on whether the rated person or an affiliate of the rate person, purchases or will purchase the credit rating or any other service or product of the NRSRO... .[29]

How one can 'prohibit' such behaviour when any pressure is usually implied is puzzling to say the least. In the case of the reinsurance firm Hannover Re, Moody's could not be held accountable because it defended its right to issue a rating that was not consistent with other rating agencies; in essence, the clear lack of appetite to prosecute agencies for the breach of regulations means that these pressures, whether perceived or real, cannot be prohibited by regulation alone.

The second form that the conflict regarding the provision of ancillary services may take is when clients may put pressure on the rating agency to award a certain rating to ensure they keep their business. There have been a number of references to this aspect in the literature,[30] with both Macey and Bai helpfully

---

26 Stéphane Rousseau 'Enhancing the Accountability of Accountability of Credit Rating Agencies: The Case for a Disclosure-based Approach' [2005] 51 *McGill Law Journal* 629; see also Deniz Coskun 'Supervision of Credit Rating Agencies: The Role of Credit Rating Agencies in Finance Decisions' [2009] 5 *Journal of International Banking Law & Regulation* 258; Lynn Bai 'On Regulating Conflicts of Interest in the Credit Rating Industry' [2010] 13 *New York University Journal of Legislation and Public Policy* 261 for the same sentiment.

27 The Credit Rating Agency Reform Act of 2006 Pub. L. 109–291, 120 Stat 1327; Markham (n 386) 725.

28 Committee on Financial Services *Credit Rating Duopoly Relief Act of 2006: Report 109–546* (GPO 2006) 13.

29 Securities and Exchange Commission *Final Rule Analysis – Securities and Exchange Commission Release No 34-72936; File No S7-18-11* (2014) [n 70].

30 Alcubilla and del Pozo (n 1) 145; Carol A. Frost 'Credit Rating Agencies in Capital Markets: A Review of Research Evidence on Selected Criticisms of the Agencies' [2007] 22 *Journal of Accounting, Auditing & Finance* 480.

linking additional services in the rating industry to additional services within the public accounting industry which came to a head with the Enron scandal.[31] The lead up to the Enron and WorldCom scandals provides a perfect example of the dangers of financial gatekeepers engaging with additional service provision and produced an abundance of scholarly work on the subject as a result.[32] The stance taken in the aftermath by legislators, predominantly through the Sarbanes-Oxley Act, will be covered in much more detail in the next chapter because it serves as some form of inspiration for the proposal that will be advanced.

Economic rent theory

While there has been plenty of research on the immediate issues with rating agencies (and, before them, accounting firms) providing additional services, there is little on placing the effects of that provision within a larger picture. It is undoubtedly true that a number of conflicts arise from the provision of ancillary services, but our aim here is to advance a proposal that sees that the provision is absolutely prohibited. Any discussion regarding the pressures within the working relationships that surround the rating industry are superficial at best when one is concerned with the dissolution of the service. For our purposes, it is enough now to state that the concept of 'excess' is the crux of the issue; it is this notion of excess that leads us to assess the theory of 'economic rent', as Hirshleifer et al. explain:

> Economists give the term *economic rent* a special meaning. It must be distinguished from the usual concept of rent as the hire-price for annual use of an acre of land, a building or a machine. Instead, economic rent is defined as the *excess return* to any input.[33]

The theory of economic rent is, arguably, directly applicable to the ratings industry. However, it would be beneficial to examine the theory before continuing because this notion of excessive return on the agencies' output is of real importance to the communication of this work. Congleton provides a very helpful analysis of the theory when he discusses its evolution. He begins by stating that the term 'rent seeking' was initially coined by Anne Krueger in 1974,[34] in

---

31 Bai (n 26) 261; Jonathan R. Macey 'The Politicisation of American Corporate Governance' [2006] 1 *Virginia Law & Business Review* 18.

32 Just a few scholarly works that are representative of the vast amount of research conducted in this area regarding accounting firms' provision of additional services are Cearns (n 16); Mike Brewster *Unaccountable: How the Accounting Profession Forfeited a Public Trust* (John Wiley & Sons 2003); Dennis Caplan, Diane Janvrin and James Kurtenbach 'Internal Audit Outsourcing: An Analysis of Self-regulation by the Accounting Profession' [2007] 19 *Research in Accounting Regulation* 3; Don E. Garner, David L. McKee and Yosra A. McKee *Accounting and the Global Economy after Sarbanes-Oxley* (Routledge 2014).

33 Jack Hirshleifer, Amihai Glazer and David Hirshleifer *Price Theory and Applications: Decisions, Markets and Information* (Cambridge University Press 2005) 402.

34 Anne O. Krueger 'The Political Economy of the Rent-seeking Society' [1974] 64 *The American Economic Review* 3.

which she argued that the competition for the 'rents' associated with import and export monopolies caused a good deal of competition for positions within a given industry that consumed vital resources – talent, time, training etc. – which she ultimately saw as a *waste* of resources depending upon the value of the rent accrued (i.e. the competition drove down the value of the rent)[35] However, unbeknownst to Krueger, Gordon Tullock had published a seminal paper almost a decade earlier which was also concerned with the quest for attaining unearned rents and the inefficiencies that came with that endeavour.[36] Congleton concludes that the early literature established the concept of 'rent-seeking' as 'the wasting of resources in the pursuit of "unearned" profits or wages, which were often obtained through public policies that were widely acknowledged by economists to be counterproductive'.[37]

This rent-seeking behaviour, which is clearly attributable to the rating agencies' adoption of ancillary services in the build-up to the financial crisis and the value that it seeks to achieve, depends on one aspect: competition. Simply put, 'economic rent is smaller the greater the range of alternatives considered',[38] which is what Krueger and Tullock were referring to as the most important factor in determining the value of the rent and therefore the efficiency of dedicating resources to its attainment. The common assertion in this regard is that industry participants would engage in concerted campaigns against policy makers to ensure that competition is kept to a level where the value of the rent outweighs both the cost of competing and of procuring the favour of the policy makers.[39] In thinking of the ratings industry it is clear to see that this aspect is inherently accounted for because the ratings industry is arguably a 'natural oligopoly'. This means that the competitive costs in attaining rents are minimal (in addition to the assistance of the SEC with its NRSRO designation process in the mid-1970s).

This particular field is extremely well researched. However, when we apply the concept to the ratings industry and its adoption of ancillary services the outcome is particularly sinister. There have been a number of references to the output of the agencies constituting what is known as a 'public good'. This is an economic term rather than one which denotes the moral nature of the ratings industry and is based upon the concept that there are certain areas or aspects of society that need to be provided for the benefit of the public, even if there is little financial benefit.[40] There are instances whereby the good needs to be produced, but the cost would be too high for the state so, where possible, the private sector would be enlisted to provide it. Yet, with little financial benefit available, the state will usually allow for the full or partial exclusion of access. This creates enough profit

---

35 Roger D. Congleton 'The Nature of Rent Seeking' in Roger D. Congleton and Arye L. Hillman (eds) *Companion to the Political Economy of Rent Seeking* (Edward Elgar Publishing 2015) 3.

36 Gordon Tullock 'The Welfare Costs of Tariffs, Monopolies and Theft' [1967] 5 *Western Economic Journal* 3.

37 Congleton (n 35).

38 Hirshleifer (n 33) 404.

39 Congleton (n 35) 4.

40 Further details were discussed earlier, see *The Impact of Technological Advancement*.

to make the provision of that good worthwhile for the private sector. To simplify this concept we can look at the example of the ratings industry and what is known as a 'public-private partnership'[41]. The growth of the capital markets, combined with the issues that stem from the state providing financial information for investors, means that the state is in no position to provide credit ratings for the marketplace. However, even though ratings are important to the functioning of the capital markets (when delivered accurately), the 'free-riding' that occurred in the late 1960s with the commercialised use of photocopiers meant that the agencies could not 'capture' the financial benefit for providing the good. The answer to this conundrum is seen in the SEC's acceptance of the adoption of the issuer-pays model, which simultaneously allows for the 'public good' to be delivered while allowing the agencies to capture the benefits of provision.

On the surface this seems to work well. However, the self-interested nature of both the issuers and the agencies means that conflict is inherent within their relationship. Furthermore, the agencies' adoption of ancillary services in the lead up to the largest crash since the Great Depression constitutes what is known as a *quid pro quo*[42] – an advantage granted in return for something – which is also attributable to the concept of economic rent and rent-seeking. It is entirely reasonable to suggest that the adoption of ancillary services in the rating industry, just two or three years after the largest accounting failure in history which was directly related to the provision of additional services by accounting firms, is a prime example of a quid pro quo; the *excess* is an unspoken stipulation of the agencies' provision of a 'public good'.

Earlier it was said that assessing the role of the state and the agencies' adoption of ancillary services would result in a sinister evaluation. This is not because of the public–private partnership theory that was advanced above, but because of an understanding advanced by Kofi Dompere, which is relatable to the rating industry situation, although it admittedly paints a particularly bleak picture when it comes to the possibility of advancing the public interest in this sphere. Dompere begins by positioning the issue of economic rent and rent-seeking as a process that requires

> the members of the principal (the State) to actively work to include in the social goal-objective set, the goals and objectives that create rent-seeking environments for social groups where specific rents may be exploited and harvested by specific groups. In this way, the members of the decision-making core (the agent) or the elected officials become nothing but economic puppets to non-politically elected salespersons.[43]

41 Helmut Willke and Gerhard Willke *Political Governance of Capitalism: A Reassessment Beyond the Global Crisis* (Edward Elgar Publishing 2012) 8.

42 The theory can be traced back to Knut Wicksell and his work on the relationship between a government and its citizens, see Knut Wicksell *Finanztheoretische Untersuchungen nebst Darstellung und Kritik des Steuerwesens Schwedens* (Jena 1896).

43 Kofi K. Dompere *Fuzziness, Democracy, Control and Collective Decision-choice System: A Theory on Political Economy of Rent-seeking and Profit-harvesting* (Springer Science & Business Media 2014) 6.

Although this is admittedly a very controversial take on the situation within society today, this should not reduce our willingness to both evaluate and incorporate it into our understanding of the ratings industry.

Dompere continues:

> The game is played with the constitution as the umpire. The whole process involves: 1) the establishment of the social decision-making core (the elected officials or the members of the agent), 2) the selling and buying of influence in order to affect the direction of votes to create the social-objective set, national interests and social vision, that define a rent-seeking environment favourable to specific interest groups and 3) the exploitation of the environment for private gains through non-wealth-creating transfers through resource allocation for output production and income-wealth production. Number one is called influence tampering; number two is called rent-creation; and number three is called rent protection and harvesting.[44]

By using this template to evaluate the ratings industry situation it becomes difficult to disagree with Dompere; we have seen instances throughout our examination of the 'revolving door' theory (influence tampering), concerted lobbying campaigns (rent-creation) and the establishment of revenue streams that are excessive (harvesting). Furthermore, we have seen how the Dodd-Frank Act, amongst a host of other legislative and regulatory moves, served to empower the agencies rather than discipline them. Dompere again encapsulates this phenomenon: 'The *political structure* offers opportunity for *rent creation* and the *legal structure* offers opportunities to *protect rent*, while the *economic structure* with the four aggregate markets offers opportunities to *harvest rent*.'[45]

Yes this version of events paints a dismal picture, but the evidence points towards it being the case. It is noted within the literature that the agencies are generating rental returns irrespective of their performance,[46] that regulations are directly allowing rent-seeking activities to take place[47] and that the NRSRO designation in the mid-1970s was a clear indication of this.[48] Chapter 2 was dedicated to the principle of focusing on the *actual* rather than being led by the quest for realising the *desired* and that principle is directly attributable here; the reality is particularly downbeat with regard to the potential for change, but to overlook the reality while attempting to make any sort of inroad is simply not the way to initiate any form of change for the benefit of the public.

---

44 ibid.
45 ibid.
46 Jonathan R. Macey 'The Nature and Futility of "Regulation by Assimilation"' in Greg Urban (ed.) *Corporations and Citizenship* (University of Pennsylvania Press 2014) 212.
47 D.T. Llewellyn 'Banking in the 21st Century: The Transformation of an Industry' in Tom Valentine and Guy Ford (eds) *Readings in Financial Institution Management: Modern Techniques for a Global Industry* (Allen & Unwin 1999) 40.
48 L.J. Rodriguez 'The Credit Rating Agencies: From Cartel Busters to Cartel Builders' in William A Niskanen *After Enron: Lessons for Public Policy* (Rowman & Littlefield 2007) 227.

Conclusion

One issue that consistently arises when researching the credit rating industry is that of moving into controversial realms. The short suggestion above concerning ancillary service subscription as constituting a reward for facilitation may indeed be viewed as controversial or fanciful, but the nature of the ratings industry dictates such actions; the way in which conservative thought views the industry simply does not tally with the output of the agencies and the scandals that consistently emerge concerning their conduct. This was demonstrated at the end of the chapter when the work of Kofi Dompere was assessed in relation to the theory of economic rent and rent-seeking. Dompere's account is extraordinarily divisive, yet when it is applied to the *actual* reality of the ratings industry it seems to fit very well. Dompere's take accounts for the lack of appetite from the authorities to make impactful changes, while it also accounts for the self-interested and mercenary nature of the rating agencies themselves.

Ultimately there are larger points raised by this chapter which serve as the culmination of the analyses that have gone before it and a foundation for all that follows. The notion of there being a divergence between the *actual* and *desired* is clearly demonstrated when looking at the response to the agencies' adoption of additional services. In the modern era, one that is centred upon the economy and the capital markets, the rating agencies are arguably as important as public accountants. Yet, while the accountancy industry was vilified for its use of additional services in the lead up to the Enron scandal, the rating agencies have received comparatively very little coverage for adopting what, in essence, are the very same services. The impact of the Enron scandal cannot be compared to the financial crisis, yet the mounds of research concerning additional services is predominantly concerned with the accounting industry, some 15 years later.

This demonstration of the common view being to ignore or downplay the *actual* version of events has contributed to a stark reality. First, as has been stated on a number of occasions, the provision of ancillary services has given the agencies an *excessive* revenue stream that directly nullifies the effects of 'record' and 'unprecedented' disciplinary measures such as the $1.375 billion fine given to S&P in 2015. Second and perhaps more importantly, the continued presence of this revenue stream not only protects the agencies from discipline, but also provides the initiative to become involved in other structured-finance-based scandals, because the authorities have demonstrated quite clearly that they are not prepared to discipline the agencies in any meaningful manner; recent developments in the structured-finance market for car sales in the US illustrate this very danger.[49]

---

49 Journalists point towards a raft of defaults within the automobile finance market as potential evidence for lax underwriting standards in the face of high ratings, see Serena Ng 'Subprime Flashback: Early Defaults are a Warning Sign for Auto Sales' [2016] *The Wall Street Journal* (13 March).

The provision of ancillary services presents conflicts and outcomes that are not acceptable when assessed through the lens of trying to increase public protection. While the issuer-pays model is justifiable in terms of allowing for the provision of a 'public good', the provision of additional services that do not have a bearing upon the accuracy of credit ratings is quite simply not acceptable. It is for this reason that Chapter 6 endeavours to position and explain a reform proposal that would bring an immediate end to these conflicts and warped outputs. The public is in real danger of being subjected to another rating industry-facilitated financial malfunction that would make mass austerity measures and a general reduction in social wealth the norm rather than a once-in-a-generation event.

Bibliography

Alcubilla, R.G. and del Pozo, J.R. *Credit Rating Agencies on the Watch List: Analysis of European Regulation* (Oxford University Press 2012).

Bai, L. 'On Regulating Conflicts of Interest in the Credit Rating Industry' [2010] 13 *New York University Journal of Legislation and Public Policy* 253.

Brewster, M. *Unaccountable: How the Accounting Profession Forfeited a Public Trust* (John Wiley & Sons 2003).

Caplan, D., Janvrin, D. and Kurtenbach, J. 'Internal Audit Outsourcing: An Analysis of Self-regulation by the Accounting Profession' [2007] 19 *Research in Accounting Regulation* 3.

Cearns, K. 'Auditors and International Financial Reporting' in van Mourik, C. and Walton, P. (eds) *The Routledge Companion to Accounting, Reporting and Regulation* (Routledge 2013).

Committee on Financial Services *Credit Rating Duopoly Relief Act of 2006: Report 109–546* (GPO 2006).

Congleton, R.D. 'The Nature of Rent Seeking' in Congleton, R.D. and Hillman, A.L. (eds) *Companion to the Political Economy of Rent Seeking* (Edward Elgar Publishing 2015).

Coskun, D. 'Supervision of Credit Rating Agencies: The Role of Credit Rating Agencies in Finance Decisions' [2009] 5 *Journal of International Banking Law & Regulation* 3.

Credit Rating Agency Reform Act of 2006 Pub. L. 109–291, 120 Stat 1327.

Darbellay, A. *Regulating Credit Rating Agencies* (Edward Elgar 2013).

Dompere, K.K. *Fuzziness, Democracy, Control and Collective Decision-choice System: A Theory on Political Economy of Rent-seeking and Profit-harvesting* (Springer Science & Business Media 2014).

Flannery, M.J. 'Supervising Bank Safety and Soundness: Some Open Issues' [2007] 92 *Economic Review* 1 and 2.

Frost, C.A. 'Credit Rating Agencies in Capital Markets: A Review of Research Evidence on Selected Criticisms of the Agencies' [2007] 22 *Journal of Accounting, Auditing & Finance* 469.

Garner, D., McKee, D.L. and McKee, Y. *Accounting and the Global Economy after Sarbanes-Oxley* (Routledge 2014).

Hirshleifer, J., Glazer, A. and Hirshleifer, D. *Price Theory and Applications: Decisions, Markets and Information* (Cambridge University Press 2005).

Krueger, A.O. 'The Political Economy of the Rent-seeking Society' [1974] 64 *The American Economic Review* 3.

Langohr, H.P. and Langohr, P.T. *The Rating Agencies and Their Credit Ratings: What They Are, How They Work and Why They are Relevant* (John Wiley & Sons 2010).

Llewellyn, D.T. 'Banking in the 21st Century: The Transformation of an Industry' in Valentine, T. and Ford, G. (eds) *Readings in Financial Institution Management: Modern Techniques for a Global Industry* (Allen & Unwin 1999).

Macey, J.R. 'The Nature and Futility of "Regulation by Assimilation"' in Urban, G. (ed.) *Corporations and Citizenship* (University of Pennsylvania Press 2014).

Macey, J.R. 'The Politicisation of American Corporate Governance' [2006] 1 *Virginia Law & Business Review* 1.

Markham, J.W. *A Financial History of the United States: From Enron-era Scandals to the Great Recession* (Routledge 2015).

McGraw-Hill Education, Inc. *Form 10-K* (SEC 2003).

McGraw-Hill Education, Inc. *Form 10-K* (SEC 2005).

McGraw-Hill Education, Inc. *Form 10-K* (SEC 2006).

Moody's Analytics *History of KMV* (2016). www.moodysanalytics.com/About-Us/History/KMV-History [accessed 14/4/16].

Moody's Analytics *History of Wall Street Analytics* (2016). www.moodysanalytics.com/About-Us/History/WSA-History [accessed 14/4/16].

Moody's Analytics *How Do You Transform Risk into High Performance? An Overview of Moody's Analytics* (2015). www.moodysanalytics.com/~/media/Brochures/AOE_Overview_Brochures/MA-Overview-Brochure.pdf [accessed 2/2/16].

Moody's *Policy for Ancillary and Other Permissible Services: Compliance* (2012). www.moodys.com/sites/products/ProductAttachments/Compliance/9-9-2011/SP13347_Policy%20for%20Ancillary%20and%20Other%20Permissible%20Services.pdf [accessed 11/10/15].

Moody's *Rating Symbols and Definitions* (2016). www.moodys.com/sites/products/AboutMoodysRatingsAttachments/MoodysRatingSymbolsandDefinitions.pdf [accessed 23/6/16].

Neuman, N.B. 'A Sarbanes-Oxley for Credit Rating Agencies? A Comparison of the Roles Auditors' and Credit Rating Agencies' Conflicts of Interests Played in Recent Financial Crises' [2010] 12 *University of Pennsylvania Journal of Business Law* 921.

Ng, S. 'Subprime Flashback: Early Defaults Are a Warning Sign for Auto Sales' [2016] *The Wall Street Journal* (13 March). www.wsj.com/articles/subprime-flashback-early-defaults-are-a-warning-sign-for-auto-sales-1457862187 [accessed 13/3/16].

Rodriguez, L.J. 'The Credit Rating Agencies: From Cartel Busters to Cartel Builders' in Niskanen, W.A. *After Enron: Lessons for Public Policy* (Rowman & Littlefield 2007).

Rousseau, S. 'Enhancing the Accountability of Credit Rating Agencies: The Case for a Disclosure-based Approach' [2006] 51 *McGill Law Journal* 617.

Securities and Exchange Commission *Final Rule Analysis – Securities and Exchange Commission Release No. 34–72936; File No. S7-18–11* (2014).

Securities and Exchange Commission *Report to Congress: Credit Rating Agency Independence Study* (2013).

Securities Industry and Financial Markets Authority *Statistics: US ABS Issuance and Outstanding (1985 to 2016)* (SIFMA 2016).

Testimony of Gregory W. Smith, General Counsel, Colorado Public Employees' Retirement Association in US House of Representatives: Committee on Financial Services *Hearing Before the Subcommittee on Capital Markets, Insurance and Government Sponsored Enterprises: Approaches to Improving Credit Rating Agency Regulation* (GPO 2009).

Tullock, G. 'The Welfare Costs of Tariffs, Monopolies and Theft' [1967] 5 *Western Economic Journal* 3.

Wicksell, K. *Finanztheoretische Untersuchungen nebst Darstellung und Kritik des Steuerwesens Schwedens* (Jena 1896).

Willke, H. and Willke, G. *Political Governance of Capitalism: A Reassessment Beyond the Global Crisis* (Edward Elgar Publishing 2012).

6   A reform proposal

Introduction

We will now conclude by establishing a reform proposal that has the potential to end the offsetting capability that ancillary service provision provides once and for all. The proposal, which in essence calls for the complete prohibition of any additional services that may be offered by the credit rating agencies, has been constructed so that *technically* it could be accepted and put into practice. However, while there are no technical impediments to the theorised adoption of this proposal, there are a number of impediments that must be addressed when we consider the *actual* world in which we live. Therefore, this chapter will endeavour to assess all of these issues and ultimately ascertain the potential for such impactful reforms succeeding in this field.

We will begin by examining the current regulations governing the provision of ancillary services because, although we have briefly touched on it earlier, doing so will allow us to see precisely where the regulatory framework falls short in this area. Once the imperfections in the current framework have been established, the natural progression will be to then establish the proposed remedy to the issues that are inherent within the provision of additional services by socially vital financial gatekeepers.

The proposal that has been referenced so far will be presented in a certain way, primarily because of the need to reduce, wherever possible, perceived complexities within the financial system. By introducing the proposal in this streamlined and direct way, the aim is to present a vision that leaves no room for manoeuvre; it is this 'room' that is continuously exploited, so we should endeavour to reduce these gaps whenever possible. This work now reaches its reason for being put together; to advance the reform proposal that ancillary service provision be fundamentally removed from the rating industry.

The imperfections in the current framework governing ancillary service provision

Within the SEC's *Final Rules* publication that details amendments to the relevant sections of the Dodd Frank Act,[1] we can see the actual constraints that surround

---

1 Securities and Exchange Commission *Final Rule Analysis: Securities and Exchange Commission Release No 34-72936; File No S7-18-11* (2014) 23.

the agencies' provision of ancillary services. As detailed earlier in Chapter 5,[2] the SEC confirms that Rules 17g-5 and 17g-6 of the Securities and Exchange Act of 1934 prohibit the agency from rating an issuer with whom they have had previous contact concerning their corporate or legal structure, assets, liabilities or activities. The agency is prohibited from conditioning or threatening to condition the issuance of a credit rating on the purchasing of additional services (i.e. tying).

The acceptance of the 'tying' process existing was developed in the CRA Reform Act of 2006[3] as a response to the many testimonies heard by Congressional committees concerning the 'abusive' industry practices such as issuing unsolicited ratings with a bill and 'notching'.[4] Rule 17g-6 is an example of the SEC's response to the legislative body instructing it to develop countermeasures to the aspects it decides need to be addressed. It was tentatively established alongside the Rule 17g-5 amendments in 2009.[5]

The only other rule that is concerned with the provision of ancillary services is Rule 17g-7, which determines that if a credit rating is issued it must be accompanied by a disclosure form by the agency which details whether or not that issuing party has paid for any additional services before the rating was paid for (there are strict limits to what the issuer may purchase *after* the rating has been paid for). Initially, the SEC had differentiated the need for disclosure between solicited and unsolicited ratings, although this was altered when a commenter on the proposed rules raised the concern that an NRSRO analyst may then have the opportunity to know whether a firm had purchased additional services from their rating firm.[6] Though this is logical in practice, there have been a number of confirmed instances where analysts have been directly involved with the marketing of ancillary services.[7] This is an extraordinarily troubling issue and is representative of the *actualities* of the rating industry.

This concept of the SEC trusting the agencies to separate the divisions within its business is very important and allows us to begin to focus upon the inadequacies of the current framework. Chapter 1 explained that the ancillary service divisions, using Moody's Analytics as an example, serve as the sales and marketing arms of the rating agencies as well as the provider of additional services. With this understanding we can see that the SEC does attempt to regulate the ancillary service divisions further when they state that 'section 15E(h)(3)(A) of the Exchange Act provides that the Commission shall also issue rules to *prevent* the sales and marketing consideration of an NRSRO from influencing the production of ratings by the NRSRO' (emphasis added).[8] This 'absolute

---

2 Chapter 5 – *Introduction* (n 6).

3 Markham (n 386) 725.

4 Committee on Financial Services *Credit Rating Agency Duopoly Relief Act of 2006: Report 109–546* (GPO 2006) 13.

5 Lynn Bai 'On Regulating Conflicts of Interest in the Credit Rating Industry' [2010] 13 *New York University Journal of Legislation and Public Policy* 278.

6 Securities and Exchange Commission (n 1) 332.

7 Bai (n 5) 261.

8 Securities and Exchange Commission (n 1) 99.

prohibition'[9] is clear and unwavering. Yet, we have already heard of testimonies of the failure of these 'Chinese walls' (or 'information barriers' as the SEC would prefer they be called).[10] The SEC itself, while conducting its examinations of the agencies in the preparation of these final rules, found that within the Big Three, it appeared 'employees responsible for obtaining ratings business would notify other employees, including those responsible for criteria development, about business concerns they had related to the criteria'.[11]

However, this was not an isolated finding. The SEC found in 2015 that 'one larger NRSRO and three smaller NRSROs did not have sufficient policies, procedures and controls to manage the issuer-paid conflict or to prevent analytical personnel's access to fee or market-share information'. It also found that 'an analytical supervisor (who was not authorised to grant such an exemption) at this (larger) NRSRO suspended analyst rotation for several months for a substantial number of ratings in an asset class without obtaining the required written exemption' and that a senior officer of the same NRSRO 'violated its policies and procedures by sending emails to analytical and criteria-development personnel concerning an issuer's decision to terminate its rating in response to revisions by this NRSRO to its criteria'.[12] The incredible violations of the law do not stop there; the SEC found instances of the agencies not reporting issuers who it suspected of committing material violations of the law, of issuing unsolicited ratings motivated by market-share considerations and of directors who were declared as being independent but also served on the non-NRSRO parent companies or affiliates.

These incredible and brazen violations of the law confirm Richard Portes' view that 'Chinese Walls will not do'.[13] However, it surely raises the question of why they feel so comfortable in breaking the law. Fortunately for our analysis, but unfortunately for society, that is a question that has a simple answer. The answer lies in the following statement from the SEC, one which is repeated consistently within the report on the findings of systemic law breaking: 'The Staff recommended that this NRSRO enhance its internal controls to ensure that all personnel adhere to this policy'. This sentiment is repeated time and time again and simply confirms the weak and pro-business nature of the SEC; that material violations are treated in this manner is nothing short of outrageous. In the same report, the SEC details the disciplinary measures at its

9 ibid 100.
10 Securities and Exchange Commission *Self-regulatory Organisations; International Securities Exchange, Inc; Notice of Filing of Proposed Rule Change and Amendments Nos 1 and 2 Thereto to Amend the Market Maker Information Barrier Requirements under ISE Rule 810: Release No 34-50197; File No SR-ISE-2004–18* (SEC 2004) 1.
11 Securities and Exchange Commission (n 1) 100.
12 Securities and Exchange Commission *2015 Summary Report of Commission Staff's Examinations of each Nationally Recognised Statistical Rating Organisation* (SEC 2015) 15.
13 Richard Portes 'Ratings Agency Reform' in Carmen Reinhart and Andrew Felton (eds) *The First Global Financial Crisis of the 21st Century* (VoxEU 2008) 149.

disposal. These include relatively small fines, limitations on activities and short-term censuring prohibitions (e.g. the Cease and Desist Order given to S&P) and ultimately the revoking of an agency's NRSRO licence. However, why none of these measures were utilised in response to these blatant violations is unknown and is, in truth, a damning demonstration of the SEC's inability to safeguard the public interest.

All in all is it very difficult to disagree with Eichengreen's assessment that 'the credit-rating agencies, legislative handwaving aside, were able to escape significant regulation and reform'.[14] The current regulatory framework that surrounds the agencies, at all levels, is incredibly weak. It is not illogical to presume that an effective post-crisis regulatory effort would result in a systemic lowering of profits within that particular sector being governed for some considerable period of time, but for the rating industry to have experienced just two or three years of contraction before resuming and surpassing record levels of revenues and profits is extraordinary and ultimately stands as the truest representation of the weakness of the regulatory framework governing the ratings industry.

It is contested here that this weakness is inherent within the SEC because of its constitution, although it must be stated that this contention could be applied to any number of agents of the state. Unnervingly, agents favour business over the public which is demonstrated by their passive response to material violations of the law. When we add this understanding to the US Department of Justice having to *negotiate* with companies like the rating agencies to find an appropriate level of fine and then championing this process as a positive result for the public, the true nature of what lies before of us is clear. The following proposal is predicated upon the notion that what is needed is not a simple reform proposal but ultimately a drastic sea-change in mindset, so that the public's protection is at the forefront of every agent of the state. The call for incremental and clearly defined reform proposals that are based upon the understanding of the agencies as they *actually* are is valid, yet the impediments to those reforms being recognised are great, as we shall see later and this is something that, although pessimistic, must not be forgotten.

For over a decade we have witnessed extensive poverty and 'austerity' that is the sole result of the actions of a few. To present an overarching proposal to eliminate this inherent problem may be academically appealing but is, in essence, useless against such an engrained adversary. So, in what is a minute attempt to initiate incremental change that will allow for the credit rating industry to be exposed to the possibility of experiencing discipline through financial penalties – the only discipline the State is willing to administer – this chapter will now present a reform proposal that calls for the absolute and irreversible prohibition of the provision of additional services by credit rating agencies.

---

14 Barry Eichengreen *Hall of Mirrors: The Great Depression, The Great Recession and the Uses-and-Misuses of History* (Oxford University Press 2014) 386.

This proposal is not complex. It is not complex because simplicity is the only way in which one can communicate the necessity of action in this regard and also because the wrongdoing that is being committed is also extraordinarily simple; the agencies incorporated a business for harvesting rent, the proposal here is that that business be removed. Also, if a proposal is advanced in such a simple but studied manner, but is not considered, we then have the foundation to ask 'why'.

A reform proposal to limit the impact of the ratings industry upon society

So far, we have endeavoured to understand the rating industry as it actually is, rather than how one may desire it to be. We have seen a number of instances where the industry *actively* operates against investors, issuers, the state and, most importantly of all, the public. It is reasonable to suggest that a private firm should *prioritise* its own advancement, because if it does not then no one else will, but to extend beyond this mandate and actively harm others in order to achieve growth is not acceptable within an advanced society. When we looked at the revenue figures for Moody's earlier, we saw how well the revenues garnered from credit ratings have rebounded after the crisis and remain as the foundation for the company; the question is 'Why is this revenue stream not enough?'

Of course, we cannot dictate to a private company how much it can earn. What we can do is dictate *how* a private company can earn. The credit rating industry is vital in today's economy that is centred upon the issuance of debt, so it is important to preserve and protect the rating abilities of the largest agencies. Rather than preserving and protecting this ability, it is preferable to propose a system whereby the quality of the ratings can actually be increased, which is a by-product of this proposal.

The proposal advanced here has been mentioned throughout so, in order to be clear, the reform proposal can be simplified by stating that it calls for the '*complete and irreversible prohibition of the provision of additional services by credit rating agencies*'. There has been enough evidence put forward to support this proposal, although in an attempt to counter the claims that may be made against it we shall now look at the individual components that comprise the reform proposal and aim to make it *absolute* and *irreversible*.

Absolute prohibition

In its 2003 report to Congress regarding the agencies' independence, the SEC made an interesting point regarding the models adopted by the industry: 'ancillary services are in some cases provided by the NRSRO, a *non*-NRSRO affiliate of the NRSRO or in other cases, by both the NRSRO and a non-NRSRO affiliate'. The SEC report continues by stating that Section 15E imposes requirements only upon the NRSRO and *rating*-affiliates designated by the NRSRO on its Form NRSRO, thus 'the Staff's ability under the current Commission rules directly to obtain information regarding and to examine, the effectiveness of policies and procedures could be affected by the choice of a non-NRSRO affiliate to provide such Ancillary Services'.[15] It is precisely these matters that we need to consider, as it details the *actual* state of the industry as opposed to how we imagine it should be.

Therefore, the first aspect of the proposal is that *no NRSRO, nor its holding company, can have any stake in a company (or division) that provides 'additional services', nor can it have any 'affiliate' associated with it which provides 'additional services'*. The definition of 'additional services' here is rather simple: *any service that is not a credit rating is deemed to be an 'additional service' and is to be prohibited*. Moody's promotes the sales of what it calls 'special reports' on its Moody's Investors Service website (i.e. not Moody's Analytics) that contains such elements as industry and sector outlooks, as well as outlooks by region; these services *can* be important to investors, but they are for sale and are not free. The initial cost of one of these reports is $750. To an institutional investor this is very low, but it may be expensive for a retail investor. However, institutional investors will not base their investment decisions on the basis of a $750 report and with the separation of ancillary services from credit rating services anticipated to create a new, albeit much smaller market, the retail investor will be able to purchase that information from another source (e.g. existing market forecasting companies); *for this reason 'special reports' will also be prohibited*.

According to Moody's website anyone can have 'free' access to 'Issuer Ratings, Events Calendars, Watchlists and Rating Methodologies', which according to this reform proposal is all that the company will be able to offer. The information contained within the ratings, the watchlists and the methodologies, is all that an investor really needs from a rating agency (i.e. what rating they have ascribed to an issuer, the short- to medium-term prospects of that rating remaining the same and the method with which the agency came to that particular decision). Only the equivalent services offered by other NRSROs, taking into account differences in title, will be allowed to be provided by a rating agency, irrespective of market capitalisation.

While one may argue that to prohibit *all* non-essential services may be extreme, the prohibition is based on two elements. First, the rating agencies have demonstrated consistently that they *only* seek to maximise their profit, so allowing for a reduced revenue stream will soon be countered by lobbying or reorganisation efforts to ensure that the small gap left by regulation is opened up and exploited. Similarly, the SEC cannot be trusted to keep the public at the forefront of its mindset and remain steadfast in the face of what is sure to be inevitable pressure from the agencies and their supporters. For this reason, the prohibition will be *absolute* and we shall see shortly that it has to be *irreversible* to counter this inevitable counter by the industry.

---

15 Securities and Exchange Commission *Report to Congress: Credit Rating Agency Independence Study* (2013) 20.

The right to choose

The next stage of the reform proposal is that the agencies will be given a choice; *either provide credit rating services only or provide ancillary services only, but not both.* If, as the agencies are adamant, the provision of ancillary service's value is not tied to the presence of the rating division, then this should not be as spurious an option as it first sounds; lest we forget this is a multi-billion dollar industry. However, unlike the historical trajectory in the banking industry, the agencies *will not be allowed to create rebranded ancillary service divisions and have partners move across from one industry to the other.* Rather, the line of business that they decline will have to be divested, as we will discuss below.

Divesture

After the agency chooses which line of business it would like to remain in, with it being highly anticipated that all NRSROs will choose to remain in the rating field, the next stage of the reform is that they will have a *maximum of two calendar years from the date of enactment to divest the declined business entirely.* The sole reason for this limitation, in addition to the point made earlier regarding rebranding and the continuation of close links between the old and new companies, is that the lobbying efforts by the agencies, even after enactment, would be extraordinary. Based upon what we have heard so far about this – and indeed almost every other financial sector – the longer it takes to implement the required changes, the higher the chance that lobbying efforts will dilute the intended effects, ultimately rendering the proposed reform inadequate.

In the event that the NRSRO does not divest the division and, indeed, any affiliate completely within the two-year period, *administrators will be appointed to complete the sale, in a manner akin to bankruptcy proceedings.* The market-research market has enough businesses to allow for the sale of the components of the divisions at a price that is not punitive to the rating agencies, so both the deadline and any penalties for not abiding by it are also fair.

Irreversibility

Unlike the Sarbanes-Oxley Act of 2002 that mandated that certain aspects of additional services as provided by accounting firms were to be prohibited, which encouraged the firms to divest their additional service divisions, this reform proposal has *clearly* prohibited the providing of any additional services by rating agencies. To counter the inevitable backlash and to cover for all caveats, the next stage of the reform is to articulate that *any service other than credit rating provision, the publication of watchlists and of rating methodologies, are expressly prohibited.* This has the effect of prohibiting any provision of additional services under a different title (e.g. 'advisory services'). *There are to be no exceptions to this rule.*

This aspect of the reform puts an end to any hopes that the agencies would have of following the lead of their accounting counterparts and establishing short-term 'non-competes' with the buyers of the ancillary divisions, so that the illusion of prohibition is met while the long-term aim is to continue with the provision at a later date when the economic cycle is more hospitable to private expansion.

These simple elements of absolute prohibition, the ability to choose which business one wants to operate in, a two-year deadline for divesture and the articulation of irreversibility within the reform, would all remove the rent-harvesting division of the rating agencies, aligning them closer to the public interest. However, we have looked at a number of different angles concerning the rating industry and one thing should stand out above all else; things are not as simple as they appear. While this reform has the potential to be effective, mostly because of its simplicity, there is a need to address the *actualities* that would stem from this proposal. So, we will now assess the potential advantages that could stem from the implementation of this reform proposal. Yet, in keeping with the call to assess the *actual* we shall also address the potential impediments to the implementation of this reform, because to challenge such an engrained and resourceful opponent will always be an extraordinarily difficult task.

Potential benefits of the implementation of the reform proposal

There are a number of potential benefits from the implementation of this proposal. Although every party that is concerned with the ratings industry, including the agencies themselves, can benefit from the effects of the proposal, the benefit for the agencies is predicated upon their accepting a short-term loss for long-term stability. Whether they have the capacity to do this is unknown, although all the evidence points to an industry that is mindful of its historical brushes with extinction and has become ruthless in its attempts to survive. The key challenge for this proposal is showing how the agencies can cement their position within the economy *and* contribute to the development of society at the same time.

The first point to make is that this proposal does not take the agencies out of business, as other proposals aim to do.[16] This is important because it would leave the agencies (using Moody's as an example) with a revenue stream in the region of $2 billion annually as it stands today, which is still an incredible position to be in. What is perhaps more important is that one element of the conflicts which hound the industry would have been entirely removed, so the *independence in appearance* will be increased considerably; this stands to be potentially more profitable than the provision of ancillary services in the long term because the increasingly negative reputation the agencies are garnering will surely reach breaking point at some point in the future, perhaps when their complicity in a crisis larger than 2007/8 forces the hand of legislators, albeit in a less conciliatory tone than this proposal.

This increase in reputation stemming from the implementation of the reform proposal would be enhanced further by understanding that the removal of additional services *tends* to result in an increased focus on the gatekeeper's primary function. However, this aspect needs to be understood in context; in relation to the response of the accounting industry to the prohibition on additional services,

16 See *The Oligopolistic Structure of the Ratings Industry* for just some of the proposals aimed at taking the industry out of existence.

Cottell tells us that the firms began to pay more attention to the risk profiles of their clients as a response to the legislative attack on their business,[17] which is clearly desirable.

For the issuers, the removal of additional services has a number of potential benefits, particularly if we accept that certain conditions exist. If the provision of ancillary services is being used by the agencies to harvest rent, which we claim to be the case, then the obvious conclusion that can be made is that issuers (and subsequently investors) are paying this rent to the agencies. In addition to this reduction in cost for issuers, the *theoretical* understanding that the issuers are not *technically* bound to the agencies means that the agencies would not be able to attempt to offset the losses experienced through the prohibition of ancillary service provision by raising the prices of their ratings. As opposed to the accounting market whereby publicly listed companies must be audited, the rating market is constricted by pricing pressures which means the agencies cannot simply alter their prices to suit their needs; it is not hard to imagine that large issuers would not take kindly to an increase in price, even by one or two basis points. Again, however, this benefit must be placed in context because it operates on the *desired* version of events being true, when we know that the *actuality* is that issuers are still bound to the agencies even after Dodd-Frank. This means there is potential for the agencies to pass the losses onto their customers (although this would arguably still be less than subscription to the ancillary services, the issue then would be that the issuers cannot buy either favour or protection).

However, the aim of this reform proposal was not to appease the agencies, but to protect the public and in this regard the objective would be achieved. The absolute and irreversible prohibition on additional services results in the limitation of the potential resources that agencies can use to negate any disciplinary measures that may be taken against it. This concept of protecting the public has to be at the forefront of everyone's thinking, because rather than a financial crash affecting the bottom lines of large multinational corporations, the financial crisis, which we know the rating agencies directly facilitated (amongst others), has resulted in the increase of global poverty,[18] homelessness[19] and suicide[20] amongst a host of other societal ills. This is not a far-fetched comparison; in fact it is important for the future of society that this comparison is made whenever possible.

17 Philip G. Cottell 'The Public Accounting Industry' in James Brock (ed.) *The Structure of American Industry* 12th Edition (Waveland Press 2013) 352.

18 Overseas Development Institute *The Global Financial Crisis: Poverty and Social Protection* (ODI 2009); Bilal Habib, Ambar Narayan, Sergio Olivieri and Carolina Sanchez-Paramo *The Impact of the Financial Crisis on Poverty and Income Distribution: Insights from Simulations in Selected Countries* (Centre for Economic Policy Research 2010).

19 Nicole Fondeville and Terry Ward *Homelessness during the Crisis: Research Note 8/2011* (European Commission 2011).

20 Karen McVeigh 'Austerity a Factor in Rising Suicide Rate among UK Men – Study' [2015] *The Guardian* (12 November).

The state may have opted to remove the deterrent of custodial sentences from the upper echelons of the financial sector, but even though this awful development has made the protection of the public that much more difficult, there is a way in which the weak deterrent chosen by the state can be turned to the public's advantage. With regard to the rating industry, that is to remove its rent-harvesting division and expose it, to a greater extent, to the fines that are given to it. Franklin Strier agrees with this position and in what seems like a fitting way to end this section, he states:

> The rating agencies' loss (in consulting revenue) could be the public's gain … From a utilitarian viewpoint, the loss of rating agency fees pales before the projected public good of more independent rating agencies.[21]

Potential impediments to the implementation of the reform proposal

There are a number of benefits that could come with the implementation of this reform proposal. However, actually getting the reform proposal implemented in the first place is an entirely different matter. This work has attempted to provide the context for the need for this reform by examining the majority of issues that surround the ratings industry today (and, to a certain extent, historically). As a result, we have been able to understand that the ratings industry is a particularly mighty adversary against the public interest. Not only does it amass incredible resources through the conflict-laden issuer-pays remuneration model, as well as the rent-harvesting ancillary service divisions, but it has also been embedded within the modern economy. Apparently generation-defining legislative attempts to remove the binds that keep the industry wedded to the modern economy *have had no effect* either on the fortunes of the industry or on its position within the economy. We have endeavoured to promote a new understanding of the ratings industry: we have to consider the industry for what it *actually* is, rather than what we may *desire* it to be. In that light, it is important that we attempt to ascertain the potential impediments to the adoption of this reform proposal.

The most obvious impediment to adoption of the reform would be the mobilisation of the industry's vast resources which, in reality, has and will again stymie impactful reform proposals. We have seen evidence that almost guarantees that the Big Three, if not other members of the rating industry, would mobilise their considerable resources to instigate a concerted and effective lobbying campaign;[22] if they mobilised for Dodd-Frank, they would certainly mobilise to protect their ancillary service divisions.

---

21 Franklin Strier 'Rating the Raters: Conflicts of Interest in the Credit Rating Firms' [2008] 113 *Business and Society Review* 546.
22 See *A Reality Check* (n 33).

The SEC has been admonished here for being ineffective with their administering of penalties for breaches of the law.[23] This raises another issue: the absolute removal of ancillary service divisions to remove the nullifying effects of the resources generated by the provision, but also upon of the inability of the SEC to effectively contain the naturally exploitative demeanour of the agencies, means that the adoption of the reform would be a massive blow to its reputation. It is certainly not unreasonable to ask how supportive the SEC would be of such a proposal given the reputational capital they would lose as a result.

In relation to the agencies, irrespective of the resources that they would commit to challenging this reform, the hurdles that would be presented by the need to present a global front against the industry and of the important aspect of timing (the regulatory fertile post-crisis era has passed), the biggest impediment to success lies in the minds of our societal leaders. What this ultimately means is that the decision to implement impactful reforms will be down to the will of societal leaders to reject the financial benefits of being captured and to protect the public from the inherently destructive nature of the financial industry; whether one believes that this may happen is down to one's outlook, as has been demonstrated by the variance in opinion regarding the best way to advance our society (e.g. free-market proponents as opposed to those arguing for stronger regulation) but one thing that is certain is that there is little evidence of this will being demonstrated by those in positions of power.

To counter this lack of willingness to protect the public from the iniquities of the financial sector, a reform proposal has been proposed here that is remarkably simple, based on clear evidence of wrongdoing and rent-harvesting behaviour that has the effect of negating any financial punishment. My claim is that the legitimacy of this reform, fundamentally, turns on the proper conception of the role of the financial sector within society. It is surely untenable to suggest that society is there to serve the financial sector. In fact, it is the other way around; this is a sentiment that must be remembered at all times, regardless of the personal benefits that come from ignoring it. Failure to address this risks repeating the mistakes of the past, leaving this and future generations susceptible to a crash from which society will perhaps not be able to recover.

Conclusion

The aim of this chapter was to present the raison d'être for this work. In attempting to present a reform proposal that would align the output of the rating industry closer to what is required by the public, the chapter contained the details of the call for the absolute and irreversible prohibition of the provision of additional services by credit rating agencies. To give this proposal the best chance of being implemented the chapter sought to show the weaknesses within the current

---

23 *The Imperfections in the Current Framework Governing Ancillary Service Provision.*

regulatory framework that governs the current provision of additional services, some historical instances of state intervention in private affairs and ultimately the strengths and weaknesses of the proposal itself.

The current regulatory framework that governs the provision of additional services is incredibly weak. We saw how the framework is built upon concessions and collaboration, aspects that have resulted in the direct exploitation by the rating agencies. The SEC has adopted a number of rules which seem to make sense: a good example is the ban on contemporaneously providing rating and ancillary services as mandated by the CRA Reform Act of 2006. This is positive, yet the mindset of the SEC undermines any advances in this area. We have seen a number of instances where the SEC's response to material violations of the law was to recommend changing the behaviour that was causing the breach. This approach would not be accepted in any other form of the justice system and ultimately is illustrative of the SEC's position – it is difficult to provide a reasoned argument that the SEC is championing the rights of the investor over the financial sector in this particular area.

So, the reform proposal which aims to redress the imbalance within the rating industry's relationship with society was introduced in a simplistic and straightforward manner. The proposal, that agencies are absolutely prohibited from providing any service other than rating services, are forced to choose between continuing in the rating or market-research industry and are banned from ever providing such services again, was developed to promote clarity in a field that has utilised conscious complexity for a number of years. We saw how the agencies would benefit in the long-run, how issuers would benefit and, most importantly, how society would benefit immeasurably from a constrained ratings industry. However, while a number of benefits came with the proposed reform, there were also a large number of substantial impediments to its implementation, all of which hinted at inherently systemic problems.

What is required, then, is further research that is conducted based on two beliefs: the need to focus on reality and the need to widen the availability of that research. By developing honest and uncompromising research into these destructive industries and then communicating this using as many public mediums as possible, the chances of enacting meaningful reform must rise dramatically when compared to the current situation. Whether the research is quantitative, qualitative or normative is immaterial – it must be based upon these two foundations. If it is, then it is conceivable that we will be in a much better position to hold up these destructive industries to the public for their derision when they inevitably become involved in the next societal breakdown. The shame of this lies in the many people who are currently experiencing extraordinary hardship as a result of these actors' callous disregard for society; in a just world they would be imprisoned for their crimes, but in this *actual* world we must be ready to develop public anger to a level that forces the hand of political leaders after the next catastrophe – the increased education of the public to the iniquities of these areas of society is crucial.

Bibliography

Bai, L. 'On Regulating Conflicts of Interest in the Credit Rating Industry' [2010] 13 *New York University Journal of Legislation and Public Policy* 253.

Committee on Financial Services *Credit Rating Duopoly Relief Act of 2006: Report 109–546* (GPO 2006).

Cottell, P.G. 'The Public Accounting Industry' in Brock, J. (ed.) *The Structure of American Industry:* 12th Edition (Waveland Press 2013).

Eichengreen, B. *Hall of Mirrors: The Great Depression, the Great Recession and the Uses-and-Misuses of History* (Oxford University Press 2014).

Fondeville, N. and Ward, T. *Homelessness during the Crisis: Research Note 8/2011* (European Commission 2011).

Habib, B., Narayan, A., Olivieri, S. and Sanchez-Paramo, C. *The Impact of the Financial Crisis on Poverty and Income Distribution: Insights from Simulations in Selected Countries* (Centre for Economic Policy Research 2010).

Markham, J.W. *A Financial History of the United States: From Enron-era Scandals to the Great Recession* (Routledge 2015).

McVeigh, K. 'Austerity a factor in rising suicide rate among UK Men – Study' [2015] *The Guardian* (12 November). www.theguardian.com/society/2015/nov/12/austerity-a-factor-in-rising-suicide-rate-among-uk-men-study [accessed 24/5/16].

Overseas Development Institute *The Global Financial Crisis: Poverty and Social Protection* (ODI 2009)

Portes, R. 'Ratings Agency Reform' in Reinhart, C. and Felton, A. (eds) *The First Global Financial Crisis of the 21st Century* (VoxEU 2008).

Securities and Exchange Commission *2015 Summary Report of Commission Staff's Examinations of Each Nationally Recognized Statistical Rating Organization* (SEC 2015).

Securities and Exchange Commission *Final Rule Analysis – Securities and Exchange Commission Release No 34–72936; File No. S7-18–11* (2014).

Securities and Exchange Commission *Report to Congress: Credit Rating Agency Independence Study* (2013).

Securities and Exchange Commission *Self-regulatory Organisations; International Securities Exchange, Inc; Notice of Filing of Proposed Rule Change and Amendments Nos 1 and 2 Thereto to Amend the Market Maker Information Barrier Requirements under ISE Rule 810: Release No 34–50197; File No. SR-ISE-2004–18* (SEC 2004).

Strier, F. 'Rating the Raters: Conflicts of Interest in the Credit Rating Firms' [2008] 113 *Business and Society Review* 4.

Conclusion

There is a power generated by activism and committed campaigning for social goals[1]

This work has endeavoured to assess the effectiveness of the discipline afforded to the rating agencies in light of their conduct before, during and after the financial crisis of 2007/8. Inspired by the spectacle of the leading rating agencies recommencing their unprecedented growth just two years after the largest financial collapse since the Great Depression, the aim was to understand how Standard & Poor's and Moody's have been able to absorb the 'record' financial penalties of $2.2 billion given to them by the US Department of Justice for knowingly defrauding investors in the lead-up to the crisis.

After analysing the effectiveness of the legislative measures taken against the agencies, just two or three years before the height of the crisis, we can conclude that the rating agencies exploited their position by incorporating additional service divisions to 'harvest' profits from the sector that would lead the world to the brink of financial ruin; this is how the agencies were able to absorb these record penalties. Yet, the analysis conducted here revealed a far more pessimistic view in that investors, issuers and indeed the state, all benefit from this warped anti-social arrangement. In fact, the only losers in this arrangement are the public, who have borne the brunt of the costs of this arrangement and have suffered a distinct breakdown in the fabric of society as a result.

While it would be easy to surrender to this reality and accept the role that the public must seemingly play in reaping no reward but receiving all of the cost, it is argued here that by detailing this reality in clear and unobstructed terms there stands an opportunity to reverse this sentiment that has taken hold. By producing research of this nature, then striving to disseminate it as far as possible within the public realm, the hope is that the next financial collapse – and the regulatory response to the last one dictates that future collapses *will occur* – will take place in a world where the actors are widely known and vilified as a result. It is only by increasing the awareness of the schemes and participants in those schemes that seek to extract wealth from society do we stand a chance of

---

1 Matthew Clement '1976 – The Moral Necessity of Austerity' in Stella Maile and David Griffiths (eds) *Public Engagement and Social Science* (Policy Press 2014) 70.

reducing the public's exposure to the harm that inevitably comes with such a venal crusade.

So, to achieve that aim we posed a number of clearly defined research questions which, when answered, would paint the picture of a system that needs to be constrained for the *protection* of the public. In answering those research questions the reason for the prohibiting reform proposal was formed, in that it was revealed that to *trust* in the agencies or indeed the regulators, to maintain a limited form of additional service provision was simply not a viable option based upon their history of exploiting gaps for their own gain, often at the expense of societal health.

In demonstrating who the agencies actually are, by way of a 'primer' and an intensive assessment of the relationships that define the industry, we were introduced to an industry that operates on two particular planes; one where they are perceived to be a vital cog in the effective running of the financial system and the other where the agencies play an incredibly vital role in facilitating the very worst aspects of that very same system. When assessing the *actualities* of the industry and its role, it quickly became apparent that the agencies operate in a manner directly opposite to that which is promoted; for us, this is the quintessential reason for the damage caused by the agencies and the very same reason why they are continuing to flourish despite being identified as being fundamentally complicit in one of the largest systemic failures on record.

By way of discussing some of the intricacies within the rating industry, the viewpoint was developed that, despite some inconsistencies in the literature, the agencies have been steadily preparing for the crisis-hit era, rather than being an innocent bystanders caught up in the malaise. By incorporating a different remuneration model, further developing their oligopolistic structure – with the assistance of the regulators – and also by establishing rent-seeking divisions, the rating agencies were primed to take advantage of the systemic degeneration in values and responsibility and we have seen that they did exactly that.

Yet, the purpose of this work was to present this account so that the agencies could be further identified as catalysts in that systemic degeneration. To add to that analysis, this work has endeavoured to add to the field by proposing a reason as to why the agencies, counterintuitively, have gone from strength to strength despite their transgressions; this has been achieved by presenting a deep understanding of the provision of ancillary services within the sector and the associated consequences attached to those developments. With that in mind, this 'story' will now end with remarks that can only be categorised under the banner of 'consequences'.

'Consequences'

> *This historic settlement makes clear the consequences of putting corporate profits over honesty in the financial markets.*

The statement opened the work and it is fitting that it also features in the closing. Towards the end of the book a conscious decision was made to examine the potential future ahead, in terms of looking at what may be achieved and how we may go about doing it. Conducting critical research and then disseminating that research widely, so that the public can be more aware of the system that is costing them so much, is a particularly worthwhile endeavour. However, the potential effect of that research will only come to fruition if we as researchers are brutally honest with our critique. The statement above says that the historic settlement makes clear the *consequences* of putting corporate profits over honesty and it is absolutely correct. The historic settlement makes it absolutely clear that there are no real consequences to putting corporate profits over honesty in the financial realm. To punish fraud – committed by divisions within S&P and Moody's with clear organisational structures so that we know who made the decision to defraud millions of investors – with a $2.239 billion fine when the profits earned from their fraud far outweigh that fine (and then some) sends a clear message to anyone wondering whether they can get away with fraud in the financial sector in future upturns. By focusing upon aspects of the rating industry that stand no chance of reducing their capability to transgress not only sends a clear message to the agencies that their transgressions can continue unabated, but should also send a message that the system, as it currently operates, does not do so in the name of protecting citizens.

If we are to see a world in which the protection of the citizen is considered in economic policy, which it should be given the centrality of the economy to modern society, then a period of *concerted* social campaigning is what is required. That is not to say that one must reject their views on how the system should operate entirely, but we must all primarily seek to eliminate the social ills that financial catastrophes create. It is simply not justifiable that the rate of suicide, homelessness, unemployment, disease and familial breakdown should increase because of the quest for *excessive* profits by multinational firms. This author has no qualms with the idea of profit or the quest for it, but it should be stated emphatically that the quest for profit *at all cost* is not capitalism, it is greed. It is not something to be lauded, it is something to condemn. It is, essentially, something that we must aim to constrain or better still eradicate, if society is to move forward. *Placing any other values at the forefront of our thinking will only lead to the continuation of the system that, in 2007/8, left a lasting and destructive mark upon society.*

Bibliography

Clement, M. '1976 – The Moral Necessity of Austerity' in Maile, S. and Griffiths, D. (eds) *Public Engagement and Social Science* (Policy Press 2014).

Index

For Product Safety Concerns and Information please contact our EU
representative GPSR@taylorandfrancis.com Taylor & Francis Verlag GmbH,
Kaufingerstraße 24, 80331 München, Germany

Printed and bound by CPI Group (UK) Ltd, Croydon, CR0 4YY
01/05/2025
01858442-0001